FROM
YEOMANETTES
TO
FIGHTER JETS

TITLES IN THE SERIES

TRANSFORMING WAR

Paul J. Springer, editor

To ensure success, the conduct of war requires rapid and effective adaptation to changing circumstances. While every conflict involves a degree of flexibility and innovation, there are certain changes that have occurred throughout history that stand out because they fundamentally altered the conduct of warfare. The most prominent of these changes have been labeled "Revolutions in Military Affairs" (RMAs). These so-called revolutions include technological innovations as well as entirely new approaches to strategy. Revolutionary ideas in military theory, doctrine, and operations have also permanently changed the methods, means, and objectives of warfare.

This series examines fundamental transformations that have occurred in warfare. It places particular emphasis upon RMAs to examine how the development of a new idea or device can alter not only the conduct of wars but their effect upon participants, supporters, and uninvolved parties. The unifying concept of the series is not geographical or temporal; rather, it is the notion of change in conflict and its subsequent impact. This has allowed the incorporation of a wide variety of scholars, approaches, disciplines, and conclusions to be brought under the umbrella of the series. The works include biographies, examinations of transformative events, and analyses of key technological innovations that provide a greater understanding of how and why modern conflict is carried out, and how it may change the battlefields of the future.

FROM
YEOMANETTES
TO
FIGHTER JETS

A Century of Women in the U.S. Navy

RANDY CAROL GOGUEN

Naval Institute Press
Annapolis, MD

Naval Institute Press
291 Wood Road
Annapolis, MD 21402

Library of Congress Cataloging-in-Publication Data
Names: Goguen, Randy Carol, author.
Title: From yeomanettes to fighter jets : a century of women in the U.S. Navy / Randy Carol Goguen, Ph.D., Cdr. USNR (Ret.)
Other titles: Century of women in the U.S. Navy
Description: Annapolis, MD : Naval Institute Press, [2023] | Series: Transforming war | "This book is a revised and updated version of my 2007 dissertation for a Ph.D. in diplomatic and military history from Temple University, "At the Tip of the Trident: Integrating Women into the Fleet.""—Acknowledgments. | Includes bibliographical references and index.
Identifiers: LCCN 2023039592 (print) | LCCN 2023039593 (ebook) | ISBN 9781682478899 (hardcover) | ISBN 9781682479087 (ebook)
Subjects: LCSH: United States. Navy—Women—History. | Yeomen (F)—History. | Women sailors—United States—History. | Sea power—United States—History—20th century. | Sea power—United States—History—21st century.
Classification: LCC VB324.W65 G64 2023 (print) | LCC VB324.W65 (ebook) | DDC 359.0082/0973—dc23/eng/20231019
LC record available at https://lccn.loc.gov/2023039592
LC ebook record available at https://lccn.loc.gov/2023039593

♾ Print editions meet the requirements of ANSI/NISO z39.48-1992 (Permanence of Paper).
Printed in the United States of America.

32 31 30 29 28 27 26 25 24   9 8 7 6 5 4 3 2 1
First printing

Dedicated to the women of the United States Navy

— CONTENTS —

— ACKNOWLEDGMENTS —

I conceived of writing *From Yeomanettes to Fighter Jets* while working on my PhD in diplomatic and military history from Temple University. That work concluded with Congress lifting the combat exclusion laws in 1994. This book brings the story to the present day. Research for the original work involved road trips to archives up and down the east coast from Skowhegan, Maine, to Princeton, New Jersey, to Annapolis, Maryland, and Washington, DC. A historian is seldom happier than when ensconced in an archive or library. When I began updating this work, the COVID-19 pandemic was well under way, and access to physical archives was restricted. Fortunately, the Internet provided a wealth of online source material. The U.S. Naval Institute's *Proceedings* was a timely and invaluable online resource for documenting contemporary debates within the service. The online portal of the Anne Arundel County Public Library in Maryland provided access to newspapers and scholarly journals as well as efficient interlibrary loan services. The online portals to holdings of the National Archives, Naval History and Heritage Command, and Library of Congress were also important resources for research.

I am indebted to a number of people for their encouragement and assistance with the dissertation that provided the foundation for this book. First and foremost, to my dissertation director, mentor, and shipmate Capt. David Alan Rosenberg, USNR, PhD, whose unwavering support and confidence in my abilities made the completion of the original study and this book possible.

I am also indebted to Capt. Linda D. Long, USN (Ret.), former Special Assistant for Women's Policy (PERS-00W), who with the consent of Vice Adm. Daniel T. Oliver, then Chief of Naval Personnel, graciously granted me access to PERS-00W historical files prior to their transfer to the Naval Historical Center Operational Archives in the summer of 1999 while I was serving as an instructor in the History Department at the U.S. Naval Academy. Captain Long also generously donated her personal collection of documentary materials she had saved from the early years of the Women in Ships program, which proved invaluable.

Thanks are also due to my colleagues in the History Department at the U.S. Naval Academy, where I served on active duty as an instructor August 1998–2000. Special thanks to academy professors Robert Artigiani, Lori Bogle, Nancy Ellenberger, and Phyllis Culham for their collegiality, insight, and encouragement. The staff at the Naval Academy's Nimitz Library always responded helpfully and efficiently to my requests, especially reference librarians Barbara Manvel and Barbara Breedon; Jennifer Bryan, head of Special Collections and Archives; and Howard Cropper at the circulation desk. Thanks also to the staff members of the Naval History and Heritage Command's Operational Archives Branch, especially Dr. Regina Akers and Kathy Lloyd. Angie Stockwell of the Margaret Chase Smith Library was also very helpful to me in my research, both at the library and by email correspondence.

Finally, a special note of appreciation for the members of my dissertation committee: David A. Rosenberg, Richard Immerman, and James Hilty of Temple University; and Dean Margaret Marsh of Rutgers University. Thank you for your forbearance and support over the years as I struggled to stay on track while being recalled to active duty in the Navy after 11 September 2001 and then accepted a full-time civilian position with the Navy after demobilization, while also continuing to serve in a demanding assignment in the Navy Reserve.

JoAnne Follmer and Debbie Thomas, the graduate secretaries in Temple's History Department, were very helpful to me in keeping my paperwork straight while I finished my studies from afar.

A special thanks is due to Professor Immerman for helping to untangle various bureaucratic glitches on my behalf in his capacity as History Department chair, and also for his willingness to serve on my dissertation examining committee following the untimely demise of Prof. Russell F.

Weigley. I am indebted to the late Professor Weigley for the exemplary standards he set for his students for research, writing, and scholarship. I still have and treasure his handwritten comments on the draft first chapter I submitted, which included: "There is always a tendency for us to want to use everything we have learned, but it must be resisted." The expertise of the editorial staff of the Naval Institute Press, especially Senior Acquisitions Editor Padraic (Pat) Carlin, Series Editor Paul Springer, and copy editor Mindy Conner, was of immeasurable help in honoring that guidance.

The views and opinions expressed herein do not represent the policies or position of the U.S. Department of Defense or the U.S. Navy and are the sole responsibility of the author.

— ACRONYMS AND ABBREVIATIONS —

ABC	atomic, biological, chemical
ACLU	American Civil Liberties Union
ACNP (W)	Assistant Chief of Naval Personnel (Women)
AD	U.S. Navy hull designator for a destroyer tender
AE	U.S. Navy hull designator for an ammunition ship
AFS	U.S. Navy hull designator for a combat stores ship
AH	U.S. Navy hull designator for a hospital ship
AO	U.S. Navy hull designator for a fleet oiler ship
AOCS	Aviation Officer Candidate School
AOE	U.S. Navy hull designator for a fast combat support ship
AOR	U.S. Navy hull designator for a replenishment oiler ship
AP	U.S. Navy hull designator for a transport ship
ARS	U.S. Navy hull designator for a salvage ship
ASVAB	Armed Forces Vocational Aptitude Battery
AVF	all-volunteer force
AVM	U.S. Navy hull designator for a guided missile ship
BB	U.S. Navy hull designator for a battleship
BuAer	Bureau of Aeronautics, U.S. Navy
BuMed	Bureau of Medicine, U.S. Navy
BuNav	Bureau of Navigation, U.S. Navy
BuPers	Bureau of Personnel, U.S. Navy
CAAF	Court of Appeals for the Armed Forces
CG	U.S. Navy hull designator for a guided missile cruiser (conventional propulsion)
CGN	U.S. Navy hull designator for a guided missile cruiser (nuclear propulsion)
CHINFO	Chief of Naval Information

CINCPAC Commander-in-Chief, Pacific
CLF Combat Logistics Force
CMR Center for Military Readiness
CNO Chief of Naval Operations
CO commanding officer
CST Cultural Support Team
CV U.S. Navy hull designator for an aircraft carrier (conventional propulsion)
CVN U.S. Navy hull designator for an aircraft carrier (nuclear propulsion)
CVT U.S. Navy hull designator for a training aircraft carrier
DACOWITS Defense Advisory Committee on Women in the Services
DD U.S. Navy hull designator for a destroyer
DDG U.S. Navy hull designator for a guided missile destroyer
DOD Department of Defense
DOD IG Department of Defense Inspector General
ELINT electronic intelligence
EOD explosive ordnance disposal
EP U.S. Navy aircraft type designator for special electronic mission maritime patrol
ERA Equal Rights Amendment
F U.S. Navy aircraft type designator for a fighter jet
F/A U.S. Navy aircraft type designator for a fighter/attack jet
FCDA Federal Civil Defense Administration
FET Female Engagement Team
FF U.S. Navy hull designator for a frigate
FFG U.S. Navy hull designator for a guided missile frigate
G-1 Personnel Department/Division, U.S. Army
GAO General Accounting Office/Government Accountability Office (post-2004)
HC U.S. Navy aviation squadron designator for helicopter combat support
H.R. House Resolution
HRM Human Resource Management

HSL   U.S. Navy aviation squadron designator for helicopter antisubmarine light

IG   inspector general

ISAF   International Security Assistance Force

ISE   independent steaming exercise

IUSS   Integrated Undersea Surveillance System

JICPOA   Joint Intelligence Center–Pacific Ocean Area

JOOD   junior officer of the deck

LHA   U.S. Navy hull designator for an amphibious assault ship

LHD   U.S. Navy hull designator for an amphibious assault ship dock

LPD   U.S. Navy hull designator for an amphibious transport dock

LSD   U.S. Navy hull designator for a dock landing ship

LST   U.S. Navy hull designator for a tank landing ship

MCS   U.S. Navy hull designator for a mine countermeasure command and control ship

MEU   Marine Expeditionary Unit

MID   Military Intelligence Division

MJIA   Military Justice Improvement Act

MJIIPA   Military Justice Improvement and Increasing Prevention Act

MLSF   Mobile Logistic Support Force

MSC   Military Sealift Command

MSTS   Military Sea Transportation Service

MTCA   Military Training Camps Association

NATO   North Atlantic Treaty Organization

NAVFAC   naval facility

NCIS   Naval Criminal Investigative Service (1992)

NCWD   National Coalition for Women in Defense

NDAA   National Defense Authorization Act

NFO   naval flight officer

NIS   Naval Investigative Service

NOW   National Organization for Women

NROTC   Naval Reserve Officer Training Corps
OCS   Officer Candidate School
ONI   Office of Naval Intelligence
OOD   officer of the deck
OP-01(W)   U.S. Navy Staff organization code for special assistant for women's policy (1979)
OPNAV   Office of the Chief of Naval Operations
PC   U.S. Navy hull designator for a patrol craft
PCS   permanent change of station
PERS-00W   special assistant to the Chief of Naval Personnel for women's policy
P.L.   Public Law
REFTRA   refresher training
ROC   Reserve officer candidate
SAPRO   Sexual Assault Prevention and Response Office
SEAL   Sea, Air, Land U.S. Navy Special Warfare
SHARP   Sexual Harassment/Assault Response and Prevention Program
SOF   Special Operations Forces
SPARS   *Semper Paratus* Always Ready Women's Reserve of the U.S. Coast Guard
SPECOPS   Special Operations
SSBN   U.S. Navy hull designator for a ballistic missile submarine (nuclear propulsion)
SWO   surface warfare officer
SWOS   Surface Warfare Officer School
TAD   temporary additional duty
TYT   type commander's training
UA   unauthorized absence
UCMJ   Uniform Code of Military Justice
URL   unrestricted line officer
U.S.C.   U.S. Code
USNR   U.S. Navy Reserve

VAQ	U.S. Navy aviation squadron designator for tactical electronic warfare
VC	U.S. Navy aviation squadron designator for fleet composite
VFA	U.S. Navy aviation squadron designator for strike fighter
VJ	Victory over Japan
VP	U.S. Navy aviation squadron designator for antisubmarine patrol
VQ	U.S. Navy aviation squadron designator for fleet air reconnaissance
VR/VRC	U.S. Navy aviation squadron designator for fleet logistics support
VT	U.S. Navy aviation squadron designator for training
VXE	U.S. Navy aviation squadron designator for Antarctic development
VXN	U.S. Navy aviation squadron designator for oceanographic development
WAAC	Women's Army Auxiliary Corps
WAC	Women's Army Corps
WAF	Women's Air Force
WASP	Women's Air Forces Service Pilots
WAVES	Women Accepted for Volunteer Emergency Service
WR	women's representative
WREI	Women's Research and Education Institute

INTRODUCTION

O n 6 September 1997, the *Arleigh Burke*–class guided missile destroyer USS *Hopper* (DDG 70) was commissioned in San Francisco. The ship was named in honor of Grace Murray Hopper, a mathematician who joined the Navy Women's Reserve (Women Accepted for Volunteer Emergency Service, or WAVES) during World War II and, over the course of an active and Reserve military career that spanned more than forty-three years, made major contributions in the fields of data processing and computer science. In the audience that day to witness this historic event was a centenarian, former yeoman third class Frieda Mae Hardin, one of the last remaining World War I women Navy veterans, in her yeoman F uniform. There were also several World War II–era members of the organization WAVES International. Among the guest speakers that day was Sen. Barbara Boxer, who said in her speech prior to commissioning the ship,

When I look at the beautiful ship and its beautiful crew, I see a Navy that Admiral Grace Hopper helped to create. A proud vessel with a crew of sailors eager to set sail aboard one of the most sophisticated ships ever built. And later on when the ship comes alive, if you look closely you'll notice three hundred men *and* women standing side-by-side as a team. The USS *Hopper* is one of the very first ships to be designed specifically to accommodate both a male and a female crew. In fact, there are forty-four female crewmembers who will perform almost every single function on this ship. There could be no better tribute to Admiral Hopper than that.[1]

Hopper was not the first U.S. Navy combatant ship named for a woman. That distinction goes to the World War II *Gearing*-class destroyer USS *Higbee* (DD 806), named for Lenah S. Higbee, superintendent of the Navy Nurse Corps during World War I. She was one of the first four women, all nurses, to be awarded the Navy Cross for their service in that conflict. The women for whom those two combatant vessels were named, those who crewed *Hopper* at its commissioning, and the women veterans who bore witness embodied the full sweep of the history of women in the U.S. Navy. The first women to serve with the Navy as nurses had no military status, but they nevertheless confronted the carnage of combat as they tended to the wounded. They deployed to combat zones in ships and aircraft; some became prisoners of war. Frieda Mae Hardin's contemporaries in the Yeomen F had military status but were precluded from serving on ships. They were primarily restricted to administrative duties until they were summarily dismissed from the ranks of the Navy at the end of World War I. During World War II, the women returned in force; some 84,000 WAVES, while still precluded from serving on ships and aircraft (except for nurses), were performing a much wider array of duties. While their civilian sisters mobilized to build weapons and equipment to fight the war, Navy women trained aircrews in gunnery, helped to build codebreaking machines, and decrypted enciphered communications so other women could track the movements of the enemy at sea. Women like Grace Hopper served literally as human computers, calibrating weaponry so the weapons would hit their targets.

Over the course of more than a century, women's contributions to the Navy were often ignored or marginalized. The interplay of technological trends, social mores, political and economic conditions, institutional culture, and military imperatives shaped the context for their service to the nation. Gradually, through patriotism, perseverance, persistence, and professionalism, and with the support of enlightened men in the military and political spheres, women broke through barriers to assume leadership at the highest levels. Navy women in the twenty-first century hold command at sea and ashore and serve in nearly every commissioned and enlisted occupational specialty. This is the story of their voyage toward equality.

Understanding women's traditional roles in American culture and how they evolved over the past century is essential to understanding the changing role of women in the Navy. Such an understanding includes the relationship of women to the state and the expectations placed upon women by society. Women's gains in the political sphere in particular have been of major significance in shaping their roles in both the civilian and military sectors of society.

Five principal trends shaped the evolution of women's roles in the Navy. First, and foremost among these, are cultural attitudes—the prevailing societal norms that determine the "appropriate" roles for women. In 1917, when women were first enlisted into the Navy, social norms dictated that a woman's place was in the private sphere, where her primary obligation was to her spouse and her children. Fulfillment of this obligation was regarded as a fundamental cornerstone of society and the state. Any woman who sought fulfillment outside the narrowly prescribed confines of the home became a subject of suspicion and ridicule. Divergence from the socially prescribed path brought with it an assumption of sexual deviancy. Those attitudes are remarkable in both their persistence and their consistency to the present day.

Cultural attitudes are in turn affected and informed by the other four trends. The consequences of political enfranchisement of women and their greater participation in public life redefined the relationship of women to the state and to society. The first generation of women to serve in Congress played a major role in creating the women's services during World War II. Military officials recognized that they could no longer ignore the political power of women and were compelled to address their concerns, either through attempts to educate women on the importance of the military or to co-opt their services into segregated reserve components with appeals to their patriotism. The political gains achieved as a result of the second feminist movement in the 1960s and 1970s compelled further concessions to women's demands for professional equity.

Women's migration into the workplace also contributed to the integration of women into the Navy. That migration began with the industrial revolution in the late nineteenth century and was well under way by the time of the establishment of the Yeomen (F) during World War I. Women's inroads into the world of business, especially in providing administrative and communications skills, would prove to be essential to the functioning of modern large military organizations.

Technological change and the resulting revision of what constituted "women's work" correlated closely with the economic advances made by women. The tools of modern bureaucracy—telephones and typewriters—came into widespread use just as women were entering the workforce in larger numbers, enabling them to lay claim to these technologies. The nascent aviation industry also provided opportunities to women, because the associated technology was too new to have become gendered as exclusively male. Their entrance into the civil aviation industry made it easier for women to be integrated into military aviation.

Finally, the changing structure and culture of modern military organizations facilitated the integration of women. As twentieth-century military institutions became larger and more complex, the need for effective administration and communication to ensure day-to-day functioning required an expanded bureaucracy where women could make substantive contributions. With the end of conscription in the 1970s and the ensuing manpower shortages, women enjoyed expanded opportunities in nontraditional fields. Communications technology provided new and sustainable career paths for Navy women in the field of intelligence, partly because restrictions on women serving at sea allowed them to dominate shore-based commands. In today's Navy women are well represented in the relatively new warfare specialty of information warfare. Originally established as the Information Dominance Corps (IDC) in 2009 and renamed in 2016, information warfare combines the disciplines of oceanography/meteorology, information professional (personnel who help develop, deploy, and operate information systems; command and control; and space systems), naval intelligence, and space cadre (personnel competent in the integration of high-end space capabilities into current operations and future plans).[2]

Conflict in the twenty-first-century cyber domain is redefining what constitutes "combat," and women are essential to fulfilling requirements for highly skilled personnel. After decades of working their way up the ranks, women are also serving in traditional combat roles at sea and ashore and are now acknowledged as indispensable to the continued success of the all-volunteer force. Cultural and institutional norms have not always kept pace with these changes, and senior military and political leaders are still grappling with policies to effectively remediate ongoing problems with sexual harassment and assault as they also vacillate on addressing the still controversial issue of universal conscription in times of national emergency.

The Four Historical Phases of Women's Status in the Navy

The trends discussed above have influenced the four historical phases of women's status in the Navy and the other branches of the military. The first phase, militarization, is defined here as the enlistment of women into the armed services between 1917 and 1947.[3] Women were permitted to serve in the Navy in strictly limited roles and in sex-segregated reserve organizations. The Navy established the Yeomen (F) during World War I and the WAVES in World War II. Public acceptance of the unprecedented idea of women in the military was partially mitigated by the prevailing national emergency and strong feelings of patriotism. Nevertheless, women's contributions were constrained by institutional adherence to traditional conceptions of gender norms.

The second phase of women's service in the Navy, occurring between 1948 and 1966, was characterized by marginalization. The Women in the Armed Services Integration Act of 1948 incorporated women into the regular branches of the armed forces but with restrictions on the number allowed to serve (no more than 2 percent of the overall manpower strength) and on rank and enlisted ratings (job specialties); women were prohibited from serving on ships and aircraft or in any duty with the potential to expose them to combat.

The third phase of integration was a transitional period between 1967 and 1993 when policies toward women in the Navy evolved in response to federal judicial rulings and legislation that struck down long-standing assignment policies; the end of conscription and the establishment of the all-volunteer military; and two highly publicized scandals (USS *Safeguard* in 1987 and Tailhook in 1991) that prompted comprehensive reassessments of internal attitudes and policies toward Navy women. Much of the progress made by Navy women during this phase was the result of Navy leadership reacting to public and congressional pressure.

The final phase, true integration, continues to evolve. The Defense Authorization Act of 1994 repealed combat exclusion laws but not all service restrictions on assignment policies. The demands of extended deployments in protracted conflicts in Iraq and Afghanistan, however, as well as contingency operations around the globe, made it impossible for military commanders to strictly adhere to policy restrictions if they wanted to accomplish their missions.

The rise of the #MeToo movement in the civilian sector in 2017 signaled a cultural sea change that renewed political pressure on the services to ensure the well-being of the women and men they placed in harm's way. Today, Navy women serve in surface warfare, aviation warfare, submarine warfare, special operations, special warfare, and information warfare communities. The first woman to successfully complete special warfare training qualified as a special warfare combatant-craft crewman in July 2021.[4] The majority of women with warfare specialties and enlisted qualifications serve in the surface warfare community. Although women now constitute more than 20 percent of the total manpower strength of the

Navy, their representation in the warfare communities is only a fraction of that. Integration is an incremental and ongoing process.[5]

The women who served in the U.S. Navy Nurse Corps, established in 1908 but not granted military status until forty years later, were in many cases the true trailblazers for subsequent generations of Navy women in all ratings and specialties. Although Congress resisted assigning WAVES overseas until near the end of World War II, Navy nurses were serving overseas in the Philippines as early as 1910. Nurses were the first women to go to sea, serving on transport ships in World War I. In World War II they came under hostile fire and began serving on aircraft as flight nurses; some were captured and held as prisoners of war by the Japanese. The highly specialized and exigent nature of the work nurses performed, and its close correlation with the traditional gender role of woman as nurturer, enabled Navy nurses to cross cultural and professional boundaries decades before their WAVES counterparts could.

Conversely, when the WAVES was established in 1942, women officers held regular commissioned rank while Navy nurses continued to hold "relative rank," a contrivance devised to prevent them from exercising authority over male personnel while performing those duties "peculiarly suited to their sex." It was not until the passage of the Army-Navy Nurse Act in 1947, introduced by Republican representatives Margaret Chase Smith and Frances Bolton, that military nurses were allowed to hold regular commissioned rank.[6]

The following chapters recount the obstacles and challenges that the first generation of Navy women confronted and overcame to pave the way for their successors, and how each subsequent generation had to deal with new manifestations of old attitudes and prejudices to secure a place for themselves in the Navy. The fundamental force driving that progress of integration was exigency. Exigency was the mother of integration.

= Part I =

MILITARIZATION

═ I ═
WRESTLING WITH WOMEN

Is there any law that says a yeoman must be a man? . . .
Go ahead. Enroll as many women as are needed in the
Naval Reserve as Yeomen, and we will have the best clerical
assistance the country can provide.
                                                    —Josephus Daniels, 1917[1]

F
ew people familiar with the history of the U.S. Navy, either through
scholarly research or lived experience, would be shocked learn that it
has never enjoyed a reputation as being in the vanguard of progressive social reform. How, then, did the Department of the Navy come to
authorize the enlistment of women during World War I? Understanding
this unprecedented departure from the prevailing cultural norms and
expectations surrounding women's role in society requires examining the
political, economic, and technological advances that created the conditions
for it in the early twentieth century. The women suffrage movement
catalyzed women's demands to participate in the affairs of government;
industrialization created opportunities for employment outside the home;
and new technologies such as the telephone and the typewriter created
niches in the modern workplace that women would come to dominate.
But the expediency of employing female labor in the private sector did not

necessarily translate into acceptance of women in the military, that most masculine of all domains. The exigent circumstances of war created the critical imperative that moderated cultural resistance to the idea of women serving in the military. As the role of women evolved over the ensuing decades, exigency proved time and again to be the mother of integration.

With its mission to deploy on long voyages to far-flung regions of the world, the Navy has traditionally been the most insular of all the armed services. Peter Karsten's social history of the Navy's officer corps in the late nineteenth and early twentieth centuries characterized the prevailing institutional culture as "a largely self-generating elite complete with aristocratic traditions and codes of behavior and armed with a self-serving philosophy. . . . [It] was a strikingly homogenous socio-professional group."[2]

Nonetheless, the Navy (and the Marine Corps, which administratively falls under the Department of the Navy) enlisted women shortly after the United States declared war in 1917. The approximately 11,880 women who served provided critical administrative support ashore that allowed able-bodied male sailors to go to sea. No women were enlisted in the ranks of the Army during that conflict.

It was the unilateral initiative of President Woodrow Wilson's Secretary of the Navy, Josephus Daniels, to enlist women. While the Navy was not a progressive organization in the political sense of the term, its senior civilian leader did support some of the Progressive movement policies within the Democratic Party. (A successful newspaper editor from North Carolina, Daniels also supported white supremacy and Jim Crow laws that disenfranchised Black Americans.) White women were the principal beneficiaries of his progressive policies, which were influenced by his wife, Adelaide Worth Bagley Daniels, who was active in the women's suffrage movement. Confronted with the need to find adequate administrative support to rapidly mobilize the Navy for war, Daniels authorized enlisting women into the Navy's Coast Defense Reserve. The federal bureaucracy in general faced an urgent need for clerical personnel, but the civil service wages offered were not sufficiently competitive to retain experienced civilian secretaries and stenographers. Historian Maurine Greenwald noted that "the first surge of patriotic fervor brought a wave of clerical workers from New York to the capital, but the disparity in salaries between the two cities sent most of them packing within a month or two."[3]

Putting women in a Navy uniform, however, entitled them to the same pay as their male counterparts. Daniels also equalized the wages of all civil service employees in his department. When Carrie Chapman Catt, president of the National Woman Suffrage Association and a friend of Adelaide Daniels, inquired whether women would be paid the same salary as men in similar jobs, as the stated policy in the Civil Service Manual was to pay stenographers and typewriters lower salaries than men, Daniels assured her, "All positions in the department are graded and the same rate of pay applies to each position, regardless of the sex of the incumbent."[4] Daniels' decision to enlist women in the Navy was clearly influenced by his personal political convictions. Such a radical idea would never have entered the mind of anyone with a traditional Navy background—or a traditional civilian background, for that matter.

President Wilson appointed Mrs. Daniels as the U.S. delegate to the Woman's Suffrage World Convention in Geneva, Switzerland, in 1920.[5] Adelaide Daniels belonged to a distinguished southern family with strong ties to the Navy. Although they shared a "romantic" and "almost proprietary attitude" toward the Navy due to family connections, the political views and convictions of Secretary and Mrs. Daniels diverged widely from the insular institutional values of the Navy.[6] Adelaide's nephews, Worth Bagley and David Harrington Bagley, would rise to high leadership positions in the Navy, serving as Vice Chief of Naval Operations and Chief of Naval Personnel respectively in the 1970s.[7]

Surprisingly, there is no documentary evidence of any reaction by the Navy's uniformed leadership to the unprecedented policy of enlisting women into its ranks. The pages of the Navy's major publications of the period, the U.S. Naval Institute *Proceedings*, an unofficial but well-connected professional society founded in 1873, and the *Army-Navy Journal*, were silent on the subject. Undoubtedly, the pressing circumstances of mobilizing for war occupied the full attention of the Navy's leaders. Lacking documentary evidence, how do we assess the prevailing institutional attitude toward women at the time?

Naval officers and their families were almost an aristocracy. They lived apart from civilian society in self-contained compounds. Within those walled enclaves, the role of women in Navy families remained narrowly defined. Naval officers sought to marry educated women, preferably of wealth and social standing, who could help their husband's career and "improve the moral fiber of her nautical mate." Peter Karsten quoted Madeleine Vinton Dahlgren, the wife of Rear Adm. John Adolphus Dahlgren (the "Father of American Naval Ordnance"), regarding women in Navy families. According to Mrs. Admiral Dahlgren, as she was often called, the naval wife's main occupation was to educate children to become virtuous and productive citizens to perpetuate the state's institutions. Daughters were taught only to be "useful and contented in the sphere in which they [were] placed."[8] The ultimate expression of institutional loyalty for a "Navy girl" was to marry a naval officer. While the husbands were at sea, wives and families exchanged social calls, learning and reinforcing the customs and behaviors befitting their proper roles. They thus remained largely insulated from, and were often openly hostile to, the social changes taking place outside the Navy yard's walls. In fact, Mrs. Dahlgren actively campaigned *against* women's suffrage initiatives. In a letter-writing campaign to newspapers across the country she appealed on behalf of thousands of "true women . . . against the oppression of having suffrage forced upon them." She argued that implicit in the civic right to vote was the civic responsibility to bear arms, "for which we are absolutely unfitted." Dahlgren warned that if suffrage for women were to become the law of the land, "*The family, the foundation of the State, will disappear*" and "the female gender will vanish into the *epicene*."[9] The sentiments expressed by Mrs. Dahlgren epitomized the rhetoric of "Republican Motherhood" and "True Womanhood," historical interpretations developed in seminal works by historians Linda K. Kerber and Barbara Welter.[10]

Kerber wrote that the concept of the Republican Mother was born from the political upheaval of the American Revolution. As the Revolution politicized all aspects of life in the new nation, the Republican Mother integrated political values into her domestic life by dedicating herself to the nurture of public-spirited male citizens to serve the state.[11] Barbara

Welter described how these values, which she termed the "Cult of True Womanhood," were perpetuated in women's magazines and literature of nineteenth-century America. The "True Woman's" life was structured around the practice of "four cardinal virtues—piety, purity, submissiveness and domesticity. If anyone, male or female dared to tamper with the complex of virtues which made up True Womanhood, he was damned immediately as an enemy of God, of civilization and of the Republic."[12]

The True Woman led a sheltered, private life removed from corrupting worldly influences. This enabled her to instill the highest moral and civic values in her children. A woman who ventured beyond the confines of her domestic domain not only threatened her identity as a True Woman, she assailed the very foundations of the ordained social order.

But just how representative were Mrs. Dahlgren's views, expressed in the last decades of the nineteenth century, of the attitudes of Navy family women in the early part of the twentieth century? The values of the various organizations with which these women affiliated themselves is one indicator. Officers' wives joined patriotic hereditary societies such as the Daughters of the American Revolution, the Grand Army of the Republic, and the Loyal Legion. Many Navy wives zealously documented their family's social pedigree so their husbands could gain access to the male branches of these quasi-military organizations.[13]

The Navy League of the United States, a private preparedness organization founded by industrial and naval interests, co-opted the national presidents of several of the nation's leading women's patriotic organizations to form its Women's Section in 1915. The roster of member organizations is instructive. Described in the press as "the first women's national defense organization," the groups represented included: Daughters of the American Revolution; Ladies of the Grand Army of the Republic; Dames of the Loyal Legion; Daughters of 1812; United Daughters of the Confederacy, Children's Auxiliary; Women's Made in the U.S.A. League; Daughters of the Union; the National Society of Sponsors; and the National Association Opposed to Woman Suffrage.[14] Mrs. Adm. George Dewey, wife of the hero of the Spanish-American War, was among the founders of the Women's Section of the Navy League. Historian Armin Rappaport wrote that "the committee . . . blanketed the nation with one million copies of a pledge to 'think, talk, and work Patriotism, Americanism, and National Defense.' . . . Plans were made for a Women's National Defense Conference and for a mammoth historical pageant to be held in the autumn in Washington."[15]

The latent tension between these culturally and politically conservative women's organizations and progressive women's organizations fully manifested itself in the interwar era. Women's patriotic groups associated with the preparedness movement allied themselves with the intelligence organizations of the Army and Navy against the progressive women's groups, whose activities and agendas were deemed culturally and politically subversive.

Cultural conservatives regarded the right to vote and the duty to bear arms as inextricably linked. In the aftermath of the Civil War, the Fourteenth Amendment to the Constitution enfranchised Black men as a reward for the faithful military service of approximately 200,000 Black soldiers who fought for the Union during that conflict. The subsequent enactment of Jim Crow laws and terror attacks on Black communities (a practice in which Josephus Daniels himself notoriously participated by instigating a massacre in Wilmington, North Carolina, in 1898) significantly curtailed voting rights for Blacks, especially but not exclusively in the South.[16] With that precedent of enfranchisement as a reward for military service in mind, many cultural conservatives assumed enlisting women in the military would also result in enfranchisement, irredeemably corrupting them and deposing them from the altar of True Womanhood.

The presumption of a reciprocal relationship between the right to vote and the obligation to bear arms discomfited many civilian government officials as well, but at least one member of Congress was inspired by Daniels' audacious example. In December 1917, just before he resigned from Congress to take another post, Rep. George Murray Hulbert (D-NY) introduced legislation "to provide for the enlistment of women in the military service of the United States."[17] The bill never even reached the floor for debate.[18] The fact that Hulbert already had one foot out the door at the time he introduced it suggests that he calculated he had nothing to lose, such as risking the antagonism and ridicule of his soon-to-be-former colleagues. As a cabinet secretary, Daniels was able to exert executive authority to impose his will on the Navy. Hulbert, however, had to rely on the support of his colleagues, which was not forthcoming. Nor were Daniels' convictions shared by his Army counterpart. A memorandum for the Army's chief of staff proposing a response to Hulbert's legislation minced no words: "The enlistment of women in the military forces of the United States has never been seriously contemplated."[19] These sentiments were conveyed in Secretary of War Newton D. Baker's formal responses to the House and Senate, to which he added, "It is requested that you use your utmost endeavor to cause said bill to be unfavorably reported."[20]

The uniformed leadership of the Navy likely shared the secretary of war's views on this subject, but Secretary Daniels had not solicited their opinions on this (and many other policies) before he acted.[21] Although the comptroller of the Treasury expressed "grave doubt as to the legality of enrolling women as yeomen in the naval coast defense reserve," he was "unwilling to make a ruling that might interfere with naval operations in connection with the prosecution of the war."[22]

Eventually, 11,880 women were enrolled and served as yeomen (F) during the war ("yeoman" is the Navy's rating for a petty officer who performs clerical duties). The (F) was added after the rating to differentiate the women from the men in that rating, in part to avoid assigning female yeomen to shipboard duty, from which they were excluded. The term was quickly corrupted into "yeomanette" in popular usage. This blatantly feminine appellation irritated Navy officials, but the yeomen (F) frequently referred to themselves by that term as well.[23] The vast majority of women served in clerical positions as intended, although some also worked in munitions plants and as "translators, draftsmen, fingerprint experts, camouflage designers, and recruiters."[24]

Daniels exploited the ambiguity in the language of the Naval Reserve Act of 1916, which did not specify sex in defining eligibility for membership, to bring the women into the Navy. The act merely stated the membership in the Naval Reserve was open to "citizens" of the United States. The authors of the legislation saw no need to make any sex distinction at the time it was written. That only male citizens would assume the civic obligation of military service was a foregone conclusion. After all, only men were afforded the civic right to vote—and with that right assumed the obligation to military service. Daniels' directive enabled women to voluntarily undertake the civic obligation of military service three years before they won the right to cast the ballot.

The exigency of the war prevented the comptroller of the Treasury from overruling Daniels' policy; this would become a common theme in World War II as well. Time and again, members of Congress who were opposed to expanding roles for women in the military complained that their resistance was characterized as an unpatriotic obstruction of the war effort when their true intentions were to protect and honor the status of True Women. Exigency again proved to be the mother of integration.

In terms of prevailing cultural expectations, what part might a woman play in warfare? In her survey of the history of women in warfare, Linda Grant DePauw identified four archetypal roles that women have tradition-ally played: victim, instigator, virago, and camp follower.[25] These concepts are useful in understanding perceptions of women's contributions to the war effort. The victim role is self-evident and needs no elaboration. The image of womenfolk being subjected to the depredations of the enemy has long been a powerful image in wartime propaganda. World War I recruiting posters were replete with such images to stir the men to enlist to fight for hearth and home.

Respectable ladies expressed their patriotism by playing the instigator role. Instigators sought to either inspire or shame men into responding to the call to war. Society and middle-class women staged historical pag-eants where women and girls elaborately costumed as allegorical figures rendered stirring paeans to patriotism. The cast of one such pageant was described in the newspaper of the Naval Training Camp at Puget Sound: "Peace, Miss Bessie Burkes; Columbia, Miss Sutherland Griffith; War, Miss Genevieve Wolfe; Belgium, Miss Pauline Bennett; France, Miss Pauline Turner; Service, Miss Helen Nesbitt."[26]

If pageantry did not achieve the desired effect on the young men, local organizations such as the Woman's Navy Recruiting Corps in Michigan employed more pointed methods by distributing pamphlets such as the one below.

★ YOU ARE WANTED ★

Don't let women and children point you out as one who ought to be in uniform and is not.

Don't let mothers who have sons in the service look at you with reproachful eyes and say: "Why aren't you where my boy is?"

Uncle Sam is going to get you; why not come now as a volunteer in the Naval Reserves?

Service for the duration of war.
High pay. Government insurance. Family allotments.

Enlist now at the
NAVY RECRUITING STATION
151 Griswold St.

WOMAN'S NAVY RECRUITING CORPS[27]

In addition to administrative duties, some civilian and Navy leaders saw potential in the virago role for the yeomen (F). Throughout history women leaders have donned military attire to inspire their troops. The most famous is Joan of Arc in France, whose image appeared on a U.S. government poster urging women to support the war effort (by buying war stamps as opposed to leading troops into battle). Other famous historical virago figures include Queen Elizabeth I of England and Catherine the Great of Russia.[28]

Rear Adm. Robert E. Coontz, commandant of the Naval Training Camp at Puget Sound, authorized training yeomen (F) to drill with rifles; they formed "the only and original company of armed women in the United States."[29] Throughout the country, yeomen (F) marched in parades to support Liberty Bond and recruiting drives.[30]

Since the idea of a woman serving in the military diverged significantly from traditional gender norms, some people regarded the yeomen (F) as analogous to camp followers. That term was originally applied to women, usually of the lower classes, who traveled with pre–industrial age armies to cook and clean for their husbands, fathers, or sons. They were often considered a necessary evil by military commanders in the field but were commonly regarded contemptuously by civilians as being little more than prostitutes. Some of them *were* prostitutes, but all of them came to be regarded as women of ill repute.[31] One female yeoman recalled with pride how her younger brother got into a fistfight with an older civilian man who made derogatory comments about the character of women serving as yeomen (F).[32]

Despite the power of these prevailing female archetypes relegating women to symbolic and subsidiary roles in wartime, the creation of the Yeomen (F) in 1917 acknowledged the effect that economic and technological changes were having on the status of women in society. By the time Americans were mobilizing to join the hostilities in Europe, the migration of working women from private homes to the public workplace was well under way. Approximately 20 percent of American women were wage earners.[33] The entry of women into the workplace was accelerated by two technological innovations of the late nineteenth century: the typewriter and the telephone. As Margery Davies noted, these technologies were relatively new and had not yet become gendered: "Without historical ties to either sex . . . female typists did not have to meet the argument that they were operating a man's machine."[34] Between 1870 and 1910 the percentage of women employed as office workers rose from 2.6 to 37.7 percent. The entry of women into the telephone industry was even more dramatic. In the first decade of the twentieth century, the number of female operators increased 475 percent. By 1917, "almost 99 percent of the nation's more than 140,000 switchboard operators" were women.[35] It was not surprising, then, that women who enlisted as yeomen (F) were quickly pressed into service as switchboard operators and typists.[36] The mobilizing Navy generated massive amounts of paperwork in the form of contracts, orders, memoranda, and other correspondence. The telephone was critical to rapid communication. This new technology and women's expanding role in working it in the civilian sector naturally transitioned to the military environment. In addition to freeing men to fight, these women made important contributions to the daily functioning of a complex institution.

The expanding "tail-to-tooth" (support versus combatant personnel) ratio was also becoming a prominent feature of modern military forces at that time. As military forces became larger and more technologically complex, the number of noncombatant jobs essential to sustaining them proliferated. The growing range and number of support positions facilitated the division of labor by sex. Women were enlisted in the Navy to provide discrete support skills that were in high demand: clerks, telephone operators, stenographers, and so on. They were immediately put to work. There was no time for basic training. They were expected to study and learn naval regulations, organization, and terminology after regular work hours. There was no military housing for women. Yeomen (F) commuted to their jobs from home daily.[37] Although the Army suffered from the same labor shortage as the Navy, Army officials approached the problem by contracting women as civilian employees on an ad hoc basis. And while none of the Navy's female yeomen could be assigned overseas or to a ship, some of the Army's female civilian contract employees did serve in France as telephone operators near the front lines.[38]

The supply officer for the Norfolk Navy Yard described the contributions of the yeomen (F) in helping the Navy to achieve "almost a miracle in the transport and supply of an Army of 2,000,000 men as well as its own naval forces overseas." Before the war, the supply department comprised approximately 66 office clerks, 36 storemen, and 115 laborers. Its workforce of Reservists and civilians expanded to approximately "500 clerks, 700 in the storehouses, and from 1800 to 2500 laborers." The storehouses operated twenty-four hours a day, seven days a week, with three eight-hour watches per day. In fact, a single watch could last sixteen hours as clerical personnel struggled to keep up with the torrent of paperwork. The women worked late into the night and then had to find their way home through congested streets with inadequate transportation services.[39] It must have been a grueling experience.

More than five hundred yeomen (F) reported for duty in Norfolk during the summer of 1918. The rapid mobilization resulted in cursory screening of recruits, and according to the supply officer, "a good deal of disagreeable weeding out had to be done." A woman counselor position was established "to receive and investigate reports raised in connection with the yeowomen, in addition to their other duties." This practice would be formalized during World War II when the WAVES established women's representative billets. Most women officers tried to avoid the assignment, which amounted to chaperone duty.

Despite initial difficulties, the supply officer concluded that for certain work yeomen (F) "were as good, if not better on the average, than men" because they were more attentive to following procedure than their male counterparts. Some were entrusted with logistics operations, while others managed departments or investigated and remediated bureaucratic snafus. While their behavior "under new and trying circumstances was excellent," they were also "more restive under Navy uncertainty as to their future."[40]

In Washington, DC, another group of exceptional women was providing excellent service under new and trying circumstances. Despite the racist attitudes and policies of President Wilson and Secretary of the Navy Daniels, there existed a tiny cadre of fourteen Black yeomen (F) who supported the Muster Roll Section in Navy Department headquarters. How this came about in the prevailing political and cultural climate of the time remains largely a mystery. What is known is that John T. Risher, a Black clerk who worked in the section, "was given plenary power to engage and select his corps of assistants."[41] Paid at the rate of "a newly enlisted man," the women were responsible for keeping the ship and deck logs up to date—no small feat at the peak of the war when the Navy was enlisting, training, and deploying men at a rate of ten thousand per day. These women undoubtedly faced far greater challenges than their White counterparts in all aspects of their service.[42]

Most of the duties yeomen (F) performed were similar to the tasks they had been performing in the civilian sector. The Navy was forced to acknowledge, at least temporarily, the reality of the feminization of certain sectors of the civilian workforce. But the militarization of women proved too radical a transgression of accepted cultural norms to many in the public and in Congress. Despite the fact that the female yeomen's duties were strictly circumscribed by their sex, women working in "the haunts of men" might "wear themselves and their better thoughts away."[43]

The patriotic impulse that motivated those women who joined the Navy did afford them a certain measure of tolerance, if not respect, from the public. As soon as the war ended, however, that tolerance evaporated. The women were rapidly discharged from the Navy, and Congress took action to ensure that they would never again be enlisted into its ranks.

Joy Bright Hancock enlisted in the Yeomen (F) during World War I. Like many women who were mustered out after the war ended, she continued to work for the Navy as a civil service employee. She worked in the Navy's Bureau of Aeronautics during the interwar era and participated in the effort to establish the Women's Reserve during World War II. She became one of the first WAVES officers and became the third director of the Women's Reserve in 1946. In her memoir of her naval career, she speculated that when Congress drafted the Naval Reserve Act of 1925, the authors "made either a slip—or perhaps a calculated effort to keep women in their place—and limited the Naval Reserve to 'male citizens of the United States.'"[44] Her second conjecture was right on the mark, but Congress' intent was adumbrated long before that in the Naval Act of 11 July 1919: "Members of the Naval Reserve Force shall not hereafter be ordered to perform active duty on shore of a kind which is ordinarily performed by civilians, and all reservists now performing such duty shall be relieved within thirty days after the date of approval of this Act."[45]

Although the legislation did not expressly use the word "women" or "female" in this provision, it was obviously crafted with the explicit aim of expelling the yeomen (F) from the ranks of the Navy. This was certainly apparent to Secretary Daniels, who in a memo to the Bureau of Navigation wrote: "It would seem proper to assume that reserves of the class referred to in said law are without proper qualifications to perform duty on shore of a kind required to be performed by officers and men of the regular service, and, not having training for duty at sea or being unqualified for such duty *by reason of sex*, the law cited has the effect of legislating such reserves as have been placed on inactive duty in pursuance thereof out of the Naval Reserve Force."[46]

Why did Congress use such vague language in the Naval Act of 1919 and then mince no words in 1925 by explicitly stating that membership in the Naval Reserve was restricted to male citizens? Perhaps it was because the naval legislation of 1919 was drafted at the same time that the debate over a constitutional amendment to enact female suffrage had reached its zenith. The House approved the amendment on 21 May 1919, and the Senate followed suit on 4 June.[47] Members of Congress probably did not want to risk antagonizing a large and soon-to-be enfranchised segment of the population.

Why, then, would Congress be so blatant in its exclusion of women in the legislation of 1925? One reason may be that once the Nineteenth Amendment was ratified in August 1920, the feminist movement fractured into factions and dissipated its energies. In the 1920s these internecine conflicts became more pronounced, and it also quickly became apparent that women voters were hardly the monolithic political bloc that many had hoped for or feared.[48] Also, as the country returned to normalcy, the belief that women, enfranchised or not, were singularly unsuited to enter the masculine domain of the military still resonated with a large portion of society. There was little public or political support for the idea of women serving in the peacetime military. The Navy's administrative history of the Women's Reserve noted that former yeomen (F) had unsuccessfully lobbied against the Naval Reserve Act of 1925.[49] Why had there been no similar protest of the Naval Act of 1919? A 1923 memo from the Historical Section of the Navy Department noted that "the placing of Yeomen (F) on inactive duty was not by an act of Congress but came about in regular routine and successive steps in demobilization at the end of hostilities."[50]

If most of the yeomen (F) were already on the inactive rolls by the time Congress passed the Navy Act in July 1919 effecting their discharges, then the long-term implications of the measure probably escaped the women's notice. Undoubtedly, most of the yeomen (F) were as anxious as their male counterparts to return to civilian life as soon as hostilities ceased. Aside from participating in parades and Liberty Bond drives, most of their time and energies were occupied in vital but tedious administrative drudgery. They worked on average ten hours a day, six days a week.[51] Most had neither the expectation nor the desire to remain on active duty. However, they probably assumed that they would have the opportunity to respond to their nation's call to civic duty in the future should the need arise.

The Naval Reserve Act of 1925 was a slap in the face to these patriots. Their government told them in no uncertain terms that their services were neither required nor desired. In yet another twist on the assumptions that had underpinned the debate over women suffrage, the yeomen (F) discovered that the right to the ballot did not include the presumption of military service. Nor can it be said that military service was an obligation that most American women aspired to incur.

Moreover, by 1925 the political energies of a substantial number of American women were being channeled into a growing international pacifist and disarmament movement engendered by collective revulsion at the horrific human toll of the Great War. In the United States and Europe, people hoped to avoid another global conflict by demanding a new international order that would give priority to arbitration over arma-ments. As these demands were pressed upon America's civilian leaders, both the Army and the Navy perceived a growing and serious threat to their institutional well-being, if not their very survival. How the leaders of the services reacted to the political pressure from various women's organizations was influenced greatly by their recent experience with the utilization of women during the war.

Although the Army had firmly and successfully resisted enlisting women into its ranks during World War I, the assistance of thousands of female civilian employees had been required to support the troops at the front. Recognizing that fact, the Army established the Women's Branch of the Army Ordnance Department in January 1918, which proved to be a major innovation in wartime labor management. Its policies represented "an amalgam of two previously independent approaches to labor manage-ment, scientific management and corporate welfare work."[52]

The Army leadership secured the services of two prominent women social reformers: industrial sociologist Mary Van Kleeck and Mary Anderson, who was active in the trade union movement. According to Greenwald, these women "saw themselves as promoting the extension of new job opportunities to women while eliminating the most exploitative features of industrial labor."[53] The policies and practices of the Women's Branch of the Ordnance Department established a precedent for future planning of the Women's Army Auxiliary Corps (WAAC) in World War II and reinforced to some Army officials the importance of cultivating and harnessing women's political and material support for the next conflict.

No similar support structure existed for the Navy's yeomen (F), who were left to their own devices. Nor was there any recognition on the part of the Navy's leadership of a need to plan the future utilization of women in wartime. In fact, Secretary Daniels' rather ham-handed imposition of the yeomen (F) on the Navy may have reinforced institutional resistance to any proposals to utilize women in the future. His departure from his post as the civilian head of the service was accompanied by a collective sigh of relief and a virulent case of institutional amnesia on the part of the officer corps concerning anything to do with women in the Navy. Hancock commented on this when the Navy leadership belatedly and halfheartedly began to address the question again during World War II. She noted that in the intervening twenty years between the world wars, flag officers seemed to have completely forgotten the successful employment of women in the Naval Reserve, while "junior officers had never hear[d] of the Yeomen (F)."[54]

In addition to the Women's Branch the Army utilized civilian women workers in the offices of the adjutant general and the quartermaster general, where they performed more traditional clerical duties.[55] While the Navy had garnered some favorable publicity and notoriety by creating the Yeomen (F), the Army actually undertook a much more serious and systematic approach to the employment of women during the war, albeit in a strictly civilian capacity. The Army's logistical needs were much greater than the Navy's, and the infrastructure to support those needs was located primarily in the "zone of the interior"—that is, the continental United

States—while the Navy's operating forces were forward-deployed in the "theater of operations," from which American women were excluded. An Army interwar report on the participation of women in war made this point. "The problem of the Navy was simple. Its needs were very small, the rates of pay were high and there were sufficient women in the country who wanted to wear a uniform to meet all demands and provide a waiting list."[56]

On the surface, there appeared to be a greater degree of institutional acceptance, within carefully prescribed limits, within the Army for the concept of wartime utilization of women. However, most officers who addressed themselves to the subject were adamant on two issues in particular: women should *not* be militarized, and they should not hold rank on an equal basis with men. "The uniform in the past has stood for a class of the population who undertakes to carry out any task in war assigned to it, up to the point of risking life itself."[57] As to the issue of rank, male officers acknowledged that women had gained access to many professions in the civilian sector, and that during a future war they were likely to exert their newly acquired political power to force their way into the commissioned ranks. In the event, Army officials should plan to channel women into "those positions for which they are better suited than men" and then "restrict them, initially at least, to the absolute minimum in other positions."[58]

This deep-seated fear of men being subjected to the exercise of military authority by women was rationalized and justified with the rhetoric of Republican Motherhood. Waging war was the duty of men, and women held the sacred responsibility of raising the next generation of citizens "along spiritual, moral, physical and educational lines." Although some war work for which women were "better suited than men" could be tolerated, *"efforts to engage in other activities should be resisted to the last."*[59] Nonetheless, during the interwar period the Army considered options for mobilizing women for a future contingency.

The Navy's files in the Naval Historical Center's operational archives, the National Archives, and inquiries to the archivist at the Naval War College Library failed to turn up any documentary record of similar interwar planning by the Navy. Given the absence of contemporaneous Navy efforts on this subject, it is instructive to look at the Army's experience, as it provides insight into the political and cultural factors that shaped the policies and perception of both services.

Senior officers attending the G-1 Course at the Army War College in 1924–25 were tasked with writing essays on the "utilization of women in the military service during war." These studies illustrate that the Army was keenly aware of the latent political power of the newly enfranchised women, warning that "it is apparent that the War Department will have to utilize the services of women in the military service whether it wants to or not."[60] Army leaders surveyed the political terrain, and with varying degrees of resignation sought to make the best of a bad situation. As one officer observed, "The Army will be in a stronger position than if it refuses to employ women at all. The latter course is apt to result in passage of legislation requiring their employment, under conditions fixed by Congress instead of by the Army."[61]

A more immediate concern than preempting radical proposals to utilize women in a future conflict was winning and sustaining their political support for the military in the face of growing public demands for disarmament and international arbitration. One of the officers at the War College noted that women had a crucial role to play in sustaining patriotic support. Toward that end, "Communists, anti-war and pacifist organizations must be put down."[62] While the civilian leadership of the Army embarked on an effort to educate American women on the importance of a strong national defense, uniformed officials kept a wary watch on women's organizations and their leaders they deemed potentially subversive. Absent the existence of a federal domestic security agency, both the Army and the Navy utilized their intelligence services to monitor the activities of women's organizations, and at times sought to play them off against each other in furtherance of the services' own interests.

In March 1920, Secretary of War Baker created the position of director of women's relations, with prescribed duties that included promoting cooperation between the Army and the women of the country and advising the War Department.[63] The second incumbent in the office (the first quit in frustration after a year, citing lack of official support), Miss Anita

disarmament. Contrary to Phipps' advice, both services' intelligence organizations sought to ally themselves with the traditional and conservative women's patriotic organizations. Army and Navy officials appealed to the leaders of these organizations to help collect and share the details of "iniquities of thought and deed" that supposedly were being perpetrated by progressive women's organizations.

In the volatile social and political environment of the interwar era, MID and ONI began dividing their efforts between addressing traditional strategic issues and ferreting out domestic "subversives." In their efforts to ensure domestic tranquility they cast a wide net. Any organization or individual whose objectives and attitudes fell outside the conservative worldview of military officials and their like-minded civilian supporters was fair game. The Army had considerably more resources to dedicate to this task than did the Navy. MID and ONI shared information with each other, but MID was by far the more active of the two organizations. MID data served as a major source for ONI's reports on domestic subversives and suspected communist sympathizers.[73]

The director of MID wrote to the leaders of various patriotic organizations requesting information regarding their "patriotic work" and asking them to aid MID by providing access to their records.[74] Many were more than happy to comply, sending press clippings, organizational literature, and personal reports on individuals and groups they found politically objectionable.[75] Both MID and ONI exchanged information with civilian organizations and individuals they knew were sympathetic to the cause of national preparedness, and referred other concerned citizens to them for information on "propagandistic activities."[76] This information was compiled along with reports from various Army and Navy field activities, and apparently was accepted at face value by uniformed officials, if not their civilian superiors.

Among the individuals who attracted the attention of MID and ONI was Hull House founder and peace activist Jane Addams, who also helped to found the Women's International League for Peace and Freedom. Her other suspect activities included "promoting federation of Religious Liberals" and being "prominently identified with the National Association for the Advancement of Colored People." One patriotic citizen, Elizabeth P. Ryder, wrote to MID to request information regarding "connections of the Women's International League for Peace and Freedom with Soviet Russia."[77]

Carrie Chapman Catt, two-time president of the National American Woman Suffrage Association and founder of the League of Women Voters, was derided as a "professional pacifist," while Margaret Sanger, advocate of the legalization of contraception, was denounced as a "birth controllist: Mentioned in list of New York Bolsheviks and other radicals."[78] Muckraking journalist Ida Tarbell came under scrutiny for her interest in the Association to Secure the Outlawing of War.[79] The International Ladies Garment Workers of America was singled out in MID files as "one of the nine unions which are revolutionary in character and are organized for the ultimate purpose of seizing industry and overthrowing the government."[80] The close scrutiny of progressive women's organizations more accurately reflected the paranoia of military officers unnerved by challenges to their culturally conservative worldview and institutional interests than any tangible threat to national security.

Director of Naval Intelligence Capt. Luke McNamee was dispatched by Assistant Secretary of the Navy Theodore Roosevelt to address a women's organization in Boston in 1923. McNamee called for the members to assist in a concerted effort to educate the citizenry, closing his speech with a biblical appeal: "If we are to guard our families and our firesides; let us keep in our hands the power that God has given us, and renounce once and forever the sophistries of the Delilahs of pacifism, that would shear the Navy of its strength."[81]

The uniformed leadership of the services believed that women who were truly concerned with the nation's well-being would recognize their patriotic duty and stay home like respectable Republican Mothers. In their estimation, suffrage had unwisely given women unprecedented political power. Because women were easily intellectually seduced and manipulated to ascribe to dangerous doctrines that worked against their own and the nation's best interests, it would be prudent to devise a preemptive plan to minimize their influence upon and within the military. However, most officers found the idea of women serving in the ranks too distasteful to give it serious consideration. Consequently, institutional inertia assisted by organized resistance from conservative civilian elements effectively quashed any planning efforts, however limited, along those lines. It would take a second global war for women to breach the ramparts of the military's resistance and secure a toehold on the ultimate masculine domain. As the government demanded unprecedented levels of political and material support from all segments of society to sustain the war effort, the wholesale exclusion of women was simply unsustainable.

= 2 =
FROM EXIGENT TO EXPENDABLE

*"I realized that there were two letters that had to be in it:
W for women and V for volunteer, because the Navy wants
to make it clear that this is a voluntary service and not
a drafted service. So I played with those two letters and
the idea of the sea and I finally came up with 'Women
Appointed for Volunteer Emergency Service'—WAVES....
I figured the word Emergency would comfort the older
admirals because it implies we are only a temporary crisis
and won't be around for keeps."*

—Elizabeth Reynard, 1942[1]

As armed conflict once again appeared imminent in Europe, the Army continued to lead the U.S. military services in considering the use of women to fulfill wartime missions. Shortly after Gen. George C. Marshall was appointed Army chief of staff in September 1939, the G-1 Staff revisited the issue. The staff's latest study took a dim view of the previous efforts of War College and G-1 officers, dismissing their studies as being "marked by a lack of factual data, rambling discussion and vague conclusions." But this new effort made no attempt to compensate for the noted deficiencies. In fact, many of the key points in the new study rehashed the concerns raised by its predecessors, especially the insistence that women should not be made part of the Army and should not hold military rank. "The advisability of making a person a member of the Army turns principally on the necessity for extreme powers to discourage desertion and cowardice. American women have never been subjected to such compulsion and no such innovation is to be expected."[2]

The proposed utilization of women's services was delineated in three major categories: ordinary civilian employees, nurses and medical technicians, and welfare workers. The British Women's Auxiliary Army Corps in World War I was suggested as a model because it demonstrated the duties for which women were "best suited": "clerks, chauffeurs, technicians of various sorts and domestic servants." Women had proved to be "especially useful in running hospital messes, and officers' cadets' and sergeants' messes in training areas; and as compared with Army cooks, they served much better food at half the cost." The author of the new study speculated that women could be utilized in complete companies to staff large activities such as quartermaster centers, or in small groups or as individuals to do welfare work for the troops. In a bold flight of imagination, the author proposed that small groups of women could be employed as "strolling minstrels."[3]

As the military situation in Europe continued to deteriorate, the U.S. government began to gear up its mobilization machinery. In September 1940 the first peacetime Selective Service Act was signed into law. Just as earlier Army studies had predicted, women's organizations across the country became increasingly insistent on being given a substantive role in the war effort. First Lady Eleanor Roosevelt proposed that American women should perform antiaircraft barrage duty, as women in Britain were currently doing. She also recommended the establishment of a pool of women under government control that could be drawn upon by all the services as needed. Army officials continued to dawdle. Neither suggestion was implemented, but they did ratchet up the pressure on the services to take some kind action to address the issue.[4]

Ultimately, Rep. Edith Nourse Rogers (R-MA) prodded the Army into action. Rogers was elected to the 69th Congress in 1925 to fill the vacancy created by the death of her husband, Rep. John Jacob Rogers. In 1941 she was one of eight female members of the 77th Congress. Democrat Hattie Caraway of Arkansas was the first and only woman senator elected by popular vote. Two of the seven female representatives in the House were Democrats: Mary Norton of New Jersey and Caroline O'Day of New York. In addition to Rogers, the other four Republican representatives were Frances Bolton of Ohio, Jessie Summer of Illinois, Margaret Chase Smith of Maine, and Jeannette Rankin of Montana, who had opposed America's involvement in both world wars.[5]

As a Red Cross volunteer during World War I, Rogers had observed firsthand the problems confronted by American civil service women and volunteers working for the Army in France. They lacked adequate housing, and as civilians were not subject to military discipline. Unlike male veterans, women who suffered debilitating illnesses or injuries as a result of their service received no compensation or benefits from the federal government. Although Rogers eventually obtained some limited relief through Congress for women telephone operators, the experience stiffened her resolve to ensure that women serving with the Army would receive the same protection as men.[6]

Rogers informed General Marshall in the spring of 1941 that she intended to introduce legislation to establish a women's corps. It was this "threat" that finally lit a fire under the planners in the G-1 Division. Resigned to the inevitable, they scrambled to produce a preemptive proposal to ensure the Army would have as much control as possible over the new organization.[7]

Rogers introduced her bill (H.R. 4906) in the House of Representatives on 28 May 1941. Despite her desire to give women full military status, she realized that insisting on such a measure might engender enough resistance from Army officials and members of Congress to kill the organization altogether. Consequently, she accepted the Army's plan to give women an auxiliary status, so that they served *with*, but not *in*, the Army. The bill was referred as a matter of course to the Bureau of the Budget for its endorsement, which initially was not forthcoming. After four months of leisurely deliberation, the War Department was informed that the bureau did not believe the proposal "was in accord with the program of the President." By this time, however, General Marshall had warmed to the idea, arguing that it would be a waste of time and valuable manpower to train men to perform duties such as typing and telephone work that women were already doing in the civilian sector. Marshall enlisted the services of Oveta Culp Hobby, who had been appointed to head the War Department's new Women's Interest Section (a position similar to the one Anita Phipps held during the interwar period). Hobby was the wife of former governor William P. Hobby of Texas. Before coming to work for the Bureau of Public Relations in the Army's Women's Interest Section, she had served in the Texas legislature for several years and as a radio and newspaper executive, publisher, lawyer, writer, and president of the Texas League of Women Voters. Hobby acted as a liaison between General Marshall and Mrs. Roosevelt, and eventually they succeeded in overcoming the resistance of the Bureau of the Budget. In this they received a little external impetus from the Imperial Japanese Navy, whose surprise attack against the U.S. Pacific Fleet in Pearl Harbor, Hawaii, four days before the bureau cleared the plan heightened the sense of urgency.[8]

After incorporating amendments proposed by the War Department, Representative Rogers reintroduced the WAAC bill as H.R. 6293 at the end of December 1941. At this point, Navy officials intervened in a last-ditch effort to dissuade the Army from sponsoring the bill. The assistant secretary of war eventually persuaded the Navy to stop obstructing the legislation, but the Navy refused to offer any support either, warning Army leaders, "You are going to take a beating and we'll wait to see what happens."[9]

Back on the ninth of December, Representative Rogers had contacted the chief of the Bureau of Navigation, Adm. Chester Nimitz, and pointedly asked "whether the Navy was interested in the passage of a bill to provide for the Navy a Corps similar to the proposed WAAC."[10] Nimitz responded that he "saw no great need for such a bill" and tried to stall for time by suggesting Rogers formally request the views of the Secretary of the Navy. In the meantime, Nimitz polled officers in the various bureaus and offices within the Navy Department for their views on the subject. Not surprisingly, few replies were in the affirmative. The Navy's unpublished official history of the Women's Reserve asserted, "Scant imagination or open-mindedness regarding the possible usefulness of women as replacements or substitutes for men was shown, and there was a complete failure . . . to foresee the coming shortage of civilian employees."[11] The

Bureau of Medicine and Surgery (BuMed) pointed out that the WAAC was limited to "noncombatant" services, and "a similar corps for the Navy would offer little in the way of practical advantages due to the differences in functions and organization of the Army and Navy." As far as BuMed officials were concerned, the Navy should "adhere to its present policy of relieving Navy personnel on shore duty where necessary by Civil Service employees."[12] Joy Bright Hancock noted in her autobiography that negative responses were also received from the Office of the Judge Advocate General, the Bureau of Supplies and Accounts, the Bureau of Yards and Docks, the Bureau of Ships, the Bureau of Ordnance, and the Assistant Secretary of the Navy. Hancock characterized such resistance as a fear of change endemic to bureaucracies.[13]

There were two exceptions to the chorus of negative responses: the Bureau of Aeronautics (BuAer) and the Office of the Chief of Naval Operations (OPNAV). Acknowledging the educational and social changes that enabled women to enter and advance in the civilian workforce during the interwar era, BuAer officials proposed expanding women's employment into more technical and skilled positions. The policies they recommended "anticipated most of the major aspects of the subsequent organization of the Women's Reserve."[14]

OPNAV, which held overall responsibility for the training, equipping, and deployment of personnel, anticipated a rising demand for communications personnel as the men currently in these positions were deployed to sea duty. A Women's Reserve could fill the billets ashore vacated by these men and also meet expanding needs. Furthermore, the nature of that work would require the women replacements to be placed under military authority and control for reasons of security. Thus, OPNAV recommended that such a program begin "without delay."[15]

In fact, it was BuAer that lobbied Navy leadership to prepare a legislative proposal permitting women to become members of the Naval Reserve. Despite rebuffs from the Bureau of Navigation, BuAer persisted in compiling studies and estimates of its own manpower needs, and all these studies pointed to the necessity of employing women. The studies cited contemporary practices in the American aircraft and related industries, as well as how women were being utilized in Great Britain and Canada. A group of senior officers in BuAer provided information for these studies: Rear Adm. John H. Towers, the chief of the bureau; Rear Adm. A. B. Cook, Tower's deputy; Capt. Arthur W. Radford, who would rise to the positions of commander in chief, Pacific Fleet and chairman of the Joint Chiefs of Staff; and Cdr. Ralph A. Ofstie, future deputy CNO for air and commander, Sixth Fleet. Joy Bright Hancock, who became a civil service employee within BuAer after her service as a Yeoman (F) in World War I, worked with all these men. Admiral Ofstie would become her third husband in 1954. (Her first two husbands, both Navy airship crewmembers, were killed in crashes.) Hancock was sent to Canada to visit stations of the Royal Air Force to gather additional information on issues such as housing, administration, and recreation for servicewomen.[16]

The attitude of the BuAer leadership toward the employment of women was markedly different from the rest of the Navy. The technology associated with aircraft was still relatively new. The industry developed rapidly during and between the world wars just as large numbers of women were entering the workforce. The aircraft industry relied on women almost from its inception, so there were no preexisting gender barriers to break down.[17] The Army Air Corps had also been among the first internal advocates for establishing a women's corps.[18]

Rear Admiral Towers had learned to appreciate the services of women working in government during his tour in the Division of Aeronautics in World War I. He depended heavily on his female civil service clerks and yeomen (F) and was therefore an ardent advocate of returning women into the Navy. He even supported the idea of a women's air corps utilizing women pilots to ferry aircraft as the British were doing. Admiral Nimitz did not share Tower's enthusiasm on either issue.[19]

Women in aviation were already in the public eye during the 1920s and 1930s as the exploits of Amelia Earhart, Jacqueline Cochran (whom Towers greatly admired), and others made newspaper headlines, but the idea of women actually serving as military pilots was too radical for most Navy men to consider. Jacqueline Cochran would eventually succeed in establishing the Women's Air Forces Service Pilots (WASP), which provided aircraft ferrying services for the Army Air Force, but in a civil service status. "WASP leadership was so keenly aware of the potential jealousy of male would-be pilots," historian Doris Weatherford wrote, "that they kept publicity to such a minimum that some people believed that existence of the WASP was a military secret."[20] When the Women's Reserve was successfully established, the history noted, it was OPNAV and BuAer "that proved to be the earliest large-scale employers" of women."[21]

The introduction of the WAAC bill brought several inquiries from members of Congress concerning the Navy's intentions. Finally, in January 1942, the Bureau of Navigation succumbed to pressure and recommended the Secretary of the Navy ask Congress to authorize establishing a women's organization.[22] While the Navy was slower off the mark than the Army, once it decided to establish a women's organization it "pushed the envelope" of cultural norms by insisting that any women's organization associated with the Navy should be militarized. The Bureau of Navigation (renamed the Bureau of Personnel in 1942) was adamant that, as in World War I, women should be serving *in* the Navy—subject to regular military control and discipline for reasons of security and organizational efficiency—rather than *with* it. "Under its urging, SecNav chose to have no women's organization at all rather than to accept an 'auxiliary' corps of the type of the WAAC."[23]

In a nod to its World War I experience, the Navy proposed to amend the Naval Reserve Act of 1938 to establish a Women's Auxiliary Reserve as a branch of the Naval Reserve. The Bureau of the Budget's response was a refrain familiar to Army officials: "the enactment of the proposed legislation in the form submitted would not be in accord with the program of the President."[24] Budget officials recommended that the Navy submit legislation to establish a Women's Auxiliary Reserve on the same basis as the WAAC legislation that had already received the bureau's endorsement. In March 1942 both the Bureau of Navigation and OPNAV asked the Navy judge advocate general to request that the Bureau of the Budget reconsider its decision.[25]

While the proposed legislation lay becalmed in the bureaucratic doldrums, external forces came into play to stir up the currents that eventually enabled a Women's Reserve bill to make headway. One of the most influential advocates working behind the scenes was Dr. Margaret Chung.

Margaret Chung, a Chinese American, was a formidable woman who had overcome substantial obstacles imposed by prevailing attitudes toward both her race and her gender to become a successful practicing surgeon in San Francisco. She was an ardent advocate of Chinese nationalism, and when the Imperial Japanese Army invaded Manchuria in 1931, Chung actively solicited American support for the Chinese cause. She spoke to women's organizations and helped to organize fundraisers, but her most noteworthy achievement was creating a network of powerful men in the military, political, and entertainment fields. Hoping to serve as a surgeon in the U.S. Navy, Chung skillfully exploited her contacts in her personal network to help establish the Navy's Women's Reserve.[26]

The origin of "Mom Chung's Fair-Haired Bastards" dated back to 1931 when an ensign in the Naval Reserve, anxious to get into the action overseas, asked Dr. Chung for assistance in securing a commission in the Chinese military. Chung invited the ensign and his six housemates, all recent college graduates and aviators, to dine with her. This arrangement evolved into a regular event, and as she and her original seven "sons" recruited others, the size of the family expanded throughout the decade. By the time of the Japanese attack on Pearl Harbor, her network numbered in the hundreds.[27]

Chung's "children" were organized into three branches and assigned numbers. Pilots were designated "Fair-Haired Bastards," non-aviators and civilians were called "Kiwis," and submariners were "Golden Dolphins." Chung bestowed small gifts on her family members acknowledging their status, and her San Francisco home was open to her military family members as a refuge for rest and recreation from the hardships of war.[28] According to Judy Tzu-Chun Wu, Chung's biographer, while Chung's personal and professional life defied convention, she skillfully presented herself as "a symbol of traditional female domesticity" that reassured men who were troubled by the social upheaval of wartime.[29] Her political strategy combining elements of maternalism, domesticity, and personal feminism proved highly effective.[30]

In March 1942, Chung offered her services as a surgeon to the Navy but was rejected because there was no organization for women at that time. This ignited her interest in establishing such an organization at the same time the proposed legislation was languishing in the Bureau of the Budget. Chung queried "Beloved Son 465," Lt. Cdr. Irving McQuiston in BuAer, who informed her that it would require an act of Congress to establish a women's organization. McQuiston asked Chung if she knew anyone in Congress who would be willing to introduce such a bill. Chung contacted her 447th son, Rep. Melvin Maas (R-MN), who was a member of the House Naval Affairs Committee, a colonel in the Marine Corps Reserve, and the father of three daughters (one of whom would become a lieutenant colonel in the Marine Corps). Maas obtained a copy of the Navy's proposed legislation from the judge advocate of the Navy and introduced it as his own bill, H.R. 6807.[31]

Chung also contacted Aliene Loveland (Kiwi 120), who was a secretary to Sen. Raymond Willis (R-IN). Through Loveland, Chung successfully lobbied Willis (Kiwi 124) to introduce a companion bill in the Senate, S. 2338. Golden Dolphin son 98, Kentucky senator Albert "Happy" Chandler, played a key role in shepherding the bill through contentious Senate hearings. In addition, Chung enlisted the support of Alice Roosevelt Longworth (Kiwi 49), the daughter of former president Theodore Roosevelt, and Mary Early Holmes (Kiwi 130), the sister of President Franklin Roosevelt's executive secretary, Steve Early, "to help lobby the 'New Deal Regime.'"[32]

Once Representative Maas commandeered the sponsorship of the legislation from the Navy, events moved quickly. The director of the Bureau of the Budget magnanimously informed the Secretary of the Navy that he no longer objected to the legislation being presented to Congress, and BuPers officials set to work drafting regulations for the Women's Reserve. Secretary of the Navy Frank Knox supported the establishment of the Women's Reserve from the outset. In fact, it was Knox's original proposal that was introduced into Congress by Representative Maas and Senator Willis.[33]

The House of Representatives favorably reported Maas' bill on 16 April 1942 and referred it to the Senate Naval Affairs Committee. The bill encountered strong opposition there because unlike the earlier WAAC legislation, this bill sought to militarize women. Although the provisions of the WAAC legislation were far more conservative, it too had encountered dogged resistance when it reached the House floor in March 1942. The strongest objections to the bill were couched in terms of the erosion of cultural values and socially prescribed gender roles. Legislators' protests— often worded in the rhetoric of Republican Motherhood—transcended party and regional boundaries. Self-appointed guardians of domestic virtues raised the specter of the humiliation of the American male and the degradation of American womanhood. Rep. Clare E. Hoffman (R-MI) protested that he and several other members of Congress were being coerced to vote for a measure "we know will not aid the war effort, because if we do not, we are sure to be accused of aiding Hitler and our enemies across the sea." Hoffman referred to the creation of the WAAC as "a diversion, a detour from the straight and narrow road." Employing the rhetoric of Republican Motherhood and True Womanhood, Hoffman asked plaintively, "Who then will maintain the home fires; who will do the cooking, the washing, the mending, the humble, homey tasks to which every woman has devoted herself; who will rear and nurture the children; who will teach them patriotism and loyalty; who will make men of them, so that, when their day comes, they too, may march away to war?"[34]

Rep. Andrew L. Somers (D-NY), a Navy veteran, called the bill "the silliest piece of legislation that has ever come before my notice in the years I served here." He found the proposal humiliating to manhood and so revolting to his concept of Americanism that it defied rational or civil discussion on the floor of the legislature.[35] Rep. Hampton P. Fulmer (D-SC) thought the bill "ridiculous," a waste of taxpayers' money on "uniforms and lipstick kits."[36]

Ultimately, the strong endorsement and personal prestige of Army Chief of Staff Gen. George C. Marshall and Secretary of War Henry Stimson rescued the WAAC bill from defeat.[37] When the Maas bill establishing the Navy Women's Reserve was introduced in the House in April, it was approved in an astonishingly fast nine days. Undoubtedly "Mom" Chung's skillful cultivation of political and naval allies had helped clear the path, and would-be opponents in the House probably thought further resistance was futile given Frank Knox's public support for the legislation.

The bill's reception in the Senate was a different matter. Senate opposition to the legislation focused on the provisions that distinguished it from the WAAC bill, namely that the Women's Reserve would be a part of the Navy as opposed to a separate auxiliary. Navy officials remained adamant on this point—not out of any newfound sense of feminism but out of desire for maximum efficiency. To win this crucial point, BuPers proposed amendments to the legislation to placate some senators' objections. Members of the Women's Reserve would not be allowed to perform duty outside the continental United States. "Congressional chivalry felt that women's 'place' was not outside the country in time of war; there was distrust of the probable efficiency of 'supervision' of the women if they went abroad" (no similar restrictions were applied to Army or Navy nurses or to the WAC).[38] The second amendment stipulated that "women shall not be assigned to duty on board vessels of the navy, or in combat aircraft."[39] Banning women from serving on these platforms, and hence with the operating forces of the Navy, imposed the greatest obstacle to facilitating the true integration of women into the service for the next fifty years.

Among the strongest opponents to the Women's Reserve bill was the powerful chairman of the Senate Naval Affairs Committee, David I. Walsh (D-MA), who attempted to derail it by prodding the Bureau of the Budget to renew its original objections and forward them to the president. Walsh nearly succeeded. On 25 May President Franklin D. Roosevelt asked the Secretary of the Navy to reconsider "the advisability of a substitute bill providing for a Women's Naval Auxiliary to serve with but not in the Navy or Naval Reserve." The Secretary of the Navy responded by asking the president to reconsider his objections.[40]

Once again, it took the covert influence of a few women in key positions to resolve the impasse. In the spring of 1942, Rear Adm. Randall Jacobs, who had succeeded Rear Admiral Nimitz as chief of BuPers, established the Citizen's Advisory Council, made up of prominent women, to make recommendations regarding the establishment of a Women's Reserve.

The council comprised presidents and deans of women's colleges and coeducational universities, and civic leaders from across the country. Virginia C. Gildersleeve, dean of Barnard College, chaired the council.[41] Dean Gildersleeve and Dean Harriet Elliott of the University of North Carolina both wrote to Eleanor Roosevelt apprising her of the dilemma and reiterating the importance of getting the bill enacted on the Navy's terms. Mrs. Roosevelt passed this information on to Under Secretary of the Navy James V. Forrestal, asking, "Can I help in any way?" Forrestal expressed his thanks for the First Lady's interest and informed her that his superior had already asked the president to reconsider his objections.

Dean Elliot received a letter from Mrs. Roosevelt on 10 June informing her that the president had seen her letter. Six days later the Secretary of the Navy informed the chief of naval personnel that the president had authorized the Secretary of the Navy to organize the Women's Reserve "along the lines I think best," and suggested "that we now press this matter to as swift an enactment as we can."[42] Secretary Knox informed Senator Walsh of the president's decision on 19 June. The bill quickly cleared the full Senate and the House and was signed into law on 30 July 1942.[43]

Despite her significant lobbying efforts to help establish the Women's Reserve, Dr. Margaret Chung never realized her ambition to serve in the Navy. In addition to the barriers imposed by her race, background investigations conducted by both the FBI and ONI turned up allegations of lesbianism, a topic of extreme sensitivity to Navy officials given the common public assumption that women who sought to enter the military were likely either promiscuous or "abnormal."[44] Chung's behind-the-scenes contributions were omitted from historical accounts until historian Judy Tzu-Chun Wu corrected the oversight.

The first Asian American woman to enlist in the Navy would be Susan Ahn, the daughter of the first Korean married couple to legally emigrate to the United States in 1902. Ahn's father was an activist who opposed the occupation of Korea by Imperial Japan. He was arrested after returning to Korea to fight for independence and died there in prison in 1938. Susan enlisted in December 1942 to honor her father and fight the Japanese. She trained as a Link flight simulator and aerial gunnery instructor. Her excellent work earned her a recommendation for a commission, and she became an officer in 1943.[45]

In addition to the amendments to the original legislation, the statutory provisions of the original act establishing the Women's Reserve fell far short of true integration. First, the Women's Reserve was authorized only for the duration of the war or national emergency, "and for six months thereafter, or until such earlier time as the Congress . . . may designate."[46] No one anticipated a need to keep women on duty after the cessation of hostilities. The stated mission of the Women's Reserve was "to release male officers and enlisted men of the naval service for duty at sea."[47] The sensitive issue of the exercise of military authority by women was "handled by Congress in the combined spirit of traditional parliamentary distrust of the ambitions of the military and masculine suspicion of the masterful female." The Women's Reserve was originally authorized one lieutenant commander and thirty-five lieutenants. "No limit was set on the total number of lieutenants junior grade, and ensigns, but no more than one third of the total number of persons holding these ranks could be j.g.s."[48]

Confining women to the lowest of the commissioned ranks created recruiting problems and unbalanced the organization. Professional women were reluctant to leave the civilian sector for a position whose rank and level of compensation were not commensurate with the level of responsibility they were accustomed to exercising and that held little prospect for promotion. Administratively, confining women to the lowest ranks of a hierarchical military organization hobbled their ability to influence policy. Command authority was also narrowly defined. Officers of the Women's Reserve could exercise military command only over other members of the Women's Reserve and in respect to the administration of the organization.[49]

Joy Bright Hancock recalled that many officers were predisposed to resist the invasion of their masculine domain by women. Sensitive to the potential for inflaming this latent antagonism, the women responsible for setting up the new organization were careful in selecting a name for it. Prof. Elizabeth Reynard of Barnard College, a member of the Citizen's Advisory Council, is credited with devising the winning appellation:

Women Accepted for Volunteer Emergency Service—WAVES. Reynard reasoned "the word Emergency would comfort the older admirals because it implies we are only a temporary crisis and won't be around for keeps."[50]

Reynard took a leave of absence from Barnard and was deeply involved in the initial planning for standing up the Women's Reserve, traveling around the country to determine what types of work women could perform. She was commissioned as a lieutenant and later served as the commandant of seamen at Hunter College in New York, where enlisted women were trained. She attained the rank of commander during her wartime service.[51] Wellesley College president Mildred McAfee, who was appointed the first director of the WAVES at the rank of lieutenant commander, characterized the prevailing attitude among the uniformed leadership of the Navy by quoting the 88th Psalm: "Thy wrath lieth hard upon me, and thou hast afflicted me with all thy waves."[52]

The women the Navy chose to serve on the Citizen's Advisory Council lent the prestige associated with their civilian institutions to the new Women's Reserve. The Navy took great pains to ensure that the Women's Reserve would project an image of dignity and professionalism. The Office of the Chief of Personnel promoted recruiting efforts that portrayed the Women's Reserve as a "somewhat independent branch." Keenly aware of the importance of public perceptions, the Navy made every effort to reassure a skeptical public that young women who enlisted would serve "under proper care and supervision."[53]

The Navy's enlistment standards for the WAVES reflected the experiences and values of the women education professionals charged with standing up the organization. WAVES officer applicants were required to have a baccalaureate degree or at least two years of college plus "no less than two years of compensating business or professional experience." Enlisted applicants were required to have successfully completed high school or business school. All applicants had to be at least twenty years of age, have no children under the age of eighteen, and "be of good repute in the community."[54]

Despite the Navy's efforts to present the new organization as highly respectable, its reputation was seriously tarnished by a malicious rumor campaign against the WAAC that appeared to start by word of mouth and private correspondence. Initially, Army officials thought it would be prudent to simply ignore the rumors because official denials would only draw more attention to them, but they were eventually forced to act when one canard became a matter of public record.[55] In June 1943 newspaper columnist John O'Donnell, a consistent critic of the Roosevelt administration, reported in a nationally syndicated column called "Capitol Stuff" that a cabal of "New Deal ladies" had forged a "supersecret" agreement with Army leadership to issue contraceptives and prophylactic equipment to WAACs. "Mrs. Roosevelt wants all the young ladies to have the same overseas rights as their brothers and fathers."[56]

Senior Army and administration officials issued heated denials and implied that those responsible for propagating the stories were providing aid and comfort to the enemy. The Army tasked its Military Intelligence Service to determine whether this slander was Axis inspired, but investigators concluded that the stories were initiated by American soldiers and sailors antagonized by the recruiting campaigns for women that called upon them to enlist and "free a man to fight." When the war in Europe progressed to actual combat in North Africa, men who were not enthusiastic about being "freed" gave further impetus to the rumors.[57]

Although an exhaustive investigation revealed little substance behind the slander, many individuals in the military and civilian spheres were ready to believe the worst about any woman who donned a uniform. Women who wrote to their sweethearts and husbands in the military seeking approval/permission to enlist often received a hostile response. One man equated WAVES with prostitutes. Other men conceded that while they thought the WAAC and WAVES were "great" and "worthwhile" organizations, they did not want their wives or girlfriends to enlist.[58]

In retrospect, Hobby concluded that the slander campaign "was inevitable; in the history of civilization, no new agency requiring social change has escaped a similar baptism."[59] The Navy's history of the Women's Reserve observed, "there is no evidence that the uniform predisposed to indiscretion, though a prurient interest to believe so among a certain part of the population was a factor which a careful public relations policy always had to take into account."[60] The legacy of the slander campaign would be institutionalized double standards for all women servicemembers and an obsessive preoccupation with ensuring they comported themselves in an appropriately ladylike manner.[61]

Given these cultural attitudes, the women's services could not simply rely on patriotic fervor to fill their ranks. A study by historian D'Ann Campbell showed that while most women who joined the services cited patriotism as a major factor in their decision, 41 percent reported having to overcome the opposition of close relatives.[62] Navy recruiting efforts took this factor into account. "A more striking respect in which this presentation differed from a men's recruiting program was that the Women's Reserve had to convince the parents, and sometimes even the church, as well as the girls."[63]

Another major factor motivating women to enlist was the desire to "try something different."[64] Both services tried to attract women recruits by emphasizing the more unusual duties available to women. Morale problems ensued when the women found themselves in substandard living conditions and assigned to menial or mundane tasks far below their capabilities.[65]

As the demands of the war effort continued to draw men away from the States for combat duty, opportunities for women to perform nontraditional work expanded; but most military women continued to perform more traditional duties. With the conversion of the WAAC to military status, the word "Auxiliary" was dropped, and the name was changed to Women's Army Corps (WAC) in September 1943. Army officials adhered strictly to Congress' instruction not to use military personnel to replace civil service employees. The Navy, on the other hand, managed to work around the congressional restriction by an arrangement in which the Assistant Secretary of the Navy would certify that civilians could not be found to fill vacancies in Washington offices, and WAVES were then assigned to those positions. By 1943 nearly a third of the entire organization was performing what was essentially civilian work in Washington.[66]

The official history of the Women's Reserve noted that "the strong weight of opinion in the Bureau among both men and women was that the officers as a body were not the indispensable part of the establishment that the enlisted were."[67] Officer recruiting was emphasized in the early months of the organization, but procurement efforts were handicapped by "completely inadequate information on the jobs which women were supposed to do."[68] An oft-heard complaint was that the WAVES officer corps contained "too many school teachers."[69] As teaching was the major professional field open to women at the time, that was no surprise. The real problem was the Navy's own vagueness as to what skill sets it needed. An initial emphasis on "experience" resulted in the accession of a large percentage of older women, many of whom lacked the flexibility of temperament to adapt to a military organization. Younger women attracted by recruiting appeals weighted heavily toward glamour and adventure performed well at indoctrination school, but their lack of work experience and special skills posed problems for assignment. Through trial and error, the Navy eventually realized the ideal officers were women between the ages of twenty-five and twenty-nine. These women possessed both "flexibility of character and useable experience." But they were also the hardest to recruit due to the "increasingly attractive competing opportunities in commerce and industry or at other war effort jobs. . . . The same thing was true on the enlisted side, but the problems were less acute because jobs were on the whole more easily defined and subject to closer supervision."[70]

Initially, WAVES officials advocated opening all enlisted ratings to women, but BuPers rejected this proposal. Dispersing women over a wide range of ratings could pose problems in arranging transfers if there were small numbers of women occupying certain rates. In addition, "the sheer weight of traditional attitudes or prejudices as to what was 'women's work' limited the practical usefulness of some of the rates which were opened." For example, at some commands enlisted women rated as mechanics were not given the opportunity to utilize their skills. Misconceptions as to the nature of the duties associated with other ratings also led to disillusionment. Consequently, BuPers liberally approved WAVES transfer requests "in the interest of morale."[71]

The official history of the Women's Reserve concluded that "morale is integration."[72] Where the work on the station was peculiarly "Navy" and different from civilian jobs, working morale was good. But Navy officials failed to impress upon the many enlisted women engaged in routine office work that they were also important to the Navy's mission. The mingling of civil service and uniformed personnel on similar work continued to supply "irritating comparisons of pay, personal freedom, and inducements. The prime difficulty, however, was the failure to take adequate steps to 'sell' the jobs to be done."[73]

Despite these problems, the WAVES and the other women's services did provide essential support to the armed forces during the national emergency. The magnitude of their achievement can be appreciated only when it is placed within the context of the formidable obstacles they had to overcome—obstacles grounded in enduring assumptions about gender roles. Challenging and then changing those assumptions proved to be a painstaking and incremental process.

The members of the Navy's Civilian Advisory Council were completely uninitiated in all aspects of naval administration and operations. They had to learn through trial and error. WAVES director Mildred McAfee and her key assistants quickly developed the skills necessary to operate in a male-dominated organization. Campbell observed that women learned to "to form networks that would supply a stream of critical information that was otherwise unavailable," while supporting the career ambitions of the regulars they worked for and dampening "ambition and rank consciousness in their own ranks."[74]

Discussing the officer detailing process, the official history of the Women's Reserve noted that due to the "novelty of the program and the prejudices which it had met," considerably more time was spent on officer assignment than would have been necessary if the women had simply been assigned in terms of their function. The report concluded wistfully, "Time may of course bring about a further integration of women into national life as to render this sort of special treatment unnecessary, and to make it in the eyes of a later generation no more than an amusing relic of outworn cultural ideas."[75]

The evolution of women's roles in the military has been inextricably linked to fundamental changes in the social structures of American society. When looking back at the first part of the twentieth century from the vantage point of the twenty-first, the progress made by women in uniform seems insubstantial at first glance. But when juxtaposed against the barriers erected by the prevailing culture, attaining military status was a remarkable development. The militarization of women could not have been accomplished without the influence of the economic, social, and political developments that preceded it. Industrialization reduced the need for women's labor in the home, facilitating their entrance into the public sphere of wage work, higher education, and political and social activism. These changes were not universally welcomed. Since the inception of the Republic, women had been completely identified with the role of wife and mother, so that any deviation from that role was deemed a threat to the entire society and contrary to the will of God. The political and social advancement of women was widely regarded as a zero-sum equation. Advancement could be achieved only at the expense of women's traditional roles—a price that many men and women found unacceptable. The breadth and tenacity of this view posed formidable obstacles to women in every field of endeavor outside the home. Furthermore, the ideal of the True Woman and Republican Mother was among the cultural values that the leaders of the armed services perceived themselves sworn to defend, while practicing the profession of arms was the quintessence of the masculine ideal.

The roles of women in the military evolved as women's relationship to the state changed. The creation of the Yeomen (F) during World War I was an anomalous event, imposed upon a resistant institution by a strong-willed civilian leader. It presaged, but did not precipitate, the achievement of suffrage. Most of the women who served were not feminists. Just as religious values animated and justified the actions of Progressive Era women in political and social reform movements, patriotic values provided the justification for military women's breach of social custom. This was reflected in the symbolic use of the yeomen (F) in virago roles in addition to their material contributions to the war effort as clerical support. The experiment ended with the emergency and was not regarded by either service as a precedent to be followed.

Economic and political changes that began in the interwar era compelled the reassessment of women's relationship with the military. The attainment of suffrage and the feminization of certain sectors of the civilian workforce were developments that the Army and Navy could not ignore. Women demanded a substantive role in defending the state. They would no longer be content with knitting socks and sweaters for soldiers and sailors or staging patriotic pageants. But in their role as the conservators of society's traditional values, Army and Navy leaders found themselves caught between defending True Womanhood and Republican Motherhood and fending off the "New Woman," who seemed hell-bent on destroying the foundations of American society. The widening civil-military political and social schism was manifested in the discrepancies in the policies of the services' civilian leadership and the practices of the uniformed personnel.

As Secretary of War Baker sought to educate and gain the cooperation of politically influential women's organizations, his efforts were undermined by his own intelligence service. The Navy made no pretense of cultivating women's support. The ONI joined with Army intelligence in forging alliances with politically and culturally conservative civilian "patriots" against the men and women who sought to turn their world upside down. Undoubtedly many acted in the firm conviction that they were defending the most sacred values of society.

The halfhearted planning efforts of Army officials—and the total absence of planning efforts on the part of the Navy—emphasized uniformed officials' inability to reconcile their traditional ideas of women's roles and capabilities with the new reality. In an era of economic, social, and political upheaval, there appeared to be no middle ground concerning perceptions of women. As the congressional debates over the legislation to establish the WAAC and the WAVES demonstrated, there was a distinct line between reverence for the female sex and contempt. Reverence was reserved for wives and mothers—women who knew their place. Equating the female sex with frailties of mind and body, men simply could not fathom the idea of women in the military. The absurdity of the concept was so intuitively obvious to them that they had no compunction about expressing their views vociferously and publicly. Militarizing women corrupted the women and humiliated the men forced to serve with them.

Largely excluded from the formal channels of power, women both within and outside the military relied on informal personal networks and indirect influence to overcome these institutionalized prejudices. It is important to note, however, that none of the breakthroughs they achieved could have happened without the support of enlightened men in key positions. Rep. Edith Nourse Rogers' WAAC bill, as conservative as it was in conception, might never have passed without the personal support of Army Chief of Staff Marshall and Secretary of War Stimson. Margaret Chung's impressive lobbying effort was founded on a network of alliances with powerful men within the government and the military such as Representative Maas, Senator Willis, Rear Admiral Towers, and Lieutenant Commander McQuiston, whose trust and regard she won through a carefully cultivated image of domesticity into which she sublimated her personal feminism. That lobbying effort might yet have foundered had it not been for the personal intervention of Eleanor Roosevelt and her husband on behalf of the women of the Civilian Advisory Council.

Mildred McAfee also relied on an informal network of women and a few key men in powerful positions to operate within the hostile Navy bureaucracy. She and her assistants achieved remarkable results in standing up the organization in a short period of time, but they were less effective in achieving true integration for women into the Navy.

Nonetheless, the accomplishments of the WAVES were many and substantial. On the third anniversary of the Women's Reserves on 21 July 1945, the Navy issued a radio and press release recounting their contributions to the war effort. There were 86,000 women serving on active duty: approximately 8,000 officers and 70,000 enlisted WAVES posted at 900 shore installations throughout the continental United States and in the territory of Hawaii. An additional 8,000 women were in training or awaiting call to duty. WAVES constituted 18 percent of the total naval personnel assigned to shore establishments in the continental United States, serving in air stations, naval hospitals, district headquarters, Navy yards, and supply depots. In Washington, the release noted, "approximately 20,000 WAVES, almost twice the original enlistment goal proposed for the entire Women's Reserve, are serving in the Navy Department and the Potomac River Naval Command in the nation's capital. WAVES compose 55 percent of the uniformed personnel in the Navy Department in Washington."[76]

WAVES handled 80 percent of the work involved in the administration and supervision of the Navy mail service and constituted 75 percent of the total personnel in "Radio Washington," the nerve center of the entire Navy communication system. WAVES provided 70 percent of the manpower in BuPers. At the Indian Head rocket powder plant, responsible for 70 percent of the testing for all U.S. rocket propellant, WAVES completely operated the laboratory, manned one of the two firing bays, and did approximately half of the ballistic calculations.[77]

Seamen constituted the largest group of enlisted women, numbering approximately 24,500 and serving in a wide range of billets. Thirty-eight ratings were open to enlisted women, with approximately 14,500 serving as yeomen. They also served as storekeepers, radiomen, specialists, telegraphers, electrician's mates, cooks, bakers, and printers. One hundred women qualified as chief petty officers.

The Hospital Corps included some 13,000 enlisted WAVES who served as hospital apprentices or pharmacists' mates working in wards, clinics, and laboratories. Thirty percent of WAVES were assigned to naval aviation—repairing planes, packing parachutes, and collecting weather data. One thousand women served as Link Trainer instructors, giving lessons in instrument flying to approximately four thousand men a day. WAVES served as gunnery instructors and operated the Link celestial navigation trainers at seventeen naval activities. They also served as air traffic controllers and flight orderlies. Thousands of WAVES served in the Supply Corps and were responsible for outfitting the fleet and handling monthly transactions in the millions of dollars.[78]

Although it was not widely publicized at the time for reasons of national security, WAVES also made important contributions in the field of intelligence. Agnes Meyer Driscoll served as a Yeoman (F) in World War I.

Unlike Joy Bright Hancock, Driscoll did not put the uniform back on for World War II, but she continued working in the Office of Naval Communications as a civilian. An Ohio State University graduate who majored in mathematics, physics, foreign languages, and music, "Miss Aggie" was a brilliant cryptanalyst. She trained most of the naval officers who received the lion's share of the credit for the Navy's codebreaking accomplishments during World War II.

Rear Adm. Edwin T. Layton, Fleet Adm. Chester Nimitz's intelligence officer during the war, wrote of Driscoll in his memoir, "She not only trained most of the leading cryptanalysts of World War II, but they were all agreed that none exceeded her gifted accomplishments in the business."[79] Those accomplishments included making critical inroads into the Japanese fleet's operational code, JN-25, which the U.S. Navy exploited after the attack on Pearl Harbor for the rest of the war. Codebreaking was critical to the American victory over the Imperial Japanese Navy at the Battle of Midway.[80] Much in the same way that exceptional women like Hancock helped pave the way for the acceptance of women into the field of naval aviation, Driscoll and other female civilians working for naval intelligence organizations proved their value and opened up opportunities for thousands of Navy WAVES.

Cooperative faculty members at women's colleges helped recruit officers by recommending undergraduates believed to possess an aptitude for cryptanalysis as well as the maturity to observe strict security measures. The students worked in secrecy on weekly problems graded by Navy officers.[81] Candidates attended a three-month training course at Goucher College in Baltimore, Maryland, or Smith College in Northampton, Massachusetts. Of the 197 college women initially recruited, 74 survived the process to report for duty in Washington, DC.[82]

There were hundreds of other positions that did not require cryptology training. Six hundred newly inducted WAVES and two hundred men were sent to Dayton, Ohio, to help build and operate the Bombe machines used to decipher the German Enigma codes. The Navy constructed 120 of these machines, and WAVES operated them 24 hours a day, 7 days a week. Most of the WAVES involved in the Navy's communications intelligence efforts were assigned to the Naval Annex on Nebraska Avenue in Washington. By February 1944, nearly three thousand WAVES were stationed there.[83]

WAVES were also assigned to the Combat Intelligence Division of the Commander in Chief, U.S. Fleet (COMINCH) headquarters in the Main Navy Building on Constitution Avenue. Here they processed the "special intelligence" derived from decrypted radio intercepts and maintained a detailed plot of German U-boat operations in the Atlantic, enabling the Allies to plan operations to break the back of the German submarine offensive. The efforts of thousands of civilian and Navy women who provided critical support to the Navy's intelligence organizations during World War II have only recently received the recognition they deserve.

Capt. Henri Smith-Hutton served as fleet intelligence officer on the staff of COMINCH Adm. Ernest J. King at Navy headquarters in Washington. He recalled being approached by the flag secretary on behalf of the chief of naval personnel to inquire if Smith-Hutton was willing to accept the first cadre of ten women officers scheduled to arrive soon at headquarters "to set an example to the rest of the Department," noting they were all graduates of the "finest women's colleges." The objective was to have these women replace the regular Navy enlisted yeomen and quartermasters so those men could be sent to sea. Smith-Hutton enthusiastically agreed to "take any or all of them." The flag secretary seemed somewhat surprised by that response, "then he leaned back in his chair and said, 'Thank God!' apparently he had been to all the other sections in Headquarters and had been politely refused." Pleased with the performance of the first four WAVES officers assigned to him, Smith-Hutton accepted several more groups of women "and soon one entire office where we plotted submarine positions, with the exception of two male officers who were not qualified for sea duty, consisted of WAVE officers and enlisted personnel. . . . What we needed in that part of my office was brains. The women had them."[84]

Capt. Wilfred J. "Jasper" Holmes, deputy officer in charge of the Joint Intelligence Center–Pacific Ocean Area (JICPOA) in Pearl Harbor, spoke highly of one of his mine warfare analysts. Lt. Harriet Borland accurately plotted the location of Japanese minefields and the types of mines deployed near Japan's home islands, which enabled U.S. submarine forces to successfully attack enemy shipping and then escape. Holmes later regretted not inviting Lieutenant Borland to the sessions where the returning sub skippers related their experiences. "I would have enjoyed standing up to introduce to that group of hard-bitten submarine skippers a beautiful and talented woman who as a mine warfare intelligence officer, made significant contributions to their success."[85]

Women assembled and operated codebreaking equipment, helped build and run the libraries and information centers that held extensive repositories of collateral information that correlated with new material, and provided the context for analytical breakthroughs. They were pioneers in information warfare, a field that today is recognized as a warfighting discipline on a par with surface, submarine, air, and special warfare.

The experience of marine biologist Mary Sears is a testament to the depth of the resistance that even the most exceptionally qualified women had to overcome. Sears was one of two women on the professional staff of the Woods Hole Oceanographic Institute in Massachusetts. She also held academic posts at Harvard, Wellesley, and Radcliffe. In the late 1930s, the Navy began providing significant funding to civilian institutions for applied oceanographic research studies to support naval warfare operations. Sears' initial attempt to follow her male colleagues into the services was derailed by medical issues. She eventually secured a waiver to receive a commission. In June 1943, after some abbreviated officer training, Lieutenant (j.g.) Sears reported to the Navy Hydrographic Office. Its mission was to produce navigation charts and collect oceanographic data, and demand for its products was burgeoning.

The Hydrographic Office fell under the Bureau of Navigation, which in April 1942 had claimed it had no billets appropriate for women. Along with other Navy bureaus, however, the office was authorized by the Assistant Secretary of the Navy to reappoint for the duration of the war employees whose service had been terminated by the Civil Service Commission for acts of fraud.[86] The commission strongly resisted allowing military women to fill any civilian billets, but ultimately it had to surrender. As historian Kathleen Broome Williams archly noted, "Apparently there were not enough employees, or law-breaking ex-employees, to handle the increased workload."[87]

Within a year after Lieutenant (j.g.) Sears arrived at the Hydrographic Office in June 1943, there were 30 officers and 332 enlisted WAVES working 3 shifts 7 days a week. As head of the oceanographic unit, Sears oversaw the collection and analysis of research data from oceanographic centers to produce intelligence for operational planning. It is no exaggeration to state that the unit's work was critical to the war effort. In February 1946 the Hydrographic Office stood up a permanent Oceanographic Division, with Lieutenant Commander Sears as officer in charge. Sears observed in one of her reports, "Military necessity does not wait for explorers and scientists to accumulate sufficient information."[88] A corollary to that observation might be that military necessity does not wait for bureaucracies to jettison gender biases.

The exigencies of World War II compelled a certain measure of tolerance for women in uniform. Their inclusion in the ranks was justified by the national emergency, but their presence was not intended to be permanent. It was statutorily required that they would be discharged as rapidly as possible at the end of hostilities. Given that such a large percentage of women in both services had been engaged in tedious administrative work at installations and commands far removed from the action, and many had been given little sense that their contributions were important to the war effort, most welcomed the prospect of demobilization. Like the men, women were anxious to return home to their families or to start their own families. Despite all predictions, the upheaval of the war did not topple domesticity from atop the pantheon of cultural values and expectations for women.

The fact that women had so successfully taken over support functions within the Navy in such areas as communications, medical, administration, and supply, however, made their rapid demobilization problematic. It was not long before Army and Navy leaders realized there would be a continuing need for women in the peacetime military.[89] The rapid transition from hot war against the fascist Axis powers to a Cold War against expansionist communism would require larger peacetime military and naval establishments than had previously existed in America. The participation of America's women was required. The way that participation would be accepted set the stage for the next phase of the ongoing struggle—the integration of women into the regular components of the U.S. armed forces.

= Part II =
MARGINALIZATION

= 3 =
READY ABOUT
From Reserve to Regular Status

The utilization of women for war, if improperly developed, has certain dangerous implications for our way of life. This subject deserves the most careful and cautious study.
—Report of the Eberstadt Committee on National Security Organization to the Hoover Commission, 1948[1]

After hostilities ceased, the U.S. government went about the task of demobilizing millions of uniformed personnel with alacrity, although never quickly enough to satisfy a restless public. Because women in the Navy had so dominated the billets relating to personnel administration, logistics, and essential medical services, they could not be abruptly discharged as they had been following World War I. Some women had to be retained on active duty to facilitate the demobilization process and care for the wounded returning from overseas. In addition, even before Japan surrendered, America's strategic focus was shifting away from a hot war against fascism to a Cold War against communist expansionism. The postwar force comprised the largest standing peacetime military force in the nation's history. War plans anticipated the massive mobilization of personnel and materiel to wage another global war. Within this context, some military leaders thought it prudent to retain a small number of women on active duty to serve as a cadre for rapid expansion in the event of war.

Despite the important contributions military women made during World War II, the desirability of retaining women in the military during peacetime was not a foregone conclusion. Military women and their proponents had to fight to justify their continued presence in the armed forces. After the initial skirmish was won, a more protracted battle was waged in Congress over the terms of women's continued participation. At issue initially was whether women would participate as a gender-segregated corps (as in the Army during the war) or in a reserve component (the Navy's practice). A number of compromises were made to appease conservative legislators' concerns over the numbers, rank structure, and acceptable duties of female military personnel. These compromises resulted in restrictions that continued to relegate military women to second-class status within their respective services. In the ensuing decades, the restrictions on assignments coupled with recruiting and retention problems led to skepticism concerning the utility of women in the peacetime military. During the 1950s and 1960s, military women and their advocates were preoccupied with retaining their tenuous foothold within the services and justifying their existence to a dubious public. The core argument in favor of military women remained the need to retain a trained nucleus of personnel to provide the basis for rapid wartime expansion.

An ancillary argument related to the issue of conscription. Following the establishment of the first peacetime draft on 19 June 1948, some military women's supporters argued that enlisting more women for voluntary service would reduce the number of men drafted for involuntary service. During the House debate on the Women's Armed Services Integration Act, Rep. Overton Brooks (D-LA) argued that rejecting women who had proven themselves able and willing to serve in the armed forces would make it difficult to justify compelling men to serve.[2]

The extremely low ceilings imposed on the overall numbers of women in the armed forces minimized their impact on the men's draft. However, women's proponents argued that should it come to total mobilization, women bore some measure of responsibility to assist in the country's defense. Lt. Cdr. Winifred Quick Collins asserted that while American women were not educated to believe that as citizens they bore an obligation to defend the nation, their military service in peacetime would foster public acceptance of the idea. "In the next war without question all woman-power in this country will have to be quickly mobilized."[3]

Such appeals did not resonate with American women in general. All the services struggled to recruit and retain women, never coming close to the low ceiling of 2 percent set for women's participation in the total force. By the end of a difficult era for Navy women characterized by stagnation and retreat, political and economic changes in the civilian sector combined with manpower shortages in the armed forces began to affect Navy policies and provide Navy women with new opportunities and challenges.

As the Navy demobilized at the end of World War II, officials originally planned to demobilize the Women's Reserve separately to ensure its members would be mustered out within six months of VJ day, as stipulated in the 1942 legislation authorizing the creation of the Women's Reserve. The Navy quickly realized that the wholesale dismissal of the WAVES might not be in the service's best interest. The concentration of WAVES in stateside administrative and logistics billets and at the separation centers made their services critical to an efficient demobilization process. Rapid demobilization of WAVES would have disrupted the entire naval organization.[4] Therefore, Navy officials decided to demobilize the WAVES at the same rate as they were demobilizing men and extended their service through 1 September 1946. WAVES recruiting operations and training activities, however, were shut down except for hospital corps schools. All contracts for WAVES uniform items were cancelled immediately, resulting in a severe shortage by January 1946. The effect of these actions further convinced WAVES personnel that the Navy wanted them gone as quickly as possible, and most of them left as soon as they became point-eligible for separation.

The outflow of experienced personnel, male and female, precipitated a manpower crisis that threatened to derail Operation Magic Carpet, the Navy's effort to transport its men in the Pacific theater back to the

United States. The civil service alone could not provide sufficient personnel in separation centers to process the massive amount of paperwork for thousands of returning veterans.[5] In October 1945 the Navy offered spot promotions up to the rank of lieutenant commander for male officers who agreed to extend on active duty for six months. In January 1946 the Navy offered a similar inducement to enlisted WAVES to advance up to pay grade A if they remained on active duty until December.

The WAVES director, Capt. Mildred McAfee-Horton, was on record as opposed to assigning women to the Navy in peacetime.[6] Her own cost-benefit analysis indicated "that it was not in the best interest of the Navy to have women on active duty in time of peace." Among the reasons not to keep women on active duty were complications in sea-to-shore rotations for male sailors since women could not serve at sea; the need to provide for the morale and welfare of female personnel to maintain the same standard of efficiency; the costs of special recruiting and training programs for women; higher attrition rates for women during wartime; and the undesirable practice during the war of using Navy women to do the same jobs civil service workers refused to take due to bad working conditions. Since the Navy appeared to be determined on its course, however, McAfee-Horton circulated an initial proposal in BuPers for the postwar utilization of WAVES. The plan envisioned creating a permanent Women's Reserve, not to exceed five hundred officers between the ages of twenty-five and thirty-five. The plan did not provide for enlisted personnel. Membership would be entirely voluntary, and the officers would serve without compensation except for travel, housing, and subsistence expenses provided for two weeks of annual active-duty training. The plan did allow for the possibility of keeping a handful of women on active duty to administer the program. Those women would receive the same pay as their male counterparts. The women would complete correspondence courses during the year and spend their active-duty periods visiting various naval installations to "to be kept conscious of military needs and trends, and not have to be hastily and inadequately educated in the event of another war." Retirement (without pay) would be compulsory at age thirty-five, at which point the retirees could join civilian committees organized for publicity and recruiting purposes.[7] As the official history of the Women's Reserve later pointed out, however, this proposal overlooked a crucial lesson learned during the war: the effectiveness of enlisted WAVES had far surpassed that of the officers.[8] McAfee-Horton also worried that the peacetime Navy would not dedicate the same level of resources to ensure the proper supervision and care of its female personnel as it had during the war.

Since the postwar plan for the Women's Reserve anticipated that WAVES would be serving in gender-segregated units, Chief of Naval Personnel Adm. Randall Jacobs directed Captain McAfee-Horton to draft a proposed reorganization plan that would emulate the WAC's wartime organization. The WAC had been established as a separate corps of the Army, with its own chain of command, while WAVES were incorporated into the organization of the active-duty forces. McAfee-Horton's plan was circulated within BuPers for comment. Her proposal was essentially a rehashing of the original organization plan for the Women's Reserve from 1942. It did not specifically address how the women would be employed as peacetime reservists (e.g., monthly drills, annual training, correspondence courses, etc.); the section on utilization simply recapitulated the practices of the last war when members of the Women's Reserve were serving on active duty full time.[9]

Among the comments on McAfee-Horton's plan as it was circulated through BuPers was a memorandum from Lt. Christopher S. Sargent, USNR, that criticized her failure to consider two key differences between the organizations, one statutory and the other organizational. The statutory difference was that WACs could by law exercise military authority over male personnel specifically placed under their command. The organizational difference was that the WAC was its own corps, with its own chain of command, while "the military authority of the WAVES has never been established except in an exceedingly fuzzy state." Sargent concluded: "Integration into the Navy is not possible because the Waves cannot be given authority over male personnel."[10] Sargent's memo asserted that despite these perceived defects, it was too late to make radical changes in the WAVES organization and recommended no further organizational shifts be contemplated.

Planning for a postwar WAVES organization continued to assume the creation of a separate Women's Reserve. There were initially no plans to allow women to serve in the Regular Navy during peacetime. As the war ended, Navy officials began to receive queries from members of Congress about plans for the postwar utilization of women. The incumbent assistant director of the Women's Reserve proposed publishing a statement in the BuPers Information Bulletin "to forestall the flood of questions now being received in the Senate regarding the use of the WAVES in a postwar Navy," stating: "The Navy has no plans for the incorporation of women into the Regular Navy after the war."[11]

The concept of a postwar WAVES organization that closely paralleled the wartime organization prevailed with senior leadership. Vice Adm. Louis Denfeld, the new chief of BuPers, announced plans to ask Congress for permission to keep a WAVES component in the Naval Reserve as well as retain some WAVES needed in certain specialties on active duty. Vice Admiral Denfeld informed Congress that requests from the "various Bureaus, Boards and Offices of the Navy Department" indicated a need for 1,367 Reserve officers and 9,426 enlisted women to serve on continuous active duty. The requests were made "on the basis that the members of the Women's Reserve would comprise part of the peacetime allowances of the activities and that the assignment of women would be made in place of male personnel, not in addition to them."[12]

In March 1946 Rep. Carl Vinson (D-GA), chair of the House Committee on Naval Affairs, introduced H.R. 5915 "To amend the Naval Reserve Act of 1938, as amended, so as to establish the Women's Reserve on a permanent basis and for other purposes." Testifying at a hearing on the bill on 9 May 1946, Vice Admiral Denfeld stated that while the Navy planned to assign "an appreciable number of officers and enlisted women to active duty in peacetime . . . whether we have them in the Regular Navy or the Reserves does not matter." Denfeld's view was not shared by Capt. Jean Palmer, the newly selected incumbent director of the Women's Reserve, who asserted that "the women would rather be in the Regular Navy."[13] Palmer's position was endorsed by another member of the Naval Affairs

Committee, Rep. Margaret Chase Smith, one of two female representatives who had been chosen for assignment to the House military service committees by House Minority Leader Joseph Martin (R-MA). (Clare Booth Luce [R-CT] was named to the House Military Affairs Committee.) Martin noted that "in singling out the women members for these assignments, the committee was guided by a realization that the women of the country take an important part in the war effort."[14]

As we have seen, Smith was a strong advocate for women in the Navy. In 1944 she sponsored a bill with Rep. Frances Bolton (R-OH) to give regular commissions, as opposed to "relative rank," to Navy and Army nurses. After three years of sustained effort, Smith eventually prevailed. She also succeeded at providing Navy women the opportunity to serve overseas (the Army had assigned women overseas throughout the war). Although Smith wanted women's overseas assignments to be unrestricted to best serve the Navy's needs, she "had to settle for a compromise bill that only allowed Navy women to serve in overseas assignments in the 'American Area' (North and South America, Hawaii, Alaska, the Canal Zone, and the Caribbean)."[15]

The legislation to establish the postwar Women's Reserve incorporated several of the points for which Smith had fought in previous legislative battles. It repealed the provision that restricted women's service to the duration of the national emergency plus six months. It allowed women to exercise supervisory authority over men, although strictly in an administrative capacity. Women could not exercise disciplinary authority over male sailors. Women would be permitted to travel outside the continental United States at the discretion of the Navy Department and would receive the same benefits as men except for dependent's benefits (the operating assumption being that women were by nature and social custom dependents).

Support for the provision to restrict women strictly to reserve status was justified by some proponents of the original bill to prevent women from counting against the Navy's total authorized active-duty strength. While women could be called to unlimited active duty on a strictly voluntary basis, they would be sent home when no longer needed. Male Reservists, as had always been the case, would remain in reserve status until involuntarily recalled to active duty for a national emergency. The effect of this proposed arrangement was to exploit the services of members of the Women's Reserve while denying them the status and benefits of a full-time career. This construct for the participation of women in the postwar Navy is reminiscent of Madeleine Vinton Dahlgren's admonition that Navy daughters should be "useful and contented in the sphere in which they were placed." The inherent inequity of this arrangement was apparent to other members of the Naval Affairs Committee, who pressed Vice Admiral Denfeld to explain "why the Navy did not ask for legislation to provide for the enlistment and commissioning of WAVES in the Regular Navy instead of just the Reserves?" Denfeld reiterated, "I have no objection to which way we have them, as long as we have them." Chairman Vinson, however, asserted that putting women in the Regular Navy was "a nice way for women to get killed. . . . You have got to recognize the fact that the Navy is a fighting military organization, and I think we are going a long ways to put them in the permanent Reserves and to call them when we need them."[16]

Navy officials had previously queried the WAVES still serving on active duty to gauge their interest in remaining in the Navy in their present circumstances. The results were not promising. An April 1946 memorandum noted that of the 1,467 enlisted WAVES currently attached to the Office of the CNO, only 815 expressed a desire to remain on active duty until September, and only 38 were interested in staying until July 1947. Among the reasons the women gave for their lack of interest were

1. Uncertainty of a business future if release delayed until mid-1947.
2. Hope of marriage to returning veterans greatly handicapped if remaining in the service.
3. Uncertainty of being actually retained beyond demobilization period.
4. Dislike of regimentation regarding quarters and hours.
5. Natural feminine desire for costume change after working hours.

6. Inability to obtain more interesting assignment if enlistment was extended; principally among which is a dislike of night watches.
7. General uncertainty as to the future for WAVES in the postwar Navy.
8. Feeling on the part of many that assigned job is unimportant—that their talents are not being employed to fullest.[17]

Capt. Jean Palmer, who succeeded Captain McAfee-Horton as director of the Women's Reserve in February 1946, had initially supported her superior officer's view that women were not needed in the Regular Navy during peacetime. As it became apparent that the Navy did need a substantial number of women to serve on active duty after the war, Palmer became an advocate for full permanent status. Commenting on the CNO's memorandum, Palmer noted, "A career in the Reserve offers no security and the women are not willing to sign up for jobs with such disadvantages when they have no assurance that they will have the advantages a Regular Navy career offers."[18]

Representative Smith would not be swayed from her insistence on permanent status for women in the Regular Navy. She stated pointedly, "Mr. Chairman, I feel that the women of the Naval Service have done an excellent job. I think that they know we feel that way, and I think we do not have to enact legislation to show our appreciation. The Navy either needs these women or they do not, and I would have a vote on that." Smith then proposed an amendment to the bill that would grant women permanent status in the Navy and Marine Corps and their reserve components "in the same manner and under the same circumstances and conditions as such laws or parts of laws apply to the appointment and enlistment of men."[19]

Vinson was not happy about Smith's proposed amendment. When it came up for a vote, he warned the other members of the committee that if they voted in favor of it, "you are killing the whole thing here." Nonetheless, the amendment passed by a vote of ten to two. Vinson refused to call a floor vote on the bill, and it languished in committee and died when the 79th Congress adjourned. An Army-sponsored bill to establish a postwar WAC organization met a similar fate in the Military Affairs Committee.[20]

When Congress next convened, the intervening election had wrought some changes. The Republicans won majorities in both houses of Congress, changing the composition and leadership of the armed services and the congressional committees. The defense unification process led to the Army and Navy combining their legislation proposing permanent status for women into one bill. The previously separate Naval Affairs and Military Affairs Committees in both houses of Congress were consolidated into Armed Services Committees. The new legislation was introduced in the Senate first as S. 1641, the Women's Armed Services Integration Act of 1947.

Capt. Joy Bright Hancock, who relieved Captain Palmer as the director of the Women's Reserve in July 1946, was instrumental in preparing the Navy's case before Congress. Early on during the Senate subcommittee hearings that ran from 2 to 15 July 1947, members of the subcommittee raised concerns about women being "incapacitated" by menopause. Hancock requested a detailed official statement from the Navy's surgeon general, which Vice Adm. Thomas Sprague, chief of the Bureau of Personnel, read into the record at the hearing. The surgeon general's statement refuted the idea that menopause "invalided" women and shocked the senators by noting that men pass through a similar physiological change. Hancock noted that thereafter, members of Congress would jokingly accuse each other of suffering from the effects of menopause.[21]

In her autobiography Hancock expressed her gratification for the support of senior Army and Navy officials for the legislation. CNO Fleet Adm. Chester Nimitz, who had not supported the creation of the Women's Reserve at the outset of the war when he led the Bureau of Navigation, admitted his error after watching the WAVES in action. The Navy had carefully studied its requirements and determined that it needed the skills its women had to run the organization efficiently.[22]

The bill passed the Senate on 23 July 1947 and was referred to the House committee. Navy officials anticipated much rougher sailing in the House, which did not take up the bill for consideration until the next session, in February 1948. The Navy's strategy was to have the senior male leadership testify on behalf of the legislation to emphasize its importance for fulfilling the needs of the service.[23] A stellar lineup testified in favor of the bill, led by Secretary of Defense James Forrestal, Chief of Staff and General of the Army Dwight D. Eisenhower, CNO Adm. Louis E. Denfeld, and Vice CNO Vice Adm. Arthur W. Radford. The chiefs of Supplies and Accounts, Medicine and Surgery, and Naval Communications added their support.[24] All spoke with the conviction of the converted. Army and Navy officials alike emphasized the necessity of giving the women status in the regular forces, stressing two major themes. First, women were particularly well suited for certain jobs and performed them better than most men. Many of these jobs were in the fields of aviation, naval communications, and intelligence, but most were administrative, medical, and clerical in nature. In his testimony before the committee, Rear Adm. Earl E. Stone, Chief of Naval Communications, reiterated a point made by others: "In work requiring manual dexterity and in long-continued performance of routine exacting tasks, the [WAVES] are equal or superior to men."[25] When some members of Congress contended that civil service workers could do the same jobs at less expense to the government, the service leaders pointed out that there were ceilings imposed on the number of civil service workers that could be hired, and even if the ceilings were raised, military personnel were not subject to the same constraints as civilians in terms of limited work hours and overtime pay requirements. General Eisenhower noted that military women were highly motivated, willing, and able to work the same long hours as their male counterparts. "They are there longer hours doing the work, but they are doing it voluntarily. You practically cannot run them off."[26]

Some opponents of regular status for women, most notably Rep. Carl Vinson, seized upon the economy argument to bolster the case for keeping the women of all the services in a reserve status, to be called as needed, without incurring the costly benefits that would accrue to the government if they had regular status, such as retirement and promotion to more senior ranks. Secretary of Defense Forrestal mounted a forceful defense against this proposal, arguing that no organization could reasonably expect to achieve its mission if people performing identical work with equal responsibility were treated inequitably. If women were not given the same status and benefits as men, the services risked losing the most competent women. "Unless there is such a nucleus of women in the Regular services there will be no springboard from which to launch a mobilization program for women."[27]

Despite the overwhelming support of the services' senior leadership, diehard opponents of permanent status for women in the peacetime armed forces nearly succeeded in derailing the bill. When it reached the Organization Subcommittee of the House Armed Services Committee, it encountered strong opposition led by the chair of the full committee, Rep. Walter G. Andrews (R-NY).

When the same lineup of senior leaders repeated their testimony in favor of the legislation, Andrews tried to further postpone consideration of the bill, imploring the service chiefs to reconsider reserve status only. He cited "considerable, not antagonism, but antipathy" to women being brought into the regular services on the same basis as men. "The history of the army shows that at one time exactly the same argument was brought up with respect to doctors, dentists, and chaplains," Eisenhower replied. ". . . We have long since outgrown that and I believe that that type of argument no longer has any validity."[28]

Despite the service leaders' unanimous support, the bill emerged from the House subcommittee with the provisions for regular status stripped out. The bill was forwarded to the full committee, where it passed by a vote of twenty-six ayes, one present, and Representative Smith's lone nay.

With the opponents of regular status believing they had won the day, the House committee listed the bill on the consent calendar to expedite its passage. This proved to be a tactical error that Smith exploited to full advantage. The consent calendar is usually reserved for noncontroversial bills reported out of committee with unanimous approval whose passage is anticipated without amendment. Therefore, a single objection can prevent the bill's consideration. As soon as the House clerk called the bill, Smith objected. Rep. Paul Shafer (R-MI) accused Smith of killing the bill. In a formal statement, Smith accepted responsibility, retracing the history of the legislation through both houses, arguing that such a discriminatory bill would not attract women with the competence that the armed services required. She concluded, "It is better to have no legislation at all than to have legislation of this type." She forced the committee to send the bill to the House floor for debate.[29]

During the ensuing floor debate, Smith proposed three amendments to the bill, only one of which carried. The first amendment was intended to force Congress to acknowledge the true nature of the legislation by changing its name from the "Women's Armed Services Integration Act" to the "Women's Armed Services Reserve Act," which was approved. The second amendment was a ploy to compel the Senate to revisit the issues by incorporating just enough changes necessitated by the Unification Act in the rejected Senate version of the bill to allow it to be reconsidered as a new amendment. This amendment was rejected by the Committee of the Whole. Her final amendment was an effort to force recalcitrant foes of regular status to face up to the consequences of their opposition by severely limiting the number of women who could serve on active duty at any one time to ten officers and twenty enlisted women. Historian Janann Sherman noted that Smith's "speech highlighted the speciousness of using women in unlimited numbers for unlimited periods of time while naming them to a contrived reserve, when the men's reserves were defined as inactive."[30] This amendment failed as well, but Smith had succeeded in forcing a floor vote in the full House.

The bill was sent to a joint conference committee where Senate proponents of regular status for women would have one more opportunity to influence the bill. While the committee was considering the bill, Smith was infuriated to learn that the services' legislative and liaison officer representatives had met with members of the committee "behind closed doors and in executive session" to oppose regular status for women as being too expensive. She cited as proof Rep. Dewey J. Short's (R-MO) statement the day before reviving the menopause argument, in which he claimed that "with the physical disabilities of illnesses that result [from menopause], the cost of the program would be stupendous if not prohibitive."[31]

In a letter to Secretary of Defense Forrestal, Smith demanded to know the identity of the service representatives who met with the committee.

In reply Forrestal reassured Smith of "the strenuous efforts which the legislative liaison officers of all the services have been making to get this legislation enacted in such form the women will be given regular status in the armed forces." He reminded her of the unanimous testimony he and the service chiefs had given in favor of regular status and forwarded copies of his letter to members of the joint conference committee.[32]

The joint conference committee restored the provisions to grant permanent status to women in the regular components of the armed forces. The House sergeant at arms was required to close the doors to the chamber and track down absent members to secure a final vote. The House passed the bill on 2 July 1948 by a vote of 206 to 133, with 91 members not voting.[33]

Representative Smith's tenacity and tactical acumen had won the day. On 12 July 1948, President Harry S. Truman signed the Women's Armed Service Integration Act (P.L. 625) into law. For her successful advocacy on behalf of Navy women, an admiring press awarded Smith the sobriquet "Mother of the WAVES," which followed her throughout her legislative career.[34] This characterization was inaccurate on two counts; first, the legislation for which Smith had fought actually effected the *dis*establishment of the WAVES as an official organization, as women were now technically integrated into the active forces with permanent military status (Navy women were called WAVES well into the 1970s, even though that organization ceased to exist in 1948). Second, if any legislator deserves to be acknowledged as the "parent" of the WAVES, that title rightfully belongs to Rep. Melvin J. Maas (R-MN), who had sponsored and advanced the legislation in 1942 that established the Women's Reserve (at the behest of Dr. Margaret "Mom" Chung). Smith was so sensitive on this point that she placed a statement with her official papers giving Maas his proper due. The cover memo on the statement directed, "When any questions come in either by personal interview or letter, be sure that we use the attached statement in explanation of the origin of the WAVES. THIS IS VERY IMPORTANT":

> As much as I would like to claim the honor and privilege of having been the "Mother of the Waves," I cannot do this, as the man who

really started that movement was a Representative Melvin Maas of Minnesota. He had a wife and daughters and was the one who did most of the work on this. He claimed to be the "Father" of the WAVES. It is true that he was the one to promote the program and deserves great credit. . . . I send this along to you only that you may know the true story.[35]

Nonetheless, Smith had won a major victory for women in the Navy in her own right. Now it was up to the leaders of the service to work out the details of the terms on which women would serve in the Regular Navy. In August 1948, two months after President Truman signed P.L. 625, Navy officials convened a conference of all the district and air command directors (W)—the senior women officers responsible for WAVES personnel at installations across the country. The conference provided an overview of the provisions of the Women's Armed Services Integration Act. Among the key provisions were several restrictions that effectively relegated women to a marginal status. The maximum enlisted strength for women in all the services was capped at 2 percent of enlisted male strength. There was also a ceiling placed on the number of women Navy officers for the next two years at five hundred commissioned officers and twenty warrant officers, to be brought into the service incrementally. The highest permanent rank a woman could attain in the Regular Navy was capped at commander. A woman lieutenant commander or commander who was selected to serve as the assistant to the chief of naval personnel (a post analogous to the director of the Women's Reserve during World War II) would hold the temporary rank of captain while serving in that position. Women were not allowed to serve on aircraft engaged in combat missions or on board ships other than hospital ships and naval transports, where they served as medical staff or administrative staff caring for wounded sailors or dependents of Navy personnel, duties considered traditional for women.[36] Carl Vinson was adamant on imposing those restrictions by amendment during the debate in Congress. "I think . . . somewhere in the bill we should write a provision . . . that no enlisted personnel or no officer of the WAVES or the Marines can serve aboard ship, except on a hospital ship. Of course, you can serve at shore establishments, but they have no place at all on ships."[37] During the discussion of the precise wording of the amendment, Vinson said, "I would not want to restrict it to combatant vessels. Put down 'serve in sea duty.' You have auxiliary ships as well as combat ships. Just fix it so they cannot go to sea at all." After a Navy official explained that the Navy hoped to use WAVES on board some transport ships carrying dependents in addition to hospital ships, to free Navy nurses from those administrative duties, Vinson relented and allowed exceptions for hospital ships and transports.[38]

In her comments to the conference, Cdr. Louise K. Wilde drew a maternal analogy to describe the challenges that lay ahead, referring to "the twins, Nucleus and Status": "Status" required constant nourishment and nurturing to develop into a "real Regular Navy person." "Nucleus" must develop diverse capabilities to ensure "that in time of national emergency she can take on the training assignment of her many cousins who would be called to join her."[39]

The new status conferred upon Navy women by P.L. 625 meant they were no longer separate from the rest of the Navy, but they certainly were not equal. The legal prohibition that kept women from serving at sea effectively marginalized their contributions to the main mission of their service component. One of the lessons Navy officials had learned from the experience with the Women's Reserve in World War II was that the women's morale was highest when the jobs they were performing were distinctively Navy in character, because they felt that they were making a unique and important contribution to the service and the nation. With that in mind, the officials developing the new methods for the training and administration of Navy women tried to introduce policies and procedures that would more closely emulate male sailors' experience, with limited success. The training program for women line officers, for example, entailed completing a five-month course at the General Line School in Newport, Rhode Island, half the time that their male counterparts were required to attend. The difference in the length of the courses was explained in terms of the "difference in aims and subject matter." Subjects of study for women included

Intelligence	10 hours
Organization and Logistics	100 hours
Naval History	20 hours
Military Law	80 hours
Personnel and Leadership	90 hours
Foundations of National Power	30 hours
Aviation	10 hours
Communications	60 hours
Operational Orientation	20 hours
Physical Education and Military Drill	200 hours

The officer corps in the U.S. Navy is divided into the categories of unrestricted line officers, restricted line officers, limited duty officers, staff corps, and warrant officers. Unrestricted line officers are authorized by law to exercise military command at sea. Restricted line, limited duty, and warrant officers are specialists in fields such as engineering and intelligence who may go to sea but are not authorized to exercise command at sea. The staff corps includes supply and medical officers, lawyers, dentists, and chaplains. Although some women officers were designated general unrestricted line officers, they were legally prohibited from serving at sea, so many of the topics that male line officers had to study—such as seamanship and navigation, and ordnance and gunnery—were not relevant. On the other hand, women officers attending the Navy's Supply Corps and Medical Service Corps training schools were fully integrated with their male counterparts because their duties were identical whether serving at sea or ashore.[40]

Enlisted Navy women received their training at the newly established Camp John Paul Jones at the Naval Training Center in Great Lakes, Illinois. Their course of instruction lasted ten weeks and included classes in history, current events and citizenship, ships, aircraft and weapons, organization, personnel, Navy jobs and training, military drill, physical training, hygiene, and first aid. Also included was a "surprise package— approximately five hours devoted to the topic 'On Being a Lady.'" John Paul Jones' name was invoked to justify this extra course of instruction because he had "stressed the need of service for gentlemen—defined as men of liberal education, refined manners, punctilious courtesy, and the nicest sense of personal honor." (The quote was excerpted from "Qualifications of a Naval Officer," an essay attributed to Jones that was in fact written by August C. Buell in 1900 in his biography of Jones. Attempts to rectify the origin of the quote have met with limited success because generations of naval officers were weaned on it and their emotional attachment to the sentiments expressed outweigh any perceived need for historical accuracy.)[41] Enlisted men received no comparable course of instruction in proper comportment during their basic training.

During World War II, most WAVES remained at the same activity or in the same geographical area for their entire tour of duty. Navy officials decided to introduce a shore duty rotation policy for women on the same basis as the sea-to-shore rotation policy applied to male sailors. Sea-to-shore rotation was a sensitive issue. Since women could not go to sea, any shore billet they occupied was perceived to be at the expense of a male sailor, which had the potential to be a major cause of resentment. During the debate on the Women's Armed Services Integration Act of 1948, Rep. James Van Zandt (R-PA), who served in the Navy in both world wars as both an enlisted sailor and an officer and was a past national commander of the Veterans of Foreign Wars, argued this point in opposition to the legislation. "For every job ashore filled by a Wave officer you deny a male officer, who, after several years at sea, the right to come ashore and occupy such an assignment."[42]

Before the Women's Armed Services Integration Act was signed into law, Navy officials studied how the 4,500 women serving in enlisted ratings would affect the ship-to-shore rotation for men and found that the impact on male personnel would be less than 0.8 percent. On issues such as this, however, perceptions were often more powerful than reality. The perceived negative impact of women taking shore billets away from men would pop up repeatedly in ensuing years. As noted previously, the slander campaign against the WAC and the WAVES during World War II was inspired largely by the fact that women were being recruited to "free a man to fight." Not all military men were champing at the bit to go to the front lines then, and not all sailors were anxious to go to sea in the peacetime Navy.

The legislative battle for permanent status for women in the armed services coincided with the activities of the first Commission on Organization of the Executive Branch of the Government, chaired by former president Herbert C. Hoover. The Hoover Commission investigated the organization and operating procedures of the executive branch of the federal government and recommended organizational changes to promote economy, efficiency, and improved service. The commission operated through functional area task forces. Issues pertaining to military women were addressed by the Personnel Problems Committee of the Committee on National Security Organization, chaired by Ferdinand Eberstadt. In September 1948, the directors of the women's services participated in a conference with Matthew Radom, the chair of the Personnel Problems Committee. The group developed nine major recommendations concerning women in the military to be forwarded to the Eberstadt Committee. The importance of cultivating favorable attitudes toward military women by both the public and by military men was the overriding concern and was reflected in six of the nine recommendations. The recommendations included mounting a public relations campaign to "increase the prestige of women"; assigning them in large groups and providing special consideration for housing, recreation, and uniforming to ensure "their good welfare"; imposing uniform educational standards for women officers that would be higher than those required for men; and allowing women, even those without prior service, to participate in the reserve components. Such measures they hoped would win the support of "fathers, mothers, and boyfriends."[43]

The final report of the Eberstadt Committee reflected these concerns, noting that "the place of women in the armed services is not completely secure. Public acceptance of the new role of women is not complete nor are the men of the armed forces—or their wives—completely 'sold' on women in uniform." Since women served voluntarily, their successful recruitment "depend[ed] fundamentally upon the opinions of men in uniform." Successful recruitment could be achieved through a public information program that provided "a clear and dignified statement of the importance of women in uniform, their past accomplishments and future hopes."[44]

The report also noted that during the war, many military women had been placed in jobs that could have been filled by men or civilian employees, and admonished that "neither political or feminist considerations must be allowed to influence policies for the proper utilization of women in the armed forces."[45] Women were utilized in that way, of course, precisely *because* men and civil service employees were not available.

In order to protect women's "fragile" morale, the Eberstadt report recommended that they be assigned in groups of not less than fifty to a post and also cautioned that any "special privileges" accorded to female personnel bore potential for arousing male resentment. One example cited of the latter was the "the requirement that male enlisted men salute women officers." The fact that the rendering of respect to a female officer was considered a "special privilege" as opposed to standard military courtesy indicates how far women in the armed forces still had to go to achieve true equality.[46]

The closing paragraphs of the section of the Eberstadt Committee's report dealing with women in the national military establishment cautioned that the utmost care had to be exercised when considering the utilization of women. The authors questioned the motivations of the "publicists in uniform—who backed the introduction of women into the uniformed forces to glamorize war, to convert the arch opponents of war in the past, women, to the service point of view."[47] Members of the committee feared that the militarization of women could result in the militarization of American society, a development that would be antithetical to American values.

To decide which ratings would be made available to enlisted women in the peacetime Navy, officials applied a sea-to-shore ratio formula. In 1951, the established rotational policy for male sailors was five years at sea to two years ashore, expressed as a sea-to-shore ratio of 2.5 to 1. Rating availability for women was restricted to those ratings with a ratio lower than 2.5 so as not to disrupt scheduled rotation to shore billets for male sailors. Women were also excluded from sea-intensive and combat-related ratings. Under this formula, approximately 40 percent of shore billets were reserved for men. From the perspective of an enlisted male sailor, this reduction in the availability of shore billets from 100 to 40 percent could hardly seem equitable, even if the relatively small percentage of women serving in shore billets did not seriously affect male sailors' rotation rates.[48] Based on this formula, Navy officials identified twenty-one enlisted ratings in which women could serve:

AC	Air Controlman	LI	Lithographer
AE	Aerographer's Mate	MA	Machine Accountant
AK	Aviation Storekeeper	PH	Photographer's Mate
AT	Aviation Electronics Tech	PI	Printer
CS	Commissaryman	PN	Personnel Man
CT	Communications Tech	PR	Parachute Rigger
DK	Disbursing Clerk	SK	Storekeeper
DM	Draftsman	TD	Training Devices Man
DT	Dental Technician	TE	Teleman
HM	Hospital Corpsman	YN	Yeoman
JO	Journalist		

Twenty-eight ratings were originally authorized for women, but seven were eliminated by this study because they had an unfavorable sea-to-shore ratio for men.[49] These ratings included

AL	Aviation Electronicsman
ET	Electronics Technician
FT	Fire Control Technician
IM	Instrumentman
OM	Opticalman
RM	Radioman
SH	Ship's Serviceman

As for the assignment of women officers, it was planned "insofar as possible, to give these women opportunities to become experts in naval shore administration and to develop technical knowledge in at least two of the fields where women officers will be utilized, such as in Personnel

Administration and in Communications," where large numbers of women would likely be utilized in a national emergency. There were no restrictions on shore billets for women officers as long as they met the qualifications and the needs of the service. Other fields in which women officers could specialize included public information, naval justice, intelligence, languages, and management.[50]

After a protracted legislative battle, women in the Navy had finally earned regular status. They achieved recognition for the important contributions they had made to the war effort, but that recognition was something of a double-edged sword. They were lauded for their efficiency and facility in performing certain tasks better than their male counterparts, including some nontraditional jobs, but they were also prized for their ability to perform tedious, repetitive tasks under less-than-ideal conditions that men and civil service personnel preferred not to do. As Secretary of Defense Forrestal noted in his testimony before Congress, "In wartime you had the appeal to every patriotic woman to render what service she could, [and] therefore, could attract and get these people of high competence. In peacetime, without the same status, the same pride of being in an organization, which is an intangible thing, it is difficult to do."[51] The first test of the nucleus concept would come quickly, with the outbreak of the Korean War in June 1950. There was no time for a shakedown cruise. Unfortunately, the statutory, cultural, and institutional restrictions imposed on Navy women would make it difficult for them to make any real headway.

= 4 =
BECALMED IN THE DOLDRUMS OF DOMESTICITY

General public apathy complicates the recruiting problem for women, and continued emphasis on the "public accep-tance" theme of military service as an acceptable career for women is believed to be the only way to counteract this national attitude.

—Cdr. Louise K. Wilde, December 1953[1]

The outbreak of the Korean War in June 1950 and the subsequent military manpower shortages led defense officials to step up mea-sures to augment American forces with new draft calls. Members of the reserve forces were recalled to active duty on both voluntary and involuntary bases, and for the first time, women were included. The involuntary recalls included enlisted Navy women with critical ratings such as hospital corpsmen (HMs) and storekeepers (SKs). An additional 15,000-plus female hospital corpsmen—nearly double the number from the previous year—were serving on active duty in June 1951.[2] Hospital corpsmen were enlisted medical technicians, while Navy nurses were commissioned officers. When the Navy Nurse Corps was first established, regulations mandated that nurses work no more than eight hours a day.[3] No such restrictions pertained to the enlisted HMs, who often put in much longer hours; and of course in the military there is no such thing as overtime. Many HMs served on Navy hospital ships in Korean waters, releasing their male counterparts to go ashore into the combat zone to serve with Marine Corps units, which did not have embedded combat medical personnel.

In addition to freeing up men to serve in combat, defense officials hoped that utilizing more women would reduce the number of draft calls for men. The Navy also suspended its policy of routinely allowing women who married while they were in the service to request and receive discharges. These policies led to some discontent in the ranks. As the fighting in Korea reached a stalemate, defense officials announced plans to reduce forces and release Reservists involuntarily recalled to active duty. One WAVES lieutenant wrote to Captain Hancock, the assistant chief of personnel for women, in May 1951 asking if consideration was being given to "unfreezing" the married women. She noted that several women at her command lost interest in their Navy careers soon after they were married and were showing signs of "emotional disturbance," adding, "I can't see where the Navy is gaining much by retaining these women." She also noted that while Navy nurses were working a standard eight-hour day, enlisted female HMs were working constantly, to the detriment of their stamina and morale. She ended her report with a plea for a WAVES administration officer to be assigned to her command. Policy designated such duties collateral; that is, assigned as additional to an officer's regular duties. The lieutenant asserted that "adequate supervision 'to ensure the maintenance of health, efficiency, morale and general welfare' has become a full-time job (and then some)."[4]

Hancock responded that the lieutenant's letter was "most timely" and that "each of the problems you presented . . . has been under active study for some time." She hoped that increased recruiting would compensate for the release of the Reservists and the married women. Regarding the proposal to lower the Navy's age for enlisted recruits from twenty to eighteen she noted, "I have recommended that this not be done, unless it is coupled with allocation of billets at places where there will be large concentrations of enlisted women for a full-time supervisory billet for a woman officer."[5] Navy officials eventually relented on the policy not to recruit women under the age of twenty. Both the Army and the Air Force had recruited eighteen-year-old women since 1948. The policy change brought more women into the Navy, but it also created a new set of problems in terms of retention and discipline.

Even as defense officials announced the first stages of a drawdown of forces for the Korean conflict, they also announced an ambitious plan to enlist an additional 72,000 women in the armed forces by June 1952. In October 1951 there were approximately 41,000 women serving in all branches of the armed forces. The Navy had ambitions of increasing its enrollment of women from 5,505 enlisted women and 906 officers to 10,000 enlisted women and 1,000 officers.[6] Just as they had in World War II, defense officials called on prominent and respected women in the civilian sector to help with the recruitment of quality women, raise the prestige of women in the services, and assuage the concerns of skeptical families, husbands, and sweethearts.

In 1950 Secretary of Defense George C. Marshall personally announced his appointment of Anna M. Rosenberg as assistant secretary of defense for manpower and personnel. A veteran of New York politics, Rosenberg had risen to prominence as a skilled mediator between businesses and labor unions on defense-related issues. She had also been a trusted adviser to President Franklin D. Roosevelt. Rosenberg was the first woman to hold a senior position in the Department of Defense. Her mandate was to support and lead a wide range of initiatives for the secretary of defense, foremost of which was an ultimately unsuccessful effort to implement a policy of universal military training. Rosenberg also actively supported President Harry S. Truman's executive order to end racial segregation in the services.[7] African Americans and women constituted two previously underutilized manpower sources that could help offset politically unpopular draft calls. To assist with the recruiting effort Rosenberg recommended establishing the Defense Advisory Committee on Women in the Services (DACOWITS), which comprised forty-nine distinguished former military and civilian women prominent in the fields of education, business, the arts, and politics. Among the more prominent members of the first DACOWITS were Sarah G. Blanding, president of Vassar;

Margaret Clapp, president of Wellesley; the stage actors Irene Dunne and Helen Hayes; Mrs. Nelson Rockefeller; Mrs. Ogden Reid, business manager of the *New York Herald Tribune*; Mrs. Arthur Hays Sulzberger; and Mrs. John Hay Whitney.[8] Rosenberg used her extensive network of business and professional contacts to enlist the support of the Advertising Council to air public service ads to educate young women, their families, and the public, "instill a sense of pride in serving the country, and urge educational institutions and civic organizations to cooperate with recruitment."[9]

Increasing the number of women in the military proved to be a formidable task. Domesticity remained firmly ensconced atop the pantheon of normative cultural values for women in the post–World War II era. Male servicemen returned to civilian life and careers in a booming postwar economy while women were expected to leave their wartime jobs, return home, and pursue the American cultural ideal of marriage and motherhood. Women and men married at a younger age and were having children sooner.[10] American women found themselves tightly constrained by gender roles founded on rigid misinterpretations of widely accepted concepts borrowed from various fields of social science that denigrated their sex and limited their potential. The popular currency of Freudian psychology, which portrayed women as inherently inferior and incomplete human beings, had a profound impact on the interpretation of gender roles. If, as Freud asserted, "biology was destiny," a woman who attempted to alter her "destiny" as a wife and mother was perverse. The child-rearing nostrums of Dr. Benjamin Spock dictated that a mother should devote herself full time and exclusively to raising her children. The pursuit of outside interests would put her offspring—and by extension society—at risk. The concept of functionalism borrowed from cultural anthropology was bastardized in its application to progressive educational policies, which channeled girls into a predetermined domestic future by creating courses in home economics, date appeal, marriage and family, and personal etiquette.[11] The Cult of Domesticity and Republican Motherhood was back with a vengeance—the former revalidated and reinforced with a veneer of broadly accepted pseudoscientific credibility, and the latter by the angst engendered by a Manichean struggle against communism and the fear of atomic annihilation.

President Dwight D. Eisenhower "himself acknowledged the family as 'a new element . . . in the total strength of the nation.'" Under the Eisenhower administration, the Federal Civil Defense Administration (FCDA) hired several female administrators "to educate the average wife and mother about her atomic-age responsibilities. . . . According to FCDA scenarios, nuclear families fought and won nuclear wars, providing . . . the symbolic unity and moral authority deemed critical to winning psychological victories over communism."[12]

In fact, when then–General Eisenhower testified before Congress in 1948 in favor of legislation authorizing regular status for women in the armed forces, he noted that accepting women into the regular components of the military should not incur significant additional expense to the government in terms of retirement benefits, because "ordinarily the enlisted individual will come in and I believe after an enlistment or two enlistments they will ordinarily—and thank God—they will get married."[13]

But for those who did dare to venture beyond the confines of the happy home, new opportunities beckoned. Labor demand generated by the postwar economic boom gave more women than ever entrée into the workforce. A history of the 1950s noted that "by 1956, 22 million women held jobs, a full third of all the jobs in the nation, and half of these female workers were married." A third of all working women were employed in clerical work.[14] Dorothy C. Stratton, former dean of Purdue University who served as director of the SPARS (women serving in the U.S. Coast Guard) during World War II, observed that when women compared well-paying civilian jobs to the demands of military life, they opted for the former. "Moreover, many young women take the position that if the nation should really need them in the armed forces, it would draft them."[15]

Indeed, Rep. Edith Nourse Rogers took to the floor in Congress to assert that she received many requests from women who wanted to enlist, and some appealed for a draft of women as well as men.[16] There was nothing stopping these women from volunteering to join the services if they so desired—except for fear of strong social disapproval. Compulsory service could help these women avoid uncomfortable confrontations with friends and family about their personal choices. But the idea of drafting women received no widespread political support and had no social appeal. Anna Rosenberg categorically rejected the idea of conscripting women and made her opposition clear to concerned members of Congress.[17]

After the Women's Reserve was established in 1942, Navy officials emphasized the importance of public information campaigns to promote the selectivity and prestige of the WAVES. But the DOD's national campaign to recruit women for all the services met with well-entrenched public skepticism.

In April 1951, Esther B. Strong, representative for women's interests and a staff member of the secretary of defense's Personnel Policy Board, asked the directors of the women's services to provide her with information. The North Carolina Family Life Council was requesting that the recruiting campaign—or worse, a draft of women—be held in abeyance until the "personality damage" military women had sustained from their wartime service was addressed. "If we can save even one girl, through our effort, from personality damage, or help in preparing her for the experience she will encounter, our efforts will not have been in vain."[18]

The Navy's senior uniformed female leaders, who had been fighting this battle since the creation of the Women's Reserve in 1942, were annoyed and frustrated by the council's request. Their frustration was succinctly expressed by Joy Bright Hancock's handwritten comments on a routing slip addressed to Louise K. Wilde, starting with the exclamation "Holy Cats." Hancock wrote that the council seemed ignorant of Navy policies for screening, recruiting, and training WAVES personnel. "I think they could well direct their concern to getting young women of N.C. prepared to meet life itself, the military being but one phase of that."[19]

The Defense Department's campaign to win public support for the idea of women serving in the peacetime military swung into high gear in November 1951. A key element of the effort was a media campaign to debunk long-standing prejudices and emphasize opportunities. Articles were published in the major women's magazines of the era.[20] *Mademoiselle* magazine included a survey to gauge young women's interest in pursuing a military career.[21] An article in the August 1952 edition of *Woman's Home Companion* was especially noteworthy for its blunt approach in directly addressing prevailing public fears and prejudices. Titled "Are Women in Uniform Immoral?" the article featured a photograph of eight smiling, attractive men and women from the four services linked arm-in-arm and striding confidently toward the camera. Above the head of each woman in the photo was a red arrow, pointing straight down. Above the photograph was a text box outlined in red:

YOU MAY HAVE HEARD
That any woman in uniform is on the make
That most girls who go into the service are tramps
That the girls who aren't tramps are abnormal

Beneath the photograph, printed in red italics: "No question, these look like fine young men and women. But then, why the tales of promiscuity and abnormality in our women's services? Here are the facts from the men who work with women in uniform."[22]

The article noted at the outset that the armed services were in the process of trying to recruit 72,000 women but that the drive lagged far behind in achieving its stated goals, primarily due to "the gossip prevalent in many areas of the country that any woman who puts on a uniform is immoral, promiscuous, or perverted—or will become so." The author quoted senior male officers and enlisted personnel from all branches of the services airing their views to the contrary. The article concluded with the comments of Air Force Chief of Staff Gen. Hoyt Vandenberg, who claimed the standards for admission to the armed forces for women were "perhaps even higher than for men," and that any woman who was deterred from enlisting by false rumors of immorality "is losing a chance for an exciting and rewarding career."[23] One of a series of articles about military women published in the *New York Journal American* featured the headline "Waves Find Stricter Moral Code in Boot Camp Than in Own Homes."[24]

Despite this concerted effort, none of the services met their ambitious goals. In her history of women in the military, Maj. Gen. Jeanne Holm,

USAF (Ret.), noted that the ill-conceived and poorly executed campaign foundered on unrealistic goals and a failure to appreciate the military and cultural contexts of the time. The higher accession standards and "cumbersome, time-consuming and expensive screening procedures to weed out possible 'misfits' . . . made it extraordinarily difficult to recruit women at all." Because the Navy and the Marine Corps had pursued a more conservative approach in their recruiting efforts, they fared somewhat better than the Army and the Air Force. By the spring of 1952, the Navy had 8,000 women on active duty, a 25 percent shortfall of its stated goal of 11,000. The Women's Air Force (WAF) fell 76 percent short of its goal of 50,000, peaking at 13,000. WAC numbers declined from 12,000 to 10,000.[25]

Authors Jean Ebbert and Marie-Beth Hall and historian Susan Godson asserted that the nucleus concept proved its worth despite the difficulties encountered in recruiting, retaining, and utilizing women during the Korean War.[26] Jeanne Holm's assessment was more critical and on the mark. She cited the inadequacy of the services' hastily updated mobilization and general war plans, which were predicated on two flawed assumptions: that large numbers of women would voluntarily enlist, and that the peacetime nucleus concept could facilitate the rapid mobilization of women for war. "World War II had proven the first assumption to be incorrect, and the experience of the fifties would prove the second to be invalid as well."[27]

The nucleus concept called for a cadre of experienced women officers with a broad professional background and enlisted women with a wide variety of technical skills on hand to train the influx of new accessions in the event of a major war or national crisis. In practice, the concept foundered on the statutory, institutional, and cultural restrictions imposed on women's utilization. Because they were not allowed to go to sea and were channeled into traditional administrative billets, women did not feel that they were making a direct contribution to the Navy's mission. There was little about their jobs that was uniquely Navy in character. Moreover, women tended to gravitate to the more traditional billets and ratings that paralleled the jobs of their female civilian counterparts—health care, administration, and supply.

At the conclusion of an armistice between North Korea and South Korea in June 1953, the Navy announced plans to gradually draw down the strength of women on active duty from 7,000 to 5,000 enlisted women, and from 900 to 500 or 600 officers through the expiration of enlistments, adjustments in recruiting quotas, and the gradual release of senior Reserve officers from active duty.[28] The number of ratings in which women were eligible to serve declined from thirty-six in 1952 to twenty-five in 1956, to twenty-three by 1960. The Navy explained the narrowing of options as a "policy for the equitable and realistic training and distribution of enlisted women . . . in order to maintain our mobilization base."[29]

Even this diminished number of available ratings was deceptive, however. Approximately 90 percent of enlisted women remained concentrated in two occupational groups: administrative/clerical and medical/dental.[30] Retention continued to be a problem. The majority of losses during four- or six-year enlistments were for marriage and pregnancy. During fiscal year 1955, more than two thousand women were discharged for reasons other than expiration of enlistment. Eighty percent of the enlisted women who were discharged were separated for the convenience of the government for marriage, pregnancy, or early reenlistment.[31]

Retention of women was not the Navy's only problem, however. The Navy's overall reenlistment rate had plummeted from 65.6 percent to 8.1 percent since 1950. Although the Navy had proudly proclaimed itself an all-volunteer force for nearly a decade, in August 1955 the new CNO, Adm. Arleigh Burke, reluctantly asked the draft board to select 56,000 men for naval service by July 1956.[32]

The peacetime draft further diminished the Navy's incentive to develop a fully functional nucleus of women to serve as a cadre for the next major mobilization. On the enlisted side, the women's program was undergoing a leadership crisis precipitated by the DACOWITS-sponsored recruiting drive in conjunction with Navy leaders' decision to release married women from their active-duty obligation and to accept women as young as eighteen for enlistment. Ebbert and Hall observed that between 1950 and 1952 the percentage of experienced petty officers had plummeted from 40 to 17 percent, which meant that "for a larger and younger force, there were fewer veteran leaders and role models."[33]

The influx of less mature junior enlisted women combined with a dearth of female enlisted leaders invariably led to problems with morale and discipline. Although the number of disciplinary cases involving Navy women remained relatively small, the prevailing cultural double standards for women were reflected in the Navy's disciplinary procedures. In 1951, Joy Bright Hancock argued vehemently against a proposal to establish detention facilities for women in the armed forces, a policy contemplated within the context of a possible major mobilization that would bring large numbers of women who were not as selectively screened into the service. In addition to being economically infeasible, given the small numbers of women likely to require incarceration, her biggest concern was the indelible stigma any woman subjected to such punishment would suffer. The most efficient and humane course of action was to simply discharge problem personnel, because "the social system and social thinking of this country places a stigma on women who have been once imprisoned, which cannot be removed."[34]

Whereas a spell in the brig might induce a male sailor to mend his ways, a woman imprisoned for a similar offense would be beyond redemption or reform in the eyes of the Navy and society. Women were expected to exert a positive moral influence on their male counterparts. After all, a WAVE was "a woman among many men with a responsibility for femininity and upholding the dignity of womanhood."[35]

The Navy's effort to convince the public that Navy women exhibited the appropriate standards of personal and professional behavior consumed an inordinate amount of the energy and resources expended on the women's program in the 1950s and 1960s. In 1951 Hancock directed the establishment of the Women's Representative (WR) system, whose origins dated back to World War I. The WR (also referred to as a Wave representative) was a collateral duty assigned to a senior female officer at a command. In addition to her regular military duties, the WR advised the base commander on issues concerning the administration of female personnel under his jurisdiction. Sometimes, an officer would be designated to serve as a WR for more than one activity at an installation. The rationale for the WR system was to emphasize the importance of proper supervision of female enlisted personnel "in maintaining military appearance, conduct and the solution of other problems peculiar to women in the service."[36] Female officers were not eager to take on the extra duty that designation as a WR entailed. Like the lieutenant who had complained to Captain Hancock in May 1951, the responsibilities imposed upon the WR constituted "a full-time job (and then some)." WR assignments were, in fact, a direct contradiction to the stated policy that female officers' assignments were made "with the intent that they fill bona fide, legalized and not necessarily 'feminized' billets." One officer detailer noted, "You would be amazed at the number of people who say I don't care where you send me or what I do, but I want to get away from the women's program."[37] It is interesting to note that Navy nurses were for the most part exempted from having to serve collateral duty as a WR. Under an agreement Captain Hancock reached with the chief of the Bureau of Medicine and Surgery, nurses assumed WR as a collateral duty only if there was no other female line officer available to do so.[38] The demands of WR duty were deemed too onerous and disruptive of the nurses' primary duties.

Navy nurses and enlisted HMs were also exempted from the prohibition against sea duty. They were permitted to go to sea to staff hospital ships and transports carrying the dependents of naval personnel. In September 1953, the Military Sea Transportation Service (MSTS) authorized sixty-three billets for enlisted women on Navy transports who were not in medical ratings.[39] Their duties were to alleviate the burden on the HMs and nurses of performing administrative duties involved with caring for the wives and children of Navy personnel on board. An earlier effort to find billets for female line officers on transports was rejected. While there were billets on transport ships for officer specialists in the fields of communications and supply, for which women line officers were trained, one transport ship's commanding officer pointed out that "there are other duties required of Communications and Supply officers which could only be performed by male officers." These duties included supervising male enlisted personnel, Shore Patrol duties, underway deck watches, and "similar collateral duties for which women are not suited on board ship."[40]

These opportunities to go to sea, however limited, did not send enlisted women stampeding to the piers. In April 1958, the head of the detailing section (the office within BuPers responsible for assigning sailors to specific jobs, or billets) noted that "the list of eligible volunteers is seldom sufficient to take care of normal rotation and unexpected losses due to discharge on account of marriage and non-returnable hospitalization cases." In addition, "the detail officer's files contain no up-to-date information on duties and responsibilities of MSTS billets and there is nothing concerning advantages or disadvantages or opportunities to the individual."[41]

The latter issue was addressed by an article in the August 1958 edition of *All Hands*, the Navy's magazine for enlisted personnel. Stretching the truth to sell these seagoing billets to female HMs, the article claimed that "sea duty has become one of the most popular duties among the women in blue as the Wave Corpsmen long waiting list for ship board duty testifies." The article emphasized the opportunities to travel and to enjoy liberty in a variety of foreign ports. The description of the seagoing HM's duties, however, made it abundantly clear that there was little "uniquely Navy" about the job. The HMs cared for dependent wives and children; manned the formula room, where there might be "as many as fifty infants on board, each with a different schedule"; assisted the medical officer during dependent sick call; and stood watches when female dependents were admitted to the infirmary.[42] Assuming that women who risked social ostracism to join the Navy did so at least partly out of a desire to escape the dictates of domesticity in the civilian world, it doesn't take much imagination to understand why serving as a 'round the clock nursemaid to someone else's wife and children on a ship from which there was no escape for "down time" would lack appeal.

In July 1961 Lt. Charlene Suneson became the first woman line officer to receive a seagoing assignment to an MSTS transport when she was ordered to USS *General W. A. Mann* (AP 112) as the ship's transportation officer. "If they don't send any more women to sea, you'll know why," she quipped to a *Navy Times* reporter on her status as a trial balloon.[43] Unfortunately for the lieutenant, her tour was not a success. She reported on board enthusiastically "with a footlocker full of seagoing pubs such as Knight's *Modern Seamanship*, Bowditch tables, nautical almanac, etc.," and expectations of underway watch duty. Instead she was assigned as an assistant to the ship's transportation officer and performed the duties of a "seagoing purser."[44] Her palpable disappointment, combined with complaints from some of the passengers with whom she interacted, led to poor fitness reports that prematurely terminated a promising Navy career. As Ebbert and Hall observed, "Only after another eleven years marked by great social changes would the Navy order women to ships."[45]

There were some modestly positive developments during this period, mostly relating to advanced training for women officers that reflected changes in American society, such as the increasing enrollment of women in colleges and universities.[46] In 1950 the Navy announced the Reserve Officer Candidate (ROC) program as a new path to a commission for both men and women. Qualified college students would spend six weeks in training during the summers following their junior and senior years, earning a Reserve commission, and then report for active duty.[47]

In 1955 the General Line School of the Naval Postgraduate School in Monterey, California, accepted the first contingent of thirteen female officers as students for advanced professional education. Their course electives included Electronics, Tactics, Nucleonics of the Navy, Aerology, ABC Warfare Defense, Psychological Warfare, Harbor Defense, International Law, Operational Planning, and Combat Information Center Training.[48] Professional educational opportunities were further expanded in 1958 when female officers were allowed to enroll in the Department of Defense Intelligence School in Washington and could be sponsored to take courses at civilian universities such as Harvard and George Washington University to earn professional degrees in fields such as business administration and comptrollership.

Additional opportunities to earn a commission were extended to enlisted women and men. In 1953, enlisted personnel with at least two years of college were encouraged to apply for commissions; the opportunity was formalized in 1955 as the Seaman to Admiral Program. The "five-term program" introduced in 1958 allowed enlisted sailors who were able to complete an undergraduate degree program in five semesters to go to school full time. Another path to a commission for enlisted members with advanced technical skills and aptitude was the Naval Enlisted Scientific Education Program (NESEP). The Navy paid tuition for highly qualified sailors to earn technical degrees at twenty-two civilian institutions while on active duty.[49] Women capable of riding the crest of the wave of advancing technology stood the best chance of breaking out of gender-stereotyped naval careers.

Completing a full twenty-year career, however, was a dimming prospect for many women officers by the mid-1950s. The provisions of the Women's Armed Services Integration Act of 1948 imposed percentage ceilings on the number of women who could serve in the various commissioned ranks. Only one female captain was allowed; commanders were capped at 10 percent of overall female officer strength, and lieutenant commanders at 20 percent. This policy resulted in a "hump" at the grade of lieutenant in the women's officer structure. Many of these officers were World War II veterans. Lieutenants who failed selection for promotion to lieutenant commander after thirteen years of active service were to be separated from the Navy with severance pay. The differences in the promotion systems for male and female officers threatened to strip the ranks of experienced women officers who would be forced out prematurely.[50]

While the Navy was authorized to have thirty-two women commanders on active duty in 1956, it had only nine. In contrast, the Army had forty-nine women serving in the equivalent rank of lieutenant colonel; the Air Force had fifty-four; and the Marine Corps, the smallest of the services, had six. The Navy promoted female officers more slowly than the other services to maintain parity in the length of service requirements with their male counterparts.[51] But lower ceilings were imposed on rank and age for women officers. Navy officials reasoned that since the top grade for a woman officer was commander (except for one captain, the temporary rank held by the assistant chief of naval personnel for women) the time-in-service requirement correlated to that of a male admiral. While a male lieutenant commander could serve until age sixty-two before being forced out, a woman could only serve until age fifty. A female commander got an additional five-year reprieve, but that was still seven years fewer than her male counterpart. Rather than following the promotion practices of the other services and promoting women to fill all thirty-two available commander billets, the Navy introduced remedial legislation in Congress that enabled the service to carry down any unused commander billets into the grade of lieutenant commander. The time-in-service limit for female lieutenants was extended from thirteen to fifteen years.[52] These measures provided only a temporary solution, delaying force-outs until 1959.[53] President Eisenhower signed the bill, H.R. 8477, into law as P.L. 585–84 in June 1956. While Reserve and temporary officers counted in the grade limitations for male officer promotions, they did not affect the women's grade limits. So women officers were encouraged to increase their overall line strength by convincing more junior officers to augment from the Reserve into the regular component of the Navy in order to justify more billets at the senior ranks.[54] That proved to be a hard sell. Throughout the 1950s and 1960s, promotion rates for female officers remained well below those of their male counterparts.[55]

The Lucas Board, an internal informal study of Navy policies and procedures governing the assignment of officer and enlisted personnel conducted in 1961 for the CNO, illustrated the conundrum confronting Navy women. The limitations imposed on the duties and assignments women officers could perform led the members of the board to conclude that the number of women officers accepted for postgraduate education should be significantly reduced. The board also recommended that the tours of duty for both women officers and enlisted personnel be extended. For officers, the board recommended tours be extended from three years to four or more. The board did not stipulate a specific length for enlisted tours, merely noted that they should be "longer." The Lucas Board's overall conclusion was that the Navy's rotation policies for officers and enlisted personnel were generally sound. The board made only four recommendations for improvements to the Navy's personnel policies. It is interesting to note that two of these related specifically to female personnel, and that they were considered "minor policies and practices [that] invite doubt as to the validity or purpose."[56]

The detailer for female Navy personnel successfully challenged the Lucas Board's recommendations, noting that the board's members apparently "misunderstood or misinterpreted" several points relating to the assignment and utilization of women personnel. The detailer's response noted that women officers filled military billets within authorized military allowances. "Thus it follows that since men and women are assigned interchangeably, *the utilization of women in the military service must follow the pattern of the utilization of men in military life rather than of women in civilian life."*[57]

As to extending women's tours, the detailer noted that women had no military obligation and came into the service as volunteers. Extending tours while simultaneously limiting opportunities for reassignment would "completely discourage the average person who is motivated toward military service because it provides a varied career pattern." Moreover, since approximately 90 percent of women officers in the Navy had no dependents, the costs incurred in moving them was infinitesimal compared with their male counterparts. Of the 27,022 permanent change-of-station orders written by BuPers through April of fiscal year 1961, only 268 were written for female personnel.[58] The CNO rejected both of the Lucas Board's recommendations pertaining to Navy women.[59]

The ongoing problems relating to the recruiting and retention of women in the armed forces inevitably led to more questions as to whether the costs involved were sufficiently justified by the purported benefits to the services. In April 1964, the General Accounting Office (GAO) published the results of its investigation into attrition rates of enlisted women in all branches of the armed forces before completing their first term of enlistment. Navy women had the second highest attrition rate, a whopping 74.1 percent (408 out of 550 cases reviewed). The only service with a worse rate was the Marine Corps with 76.2 percent (61 out of 80 cases reviewed). The Air Force came after the Navy with 69.3 percent (319 out of 460 cases reviewed). The Army had an attrition rate of 64.6 percent (388 out of 600 cases reviewed).[60] The group in the armed forces with the worst overall attrition rate was enlisted male draftees.[61]

Whereas men who enlisted voluntarily were obligated to complete their tour of service, women were able to secure an early discharge by getting married or becoming pregnant. Their decisions to do so reflected the zeitgeist of the era, and the high turnover rate was a source of frustration for commanders. The commanding officer of Naval Air Station Norfolk wrote to the chief of naval personnel in May 1950 proposing that the BuPers manual be amended to prevent junior enlisted personnel (male and female) in the pay grades of E-1 to E-4 from marrying unless they had already served two years on active duty, were at least twenty-one years of age, and had received the written permission of their commanding officer. The Naval Air Station (NAS) Norfolk commanding officer made specific reference to the high turnover rate among female enlisted personnel who were granted discharges for the convenience of the government for marriages contracted after enlistment.[62]

In her response rejecting this proposal, Cdr. Louise K. Wilde acknowledged the higher attrition rates for women but insisted that given "the importance of the establishment of the American home . . . in accordance with accepted religious and sociological views" marriage should continue to be a valid reason for requesting a discharge after completing a period of obligated service (i.e., one year of active duty during an enlistment).[63]

Although the "needs of the Navy" was the overriding concern with respect to policies concerning all male personnel, for women, the obligation to marry and raise a family—the essence of Republican Motherhood—superseded all others. While the Navy would have preferred to have a more dependable source of womanpower, it reaped the benefits of utilizing women to efficiently perform tedious, low-status administrative duties without incurring the long-term costs that came with sailors who made a career of naval service. The GAO report, however, contended that the high attrition rate of enlisted women during their first enlistment constituted a waste of taxpayers' money and recommended that the services take immediate remedial action to reduce the high attrition rates for enlisted women; failing that, the services should consider replacing them with civil service personnel.[64]

The services' response to the GAO report assailed aspects of the agency's methodology, asserting that it did not sufficiently validate or support its conclusions and recommendations. Specifically, the secretary of the Air Force countered the GAO by citing the report issued by the President's Commission on the Status of Women in October 1963. Civil service women under the age of twenty-five in the lower grades of the stenographic and clerical fields had an even higher turnover rate than enlisted military women (3 to 1 in the civil service as opposed to 2.5 to 1 in the armed forces). Moreover, when the costs of civilian overtime pay were factored into the equation, civilian workers were more expensive on a per capita basis.[65]

Defense officials pointed out yet again that although the type of work being performed by Navy women and civil service employees was substantially the same, the context within which that work was performed was not. Military women could be transferred rapidly to fill emergency requirements in war and peace. "This mobility for both peacetime and mobilization situations is a key reason for maintaining a cadre of military women in the Services."[66]

Rear Adm. Walter V. Combs, assistant chief of naval operations for manpower, noted that the Office of the Secretary of Defense conducted a study in 1964 that analyzed every military billet merely on the basis of whether a military person was required to do the job, with an eye toward maximizing the number of civilian substitutes so that military personnel could be deployed and draft calls reduced. This study also failed to consider the circumstances unique to military service that made the wholesale substitution of civilians infeasible.[67]

Jeanne Holm observed that the GAO report "might well have scuttled the women's programs" had it been published a few years earlier. But the final version of the report was not released until May 1966, when DOD was urgently seeking ways to avoid increasing politically unpopular draft calls for men as it continued to build up U.S. forces in Vietnam. The exigent circumstances of the new military buildup granted servicewomen a reprieve from the ranks of the expendable.[68]

In October 1965, DACOWITS recommended that separate legislation be drafted to correct the inequities in the personnel and promotion policies affecting women in the armed services, reviving its previous efforts dating back to 1960 to amend the Officer Personnel Act that had languished on

Capitol Hill. The bill, H.R. 16000, introduced by Rep. L. Mendel Rivers (D-SC), successfully cleared the House Armed Services Committee, which he chaired in October 1966, but Congress adjourned before it could be considered by the full House. Reintroduced into the 90th Congress as H.R. 5894, the bill was once again reported favorably by the Armed Services Committee. DACOWITS members organized a well-coordinated national campaign to support the legislation, and it passed the House on 1 May. The bill also quickly cleared the Senate with the support of Sen. Strom Thurmond (R-SC), a powerful member of the Senate Armed Services Committee and a major general in the Army Reserve. President Lyndon B. Johnson signed the bill into law on 8 November 1967. Public Law 90–130 was the first major policy change affecting women in the services since the Women's Armed Services Integration Act of 1948.[69]

While the legislation that would eventually result in P.L. 90–130 was wending its way through Congress, developments elsewhere influenced its ultimate outcome. In April 1966 DOD officials informed members of DACOWITS that thousands of women volunteers were being turned away and new recruits were confronted with long delays because of artificial ceilings imposed by the services on the numbers of women they would accept. The following month, DOD established an interservice working group to study women's programs in the services. The group recommended expanding women's line components to reach the full 2 percent legal ceiling within three to five years by expanding recruiting efforts and initiating a public information program.[70]

In the meantime, the Johnson administration was pondering how to address the pending expiration of induction authority for the Selective Service in June 1967. The president appointed the National Advisory Commission on Selective Service, chaired by Bruce Marshall, former assistant attorney general for civil rights, to study the issue and advise him.[71] In February 1967 the Marshall commission recommended continuing the draft. The report noted that women had an important role to play in the nation's defense and pointed out that there were far more women willing to serve voluntarily "than the services will accommodate."[72] The commission's report gave a boost to the proponents of the legislation. It was also helped by a concerted lobbying effort by several women's organizations. P.L. 90–130 corrected many long-standing inequities. The artificial grade restrictions imposed on women officers had led to stagnation in the ranks, and an attrition crisis loomed within the women officers' ranks. Navy officials projected a 50 percent or higher forced attrition rate among female lieutenants over the next five years and predicted suspension of promotions to commander for the next four or five years if Congress failed to redress the restrictions.[73] Among its most significant provisions, P.L. 90–130 eliminated artificial ceilings on the numbers of regular officers in the various permanent commissioned ranks; established better parity in retirement rules; eliminated the 2 percent ceiling on overall regular line officer and enlisted strength; and made women eligible for promotion to the general officer and flag officer ranks. In the Navy and the Marine Corps, however, women could receive only temporary "spot" promotions to the ranks of rear admiral and brigadier general, whereas women in the Army and Air Force could be promoted to permanent ranks of brigadier and major general. During the debate on the bill in Congress, members of the Armed Services Committee reiterated that women could not expect to achieve full parity with men in their military careers because they were exempted from "the stern commands of combat, sea duty and other types of assignments directly related to combat."[74]

When military women first won the fight for regular status in the armed forces back in 1948, it was with the support of men who attested to the ability of women to perform "duties peculiarly suited to their sex" as well as or better than men. This concept worked to the advantage of military women at the outset because it gave them a foothold in the regular components, but it soon became a liability. The technologies that had propelled women into the ranks at the beginning of the twentieth century—the telephone, the typewriter, and certain aspects of aviation technology—by midcentury had become an albatross. A demonstrated aptitude for performing important but often tedious and low-status tasks came to be regarded as biologically determined, as if women were genetically programmed to type and file and teach. All women officers in the Navy were required to learn to type. There were exceptions, dictated by expediency, when the needs of the Navy superseded assumptions about appropriate gender roles, but they were few and far between.

The Navy's oft-stated "moral obligation" to practice a "parental-type concern" for the welfare of its women personnel militated against true integration. The Women's Representative system was a case in point. While WR duty was defined as collateral, it was precisely the kind of "feminized" billet the Navy wished to avoid creating. But given the tenor of the times, it is difficult to see how things could have been done much differently. Although this period is looked upon as one of stagnation and retreat for women, women's programs in all the services were able to survive. The tension between the needs of the Navy and the dictates of cultural norms was reflected in the Navy's ambivalence in its marriage policies. Senior Navy officials realized they could not move too far ahead of cultural expectations when it came to the utilization of women. Those at the lower levels of the organization, however, had to deal with the attendant frustrations of the restrictions placed on the employment of female personnel and the need to accomplish the mission at hand. The recommendations of the Lucas Board, which would have severely curtailed educational opportunities for women officers while extending the tours of female officers and enlisted personnel, is one example. The shore installation commander's proposal to prohibit marriage prior to a certain age is another illustration of the clash of institutional and societal expectations of women.

Toward the end of the 1960s a confluence of events would lead to dramatic social changes that would have a profound influence on the role of women in American society as well as women in the U.S. armed forces. The disintegration of the long-held cultural consensus over core values affecting gender roles and work and family life would be foremost among these changes. A freshening breeze of social change propelled Navy women at an unprecedented speed into uncharted waters. Close behind it would come a series of squalls and tempests that would test the mettle of these women and the institution in which they served.

= Part III =

TRANSITION

═ 5 ═
SEA CHANGE IN THE SEVENTIES

I guess I can put up with this race thing, but don't push so hard for the women.

> —President Richard M. Nixon
> to Chief of Naval Operations
> Adm. Elmo Zumwalt Jr., 1972[1]

The end of the 1960s was punctuated by sweeping waves of social and political change. The publication in 1963 of Betty Friedan's seminal indictment of the cult of domesticity, *The Feminine Mystique,* gave voice to the frustrations of generations of American women and animated a second wave of feminism that was also propelled by the momentum of the civil rights and antiwar movements. As during the Progressive Era, women found a public voice through social and political activism—and that voice reverberated through all three branches of the federal government. Incumbents and candidates had to factor women's demands for equality into their political strategies to gain or remain in office. Federal court rulings played a key role in dismantling institutionalized sex discrimination in the civilian and military sectors of society.

The most significant factor that lent an inadvertent impetus to unprecedented change for military women was ending conscription. When men were being drafted mostly for service in the Army, the other services reaped significant secondary benefits through the voluntary enlistment of individuals who preferred to serve in another component of the armed forces. The end of the draft deprived the services of a steady and reliable source of manpower. The new all-volunteer force required new policies. Once again, exigency would open the doors of opportunity for military women, and some of those doors would be ship's hatches and aircraft canopies.

In the early 1970s, a series of events led to a reassessment of the role of women in the military. Congress passed the Equal Rights Amendment in 1972, and the proposed amendment to the Constitution went to state legislatures for ratification. The initial momentum behind the amendment, which thirty states ratified within the first year after it passed Congress, lent it an air of inevitability. The following year, President Richard M. Nixon announced the end of the draft. This posed a challenge to the armed forces—how and where would they find the recruits needed to man the new all-volunteer force?

The disintegration of the draftee military toward the end of the Vietnam War had seriously eroded the reputation of the armed forces with the American public. The accounts of troops "fragging" their own officers, rampant drug abuse, and a poisonous racial climate had taken their toll.[2] It was with this challenge in mind in the summer of 1970 that the new CNO, Adm. Elmo R. Zumwalt Jr., turned his attention to devising policies aimed at redressing the inequities associated with racial and sexual discrimination in the Navy.

On the latter issue, Zumwalt convened two Wave retention study groups tasked to develop a comprehensive proposal to improve women's presence and utilization in the Navy. Zumwalt conveyed the findings of the groups in the December 1971 *Flag Officers Newsletter*, stating he had been "sadly enlightened . . . as to how frequently our Navy women are still being used as receptionists, coffee runners and such, despite their technical training and competence." The problem was particularly egregious for enlisted women, "although . . . by no means confined to them."[3]

During his four-year tenure as CNO, Zumwalt issued 121 policy directives, referred to informally as "Z-grams." Among the best known of the

Z-grams were Z-gram 66 related to equal opportunity for minorities, and Z-gram 116 relating to equal rights and opportunities for women in the Navy.[4] In the opening paragraph of Z-gram 116, Zumwalt laid out his rationale for the momentous changes he planned to implement. Acknowledging the contributions women had historically made to the Navy's mission, Zumwalt contended that expanding opportunities for women would further benefit the service as well as enable women "to achieve full professional status." The advent of the all-volunteer force rendered the talents of women even more critical to mission success. Zumwalt concluded: "I foresee that in the near future, we may very well have authority to utilize officer and enlisted women on board ships."[5]

Z-gram 116 authorized the limited entry of enlisted women into all ratings and established a pilot program assigning women as ship's company on board USS *Sanctuary* (AH 17), a hospital ship undergoing conversion to a dependent support vessel, with the goal of regularly assigning women to sea duty.[6] Z-gram 116 also authorized expanding the types of billets and assignments available to women officers and made them eligible for command ashore and for admission to the command and staff colleges of the armed services and the Naval Reserve Officer Training Corps (NROTC).[7]

Highly cognizant of women's growing demands for equity, the Nixon administration directed the services in April 1972 to "ensure that women were given equal opportunity and to eliminate treatment and regulations which precluded adequate career opportunities for women."[8] There were limits to the president's commitment on this issue, however. In his memoir Admiral Zumwalt described the attitudes with which he was confronted, stating "it was impossible to discuss the matter rationally with some people" who raised the specters of "unisex showers and floating orgies." Zumwalt claimed that President Nixon told him after the end of a meeting with the Joint Chiefs of Staff, "I guess I can put up with this race thing, but don't push so hard for the women."[9]

In many ways, Zumwalt's activism was evocative of Josephus Daniels' push against the prevailing institutional currents to bring the first women into the Navy in 1917. Fifty-five years had passed, but cultural attitudes had changed little, and the higher echelons in the Navy showed a similar lack of enthusiasm. Toward the end of Zumwalt's tour as CNO in the spring of 1974, Congress had begun considering repealing the ban on women attending the federal service academies. Zumwalt related in his autobiography that he was instructed not to serve as the Navy's spokesman in congressional hearings because he supported changing the law. Opposition was so widespread in the Navy's senior ranks that Zumwalt "had only to turn to the newly installed number two Vice CNO Admiral Worth Bagley, to find someone who was able to testify against women at Annapolis with a clear conscience."[10] Ironically, Vice Admiral Bagley was the nephew of Josephus Daniels and Adelaide Worth Bagley. His brother, Vice Adm. David Bagley, was chief of naval personnel. Both men argued against the admission of women to the Naval Academy. When it came to progressive attitudes, environment held the upper hand over heredity.

Even more surprising, Vice Adm. David Bagley's position was endorsed by his assistant chief of naval personnel for women (ACNP [W]), Capt. Robin L. Quigley. Captain Quigley's tour in that position was controversial, as much for who she was as for what she did. The Zumwalt-Quigley controversy is worth exploring in detail because it reflected the political, institutional, and cultural flux that characterized the Navy and the country at the time.

Quigley was commissioned in 1954. Her first tour of duty was as administrative secretary of the Strategic Plans Division in the Office of the Chief of Naval Operations (OPNAV). Her subsequent tours included two years on the staff at the Naval War College and a field recruiting tour in San Francisco. She was subsequently assigned to the personal staff of CNO Adm. George W. Anderson and also worked briefly for his successor, Adm. David L. McDonald. In October 1963 she was ordered to duty on the Joint Staff in Paris, France, where she served as senior aide to the deputy commander, U.S. European Command. A three-year tour in the recruiting management division at BuPers in Washington was followed by two years on the staff of the Naval Submarine School in New London, Connecticut. When she was selected for the assignment of assistant chief of naval personnel for women in 1971, she had held the rank of commander for only nine months. Since the ACNP (W) position was a captain's billet by statutory requirement, Quigley was effectively "deep selected" for promotion when she won the assignment. The chiefs of the women's services in the Army and the Air Force had recently been promoted to general officer rank, and there was every reason to believe that Quigley would soon be pinning on the stars of a flag officer as well.[11]

When Zumwalt came into office as CNO, he wanted to cultivate new thinking by selecting personnel from further down in the rank structure to fill key billets. At age forty-nine, Zumwalt himself was the youngest officer with the least time in the flag ranks (less than five years) to be appointed CNO. Quigley was an exceptional woman who had earned a reputation as a highly competent and effective officer and manager. Her assignments at the top levels of the Navy's hierarchy from the very outset resulted in an atypical career pattern that gave her a solid understanding of how the Navy worked from the top down and the inside out. It also led her to thoroughly identify with the traditional institutional mindset of the Navy's exclusively male senior leadership, with the notable exception of the new CNO, whose thinking on issues concerning women in the Navy was radical for the day.

At the outset of her tenure as ACNP (W), Quigley was called to testify before the House Armed Services Committee's Special Subcommittee on the Utilization of Manpower in the Military, known as the Pike Committee after its chairman, Rep. Otis Pike (D-NY). Asked whether women should be admitted to the service academies, Quigley noted that she had recommended against it to the chief of naval personnel based on a sound fiscal management posture. The Navy, like all the services, was operating under severe fiscal constraints. Quigley advised that the Navy was already accessioning enough women officers through Officer Candidate School (OCS) at a cost of about $2,000 per person as compared to the cost of accessioning an officer through the Naval Academy, which totaled approximately $120,000. Additionally, since women officers were legally barred from serving at sea—the raison d'être for training officers at the Naval Academy—accepting women who could not fill seagoing billets would constitute a misuse of limited resources.[12]

Representative Pike queried Quigley on her personal views about whether women should be admitted to the Naval Academy. She answered with the Navy's official position. He asked her twice more, and each time she gave the Navy's position. Finally, an exasperated Pike said, "Damn it, Captain, I want to know what your personal view is!" The opinion Quigley gave as her own was consistent with the Navy's official position. The *New York Times* subsequently labeled Quigley a "female chauvinist pig."[13]

Representative Pike introduced an article into the record of the hearings from the *Naval War College Review* written by Lt. Cdr. Beth F. Coye on the status of the Navy's female unrestricted line officer community that was obviously intended to serve as an indictment of Quigley's views. In describing the milieu of the contemporary female line officer, Coye asserted that support for changing the traditional viewpoint of women's roles in the officer ranks was concentrated among the junior officers, who were a minority. As was true for working-class women in the feminist movement, "those women who most feel the need for reform are powerless to achieve it, and the women most able to work for such reform are slow to recognize that times have changed."[14]

Coye also noted the tendency of "women policymakers in the Wave program to react rather than to initiate new programs for women in the Navy." The conservative approach grew out of recognition that women's status was historically perceived as tenuous, as "a wartime phenomenon rather than as a permanent component." Women line officers, like other minorities, had been psychologically conditioned to identify with the prosperity of the majority to ensure their survival.[15]

Joy Bright Hancock had often been put in a position to explain how she confronted the apathy and obstructionism of recalcitrant male Navy officers. She would open conferences by stating she was acting at the direction of the chief of naval personnel, and that she would be happy to forward (with attribution) the views of any officer who desired "to work from an absolutely negative recommendation."[16]

Hancock knew how to wield the support of her superiors to effect policy even though she was only a lieutenant commander at the time and was part of a WAVES organization that had never been effectively integrated into the Navy bureaucracy. Thirty years later, when the CNO directed Captain Quigley to dramatically expand the role of women in the Navy, she refused to comply, standing on bureaucratic procedure and citing the fact that her position as ACNP (W) did not have the "line" or "vertical" authority to implement the recommendations from Wave retention study groups or Z-gram 116. Quigley asserted that the CNO did not understand the process. Most of the actions Zumwalt ordered had to be implemented by the functional organizations, not Pers-K (the branch of BuPers concerned with women's issues). Although she may have been technically correct in her insistence on proper bureaucratic procedure, Quigley failed to appreciate the primacy of the political imperative and the prerogative of the CNO to set policy.[17] To argue that she did not have the authority to carry out the directives of the CNO was disingenuous.

When she reported to her new position, Quigley first set about determining the substantive aspects of her job. As she reviewed the paperwork crossing her desk, she realized "a great deal of the paperwork in that office belonged to the functional sections of the Bureau, whether it was detailing, reserve planning, promotion policies, etc." The only reason it was sent to her was because the personnel involved were women. This struck her as highly inefficient, and she immediately set about transferring that paperwork to the appropriate sections within BuPers.

She then traveled to approximately 159 major Navy commands to meet with women officers and enlisted personnel. Her tour focused on "hot and heavy rap sessions with enlisted women," because enlisted retention was a major problem at the time while "women officers could swim for themselves; they were doing fine." A common theme that emerged during these rap sessions irritated Quigley. On the one hand, female sailors expressed a desire for equality with their male counterparts, but on the other, they expected "special and different treatment because they were women." An exasperated Quigley asserted, "You cannot walk down both sides of the street at the same time. . . . Life won't let you, no matter what arena of life we are talking about."[18]

After reorganizing her office and soliciting the views of hundreds of enlisted women, Quigley found the answer to the rhetorical question she had asked herself upon taking the position of ACNP (W): "What am I?" The enlisted women regarded her as a being invested with superpowers, a perception she characterized as "a personal trauma." She resolved to slay the myth, "and to do it post-haste."[19] The way to do that was to educate the rank and file as to what BuPers really did.[20] On 23 February 1972, she issued a memorandum that bluntly and abruptly apprised Navy women of their place in the organization. First, she directed Navy women to stop referring to themselves as WAVES. That organization had ceased to exist in 1948, and "continued use of an outmoded acronym implied they were a ladies' auxiliary of the Navy."[21] Second, Quigley abolished the Women's Representative system and directed women to use the same chain of command as their male counterparts. If women wanted to achieve full status as professionals, they had to accept and abide by the policies and standards of their profession. If they wanted to enjoy the comforts of an auxiliary status, they must accept a subordinate position. "But you must commit yourself one way or the other, because you cannot have the best of both worlds."[22]

The memo generated consternation among the ranks of Navy women and displeasure from CNO Zumwalt, but Quigley was unflinching in her conviction. "Neither I nor anyone else can make things happen for women in the Navy faster than or out of context with what is happening for people in the Navy today."[23] And that was the crux of the conflict between Quigley and Zumwalt. While they shared a common goal to advance the interests of Navy women, they differed on how and when that goal should be accomplished. Quigley focused on maintaining the integrity of the institutional process, and Zumwalt focused on quick results to be responsive to the demands of his civilian overseers.

Quigley was disdainful of the Wave retention study group, which consisted of twelve to fifteen young enlisted women and officers (all lieutenants, j.g.), who conferred for a week and generated a list of some fifty to sixty recommendations to be briefed to the CNO. Sponsors could attend the briefings but were not allowed any input. Quigley, the sponsor for Navy women, was frustrated that many of the recommendations were shallow or infeasible. The women were too junior and did not understand existing policies or how personnel functions operated.[24] Quigley returned from leave in July 1972 to discover that Admiral Zumwalt had signed a memorandum creating an ad hoc committee on equal rights for women in the Navy. Her name was conspicuously absent from the roster.[25] Quigley's boss, Assistant Chief of Naval Personnel for Personnel Affairs Rear Adm. Charles F. Rauch, asked Quigley to sit on the committee anyway. She refused. "Not only no, but hell, no! Don't you understand that the whole purpose of this was to end-run me?" She eventually agreed to send her deputy to attend in her place.[26] The final list of recommendations that emerged from the committee formed the essence of Z-gram 116, which Quigley believed "was absolutely so political in its context."[27]

Quigley objected to the "lumping together of all 'minority' problems into one bag." Although the problems of women might bear some superficial resemblance to the problems of racial minorities, the root causes of discrimination against the two groups were different.[28] Nor did she concur with the policies promulgated in Z-gram 116 that would send women to sea and allow them to receive flight training. She viewed the programs as nothing more than tokenism that would incur needless expense to the Navy. Opening aviation training to women with the combat ban still in effect would relegate them to patrol and transport squadrons, assignments that were regarded as "promotion fodder" in the aviation community because pilots flying combat aircraft were preferred for advancement up the ranks.[29] As far as sending women to sea was concerned, Quigley feared that all the positive progress that women had made up to that point was in danger of being lost.[30]

Quigley was highly aware of the sea-to-shore-rotation issue. The facts did not support enlisted men's perception that women were occupying too many shore billets and forcing men to spend more time at sea. Substituting civilians in military shore billets had the most impact on that.[31] But Navy women continued to be blamed and resented for "taking up" all the desirable shore billets.

Quigley informed the chief of naval personnel, now Rear Adm. David Bagley, that she could not support Z-gram 116 and asked to be relieved from her billet. He directed her to write a nonconcurring endorsement to the Z-gram, which she did. Bagley's deputy tried to convince Quigley to support the CNO's position, but she refused. The day the Z-gram was released, Quigley received a call from the chief of navy information (CHINFO) requesting her presence at a press conference Admiral Zumwalt was holding. Quigley explained that given her views, that would not be advisable. Following the news conference, Admiral Zumwalt called Quigley and offered her the billet of assistant for Pers-P, the "People Programs" division of BuPers, where she would be responsible for implementing Z-gram 116. She declined.[32]

According to Quigley, Secretary of the Navy John Warner had been blindsided by Z-gram 116 and was also upset about the "very ugly and very unpleasant" press coverage of the women-at-sea aspect. The firestorm of adverse publicity that focused on the salacious aspects of women at sea following the release of Z-gram 116 made Quigley feel that her tour as ACNP (W) was a failure.[33]

In order to dispel the perception that she was being fired, the Navy offered Quigley a shore command. Because she had not served the minimum two and a half years required to make her captain's rank permanent, Congress would have to approve legislation making an exception for the time-in-grade requirement to allow her to fill the new assignment. Quigley's functions as ACNP (W) were being reallocated throughout BuPers, as she wanted. When the proposed bill reached the desk of Secretary of Defense Melvin Laird, he was shocked and surprised.[34] The Army and the Air Force had recently promoted the heads of their women's branches to general officer rank, and here was the Navy abolishing their counterpart.

Admiral Zumwalt related in his memoir that before Z-116 could be formally promulgated he had to mediate the bureaucratic impasse that had developed between Secretary of Defense Laird and Captain Quigley. Zumwalt wrote that Quigley had taken the "theologically correct" position that if the Navy intended to treat women as equals, there should be no "pope" over them—a reference to her own position, still referred to informally as director of the Waves. Laird was loath to make a decision that would cause Navy women to disappear as a distinct entity, especially within the context of the contemporary political and media debates raising the specters of "floating orgies and unisex showers" if women were sent to sea. The secretary held the leeward gauge in this fight, however. It would be awkward to insist on the perpetuation of a position that the occupant herself had deemed superfluous.

According to Zumwalt, following months of negotiations, the parties involved agreed to the arrangement that upset Secretary Laird.[35] Captain Quigley characterized Admiral Zumwalt's account as "an unbelievably preposterous misrepresentation of the facts." She objected to his "pope" analogy, a term she never used to refer to herself, and his account never mentioned the conflict between himself and Quigley.[36] Ultimately, Quigley assumed command of the 4,500-man service schools command in San Diego, from which she retired in October 1974.[37]

Quigley was a woman who acted from strong personal and professional convictions. She correctly anticipated many of the problems that would arise within a decade of the promulgation of Z-gram 116, namely stagnant or nonexistent career patterns for female line officers in the surface warfare and aviation communities. Ratings that had been opened to enlisted women would subsequently be closed again. Her proposed incremental approach might have worked if the Navy had the luxury of time to proceed more deliberately. But historically, all the advances achieved by Navy women had been driven by exigency. The exigent force in Quigley's time was not a war but a political and social movement. She, like many other officers, did not believe such issues should drive the priorities of the Navy. But the services must defer to the judgment of their civilian overseers in Congress, who in turn reflect the will of the people. Quigley could not transcend the parochial views of the male leadership of her own service.

Within a few years both the Air Force and the Army disestablished the last remnants of the women's support infrastructure for their services, as well as the positions of the Women's Air Force (WAF) and Women's Army Corps (WAC) directors. The Air Force eliminated the WAF director's billet in June 1976, and a Defense Department reorganization eliminated the WAC director's position in April 1978.[38]

Although women could not yet make their mark in aviation and sea commands, there was one operational billet in a designated warfare specialty where women made a significant breakthrough. Because the mission was highly classified, however, few people outside the community were aware of this breakthrough, or if they were aware, were not authorized to discuss it publicly. The sound surveillance system developed in the 1950s as a collaboration between the Navy and private industry adapted telecommunications technology to track submarines by detecting and classifying their low-frequency sound signals. The signals were interpreted by highly trained personnel in installations called Naval Facilities (NAVFACs). Both officer and enlisted billets were shore-based and required extensive training.

The telephone industry, which had provided women with large-scale entrance into the civilian workforce and later the military, was now facilitating opportunities for Navy women to conquer new professional terrain. The Navy's World War II experience with women serving in the submarine tracking room established a successful precedent. As then, the prohibition against women being assigned to ships actually worked to their advantage. Navy policy required male personnel to rotate periodically to sea, while the demand for personnel on shore to support this critical new Cold War mission was growing. But unlike their WAVES predecessors, women serving in the Integrated Undersea Surveillance System (IUSS) specialty had a viable career path.

In 1972, the first eleven Navy women—one officer and ten enlisted ocean systems technicians—reported to the U.S. Naval Facility in Eleuthera, Bahamas. Naval historian Gary Weir noted that "for the entire history of the OT [Ocean Systems Technician] rating, extending from 1969 to 1997, any day would find as many women on a NAVFAC operations floor as men."[39] The system mission remained classified until 1991, and unlike other warfare communities, IUSS specialists were not authorized to wear a warfare specialty insignia on their uniforms until 1990.[40] The intelligence and communications specialties continued to offer women more opportunities for professional advancement in the ensuing decades.

The Navy took its first tentative step toward sending women to sea in 1972 with the assignment of fifty-three enlisted women (twenty-one attached to the hospital and the rest assigned to ship's company as members of the deck, supply, operations, resale and administration departments) and two women officers to *Sanctuary*, a hospital ship scheduled to be decommissioned by 1975. One woman line officer was assigned the primary duty of administrative assistant, with additional duties as X Division officer, personnel officer, legal officer, postal officer, officer of the deck (OOD) in port, and junior officer of the deck (JOOD) at sea. A female Supply Corps officer was also embarked. Berthing accommodations were essentially the same as for the men.

Once the ship was under way, women got their sea legs just as fast as their male counterparts did; they also got seasick about as often in rough weather. In terms of disciplinary action, during the period from October 1972 to October 1973, fourteen women went to Captain's Mast (a disciplinary hearing before the ship's commanding officer). Prior to sailing, one woman deserted and two were transferred with disciplinary action pending. During the same period, 189 cases involving enlisted men were processed. When expressed as percentages, 17 percent of enlisted women went to Captain's Mast versus 19.8 percent of enlisted men. Eleven of the fourteen women's cases involved an unauthorized absence (UA). Only two of the fourteen women were repeat offenders. Of the eighty-six men who went to Captain's Mast, twenty-four were repeat offenders; some had four or more appearances. Seven of the nine women who received discharges for the convenience of the government (12.7 percent) were pregnant. The other two were discharged for unsuitability. Eight (1.8 percent) of the enlisted men were discharged during the same period.[41]

Nine women were assigned to the Deck Department, where they worked the same long hours as the men and showed "a better than average sense of responsibility." Among the problems noted were lost work hours due to increased socializing and attempts by some women to manipulate the junior male petty officers. If male supervisors allowed women to avoid the more demanding tasks, either out of favoritism or for lack of confidence in the women's abilities, crew morale suffered. Although the women assigned to the Deck Department had clerical backgrounds, "they responded quite negatively to the prospect of clerical assignments."[42]

Women assigned to the Resale Department were reported to try harder than their male counterparts and were more "respectful, courteous and cheerful." The eight women assigned to the Administration Department, including the female line officer and a chief petty officer, were reported to perform in an exemplary manner. The two petty officers assigned to the Supply Department were rated as outstanding, and two female strikers (nonrated seamen in training for a specific rate, such as storekeeper) were deemed satisfactory. The five women assigned to mess duty, never a popular job on a ship, griped equally with their male counterparts. While the men complained about early reveille and long hours, the women complained about the heavy lifting the job required. Smaller garbage cans and special slings that made it easier to handle heavy loads while negotiating the ship's passageways and ladders remedied the problem.[43]

Sanctuary's report noted that the high visibility caused by news coverage that focused on sex and accented the negatives caused tension among the officers and crew. Once the novelty of having women on board wore off, men and women merged into a disciplined crew. During one underway period with warm weather and smooth seas, increasing instances of public displays of affection between crewmembers of the opposite sex during after-hours and holiday activities on deck led to morale problems. This was addressed by enforcing a policy banning such behavior and subjecting violators to nonjudicial punishment. "Not so much as hand-holding could be seen afterwards."[44]

During the first thirteen months of the integration period, *Sanctuary* spent a total of forty-two days under way on sea trials, independent steaming exercises (ISEs), type commander's training (TYT), and refresher training (REFTRA). The ship sailed to Buenaventura, Colombia, transited the Panama Canal, sailed to Port-au-Prince, Haiti, then made port in Mayport, Florida, where it was decommissioned. In the intervening sixteen months between the commanding officer's evaluation and the decommissioning in March 1975, the ship got under way quarterly for training. Several additional observations were made during this period. The sea duty experience enhanced the skills of the female petty officers and gave the male petty officers experience in supervising women, resulting in a significant decline in division management problems. Subsequent to the commanding officer's initial evaluation report, no other women were reassigned or discharged due to pregnancy. The number of disciplinary actions for women relative to men was consistently lower. The concerns initially expressed by the wives of male sailors had largely abated due to the Navy's efforts to counter the "abnormally high media exposure to hypothetical problem areas."[45] The ship sponsored a vigorous program of informative meetings on board with enlisted wives and held a family cruise. The wives' insecurities decreased and were an insignificant factor after the first several months. Women line officers qualified as underway OODs. It is significant to note that the Navy had not stacked the deck to ensure a positive outcome. There was no careful prescreening of the women selected for assignment to *Sanctuary*. "While all volunteered for naval service, many had not volunteered for sea duty. *Sanctuary* also received its share of less qualified personnel, including apprentice failures, both male and female."[46] The overall evaluation of *Sanctuary*'s CO stated that enlisted women performed generally as well or better than men with equal experience, and performed their duties with an "inspiring enthusiasm that invites a man to do his best."[47] Despite the relative success of the *Sanctuary* pilot program, the legal constraints barring women from sea duty remained intact, and despite the Navy's need for personnel, its leaders were not inclined to seek a change in the law.

Although Z-gram 116 did not address the issue of women in naval aviation, the subject had been raised in the course of the Pike Committee hearings. Pike upbraided the chiefs of the Air Force and Army women's programs for passively accepting inequitable treatment from their services, noting, "I have been frankly amazed at the equanimity with which you all have addressed the problems of, for example, the grades and the opportunities for promotion which are open to women in the service."[48] The committee's final report expressed concern that the DOD and military services were practicing tokenism in their policies toward women and urged them "to develop a program which will permit women to take their rightful place in serving in our Armed Forces."[49]

Following the subcommittee hearings, Brig. Gen. Jeanne Holm, the director of the Women's Air Force, briefed the Air Force secretary and chief of staff and urged them to take the lead in opening aviation training to women. "If we don't," she threatened, "the Navy under Zumwalt will."

But the Air Force's top leaders did nothing.[50] In October 1972, Secretary of the Navy John Warner announced that naval aviation training would be open to women to fill noncombat flying billets. Six out of eight women who were recruited successfully completed pilot training between February and June 1974. Four were trained to fly multiengine fixed-wing aircraft; two were assigned to transport squadrons. One flew a modified RP-3 Orion patrol plane with a weather reconnaissance squadron, becoming the first woman to fly into a hurricane, and one was assigned to a fleet composite squadron. The other two women became helicopter pilots and served with helicopter combat support squadrons. The performance of these first women pilots was closely monitored by Navy officials. "After the women had completed approximately eighteen months of training, had received their wings and served six months in flying billets, the program was to be evaluated to determine its success and future participation levels."[51] Their success or failure could determine whether more women would be allowed to serve in naval aviation.

In January 1973, shortly after the two pilot programs to send women to sea and to aviation training began, President Nixon announced a cease-fire agreement with Vietnam and an end to the draft, six months before induction authority was due to expire in June.[52] Whatever the president's personal opinions may have been about the proper role for women in the military, the recruitment and retention of women would be critical to maintain the all-volunteer force (AVF) that would become effective on 1 July 1973. With demographic trends indicating that the pool of eligible males would decline during the 1980s,[53] the Office of the Secretary of Defense took a leading role in prodding the services to reassess the utilization of women. The Navy established goals of 2,000 women unrestricted line officers and 20,000 enlisted women to support the AVF.[54] In 1972 slightly over 6,000 enlisted women and slightly over 3,000 women officers (three quarters of whom were nurses) were on active duty.[55]

There were other milestones for Navy women in 1972. The Navy Nurse Corps got its first female admiral when Capt. Alene Duerk was selected for flag rank. Lt. Ann J. Moriarity reported for duty with Naval Advisory Forces in South Vietnam as the Navy's first woman naval adviser. Nine female line officers served in the combat zone in Vietnam, challenging the assumption that there was no place in a combat zone for military women other than nurses.[56]

The imperative for volunteer manpower led to more changes. In 1973, OCS training was integrated at Newport, Rhode Island. Prior to integration, women spent half their time training as officer candidates and the other half as ensigns. This discriminated against the men, who were officer candidates the whole time they were in training.[57] The following year Congress passed P.L. 93–290 to equalize women's age eligibility for enlistment with men's. DOD changed the policy on separation for pregnancy in 1975: "Instead of being required to get out unless they are asked to stay in, pregnant women were to stay in unless they asked to get out. Normally discharge requests were granted on a routine basis."[58]

Nineteen seventy-three also saw the first example of a new external force for change—the federal judiciary—when Air Force lieutenant Sharron Frontiero filed a suit challenging the different qualification criteria for male and female spousal dependency. Wives of military men were automatically considered dependents, but husbands of female military personnel had to prove that they were dependent on their wives for more than one-half of their support. The U.S. Supreme Court ruled in May 1973 that the law violated the due process clause of the Constitution by commanding "dissimilar treatment for men and women who are similarly situated." Ruth Bader Ginsburg argued the case for the American Civil Liberties Union as amicus curiae (a friend of the court).[59] As historian Linda Kerber noted, this case would mark the beginning of "a time of extraordinary expansion of the meaning of equal treatment under the Constitution."[60] As more military women challenged discriminatory policies through the legal system, the services found it increasingly difficult to justify their policies.

By 1976, sustained congressional pressure had opened admission to the federal service academies to women as well. In 1972, Sen. Jacob K. Javits (R-NY) nominated a woman to the Naval Academy and made a public issue of her rejection. In September 1973 two House members from California, Democrats Jerome R. Waldie and Don Edwards, filed a federal lawsuit on behalf of their female constituents who sought admission to the Air Force and Naval academies. The Defense Advisory Committee on Women in the Services (DACOWITS) took up the call to admit women to the service academies during its spring 1974 conference, affirming "its belief in the eventuality of the admission of women to the service academies when the question has been resolved in the Congress and/or the court."[61] Judge Oliver Gasch of the U.S. District Court in Washington, DC, ruled against the plaintiffs in June 1974, citing laws and customs preventing women from serving in combat and a "legitimate government interest" in denying women admission to the academies, whose missions were "the preparation of young men to assume leadership roles in combat where necessary to defend the nation."[62] Members of Congress who had testified in favor of admitting women to the academies rejected the combat argument as a smokescreen for military intransigence, and the stage was set for confrontation.

In March 1974, Rep. William D. Hathaway (D-ME) offered an amendment to a bill under consideration to improve the military bonus system. The amendment, which authorized women to attend the service academies, was adopted by a voice vote. The amendment was cosponsored by Democratic Majority Leader Mike Mansfield of Montana and Republican senators Strom Thurmond and Jacob Javits. The amendment was stripped out of the final legislation by the chair of the House Armed Services Subcommittee, Samuel S. Stratton (D-NY), who asserted it was not germane to the point of the legislation under consideration and that the issue needed further study. The full committee upheld his decision. The chair of the Armed Services Committee, F. Edward Hebert (D-LA), promised to hold hearings on the amendment. The hearings took place in May and June 1974 before the House Armed Services Subcommittee on Military Personnel.

During those hearings, defense officials protested the admission of women into the service academies on the same old grounds. The service academies' mission was to train leaders for combat, and since women were excluded from serving in combatant roles, their admission would deprive deserving men of admission and degrade the military readiness of the service. The military witnesses defined combat broadly as any activity in which there was a possibility of enemy attack. Pressed by the subcommittee members to explain why women were not qualified for combat, the witnesses cited "biological and emotional differences, 'the American ethos' and the need to preserve the all-male 'Spartan atmosphere' of the academies."[63] Vice Adm. William P. Mack, the incumbent superintendent of the Naval Academy, provided the sole dissenting personal view among the ranks of the military witnesses, asserting, "If the law were changed, in my mind women could do anything men could do at Annapolis." Rep. G. V. "Sonny" Montgomery (D-MS), who was opposed to the admission of women, provided some comic relief during the hearings by observing, "I haven't had very much experience with women. I haven't been married so I don't know how they stand up in combat."[64] In May 1975 the House approved an amendment introduced by Representative Stratton to the Defense Authorization Act to admit women to the service academies starting in the fall of 1976 by a vote of 303 to 96.[65]

The opponents of integrating women into the service academies had justified their resistance in terms of protecting women from the dangers of "combat," ignoring the fact that women, especially military nurses, had been routinely serving in combat zones since World War II, and some had been captured and held as prisoners of war. Eight female nurses were killed in Vietnam. The real issue was not whether women should be protected from exposure to combat per se; military necessity historically allowed exceptions, nursing the wounded being the major one. The true issue, as it had been with the initial arguments against the militarization of women, was which expanded roles would be deemed acceptable for women in a combat environment. Nonetheless, determining the exact meaning of combat became the next phase in the ongoing campaign to achieve professional equity for military women. At its spring 1975 conference, DACOWITS recommended the Defense Department clearly define the meaning of the terms "combat duty" and "combat assignment" in order to standardize policies for the status of enlisted and officer personnel "as well as the mission and function of the service academies."[66]

In addition, DACOWITS recommended that DOD propose amending Title 10, U.S.C. section 6015 to permit assigning women to vessels other than hospital and transport vessels. This would allow men and women to be assigned according to their individual qualifications and the mission to be performed.[67]

Section 6015 originated with an amendment that Rep. Carl Vinson insisted be added to the Women's Armed Services Integration Act of 1948 granting military women permanent status in the armed forces. For Navy women especially, section 6015 was the biggest impediment to advancement because it prevented them from directly supporting the Navy's mission by deploying with the fleet.

Capt. Kathleen Bruyere (formerly Byerly) recalled being told she could "do anything the men could do except go to sea" when she enlisted in 1966. After serving with various shore activities, she began to inquire how she could compete for command opportunities ashore. She was told that Navy regulations required officers to be qualified for command at sea in order to qualify for command ashore. She spoke with Rosemary Mariner (who was also a surface warfare officer) and helicopter pilot Jo Ellen Drag, who were also seeking to expand their career prospects. Drag complained that her squadron's mission was to deliver supplies to ships but she "was not allowed to hover over an aircraft carrier, and god forbid if she had to land on one." Another young woman who wanted to go to sea told then-Lt. Byerly, "I can't get there from here."[68]

Enlisted women confronted the same dilemma regarding advancement. In 1976 four enlisted Navy women, with the support of the ACLU's Women's Rights Project (Ruth Bader Ginsburg again) and the League of Women Voters Educational Fund, took the initiative and filed a suit against the Navy contending that section 6015 excluding women from serving on most Navy ships was unconstitutional. Lt. Kathleen Bruyere, Lt. Jo Ellen Drag, and one other officer were independently looking into challenging the law. When they learned of the enlisted women's suit, they decided to join it. The case was amended in February 1977 to include the officers and became a class-action suit. The plaintiffs held a press conference to announce their suit. Immediately afterward, Lieutenant Bruyere, who had appeared in *Time* magazine's "Man of the Year" issue just the month before, wrote to the secretary of defense, the Secretary of the Navy, and the chief of naval personnel to explain her suit. "I said, we are not challenging the Navy, we are trying to get the law changed, and this is the only way we can do it."[69]

While the case was wending its way through the legal system, Lieutenant Bruyere and her husband, a surface warfare officer, were both awaiting permanent change of station (PCS) orders to move from San Diego to Newport, where they would be attending the Naval War College together—another first. Her husband's orders arrived, but Lieutenant Bruyere's did not. When she inquired about the status of her orders, she learned that they had become the focus of significant debate, with some arguing that the War College might "not be worthy of someone who had done such a mutinous thing. Eventually, cooler heads prevailed," and Bruyere reported to the Naval War College as planned.[70]

A month after the Navy women held their press conference announcing their class-action suit, Defense Secretary Harold Brown and Navy Secretary W. Graham Claytor announced that the Carter administration was endorsing a proposal to Congress to change the law, "substituting language that would allow women to serve temporarily on warships not in combat and fill full-time jobs on research and oceanographic ships as well as transports."[71] Brown noted that right after he took office he had ordered a study on the utilization of women in the services. The study concluded that "there are more high-quality women willing to enlist than are now accepted." Claytor even raised the possibility of "manning" a destroyer with an all-female crew, insisting, "I am perfectly willing to take a shot at that; no reservations about the abilities of women."[72]

Navy leaders immediately began planning for the potential assignment of women to sea duty even though neither Congress nor the courts had decided the issue. On 29 June 1978, the CNO issued a message describing the proposed amendment; its language was adopted by both the Senate and House Armed Services Committees for inclusion in the fiscal year 1979 DOD Authorization Bill. The message also provided "advanced planning to permit near-term implementation in the event the amendment is enacted."[73]

The federal court ruled on the lawsuit before Congress took any action on the Carter administration's proposed amendment. In July 1978 Judge

John J. Sirica of the U.S. District Court in Washington ruled in favor of the plaintiffs. Sirica stated in his ruling that in adopting the amendment that created section 6015, Congress "acted without serious deliberation, against the expressed judgment of the military, and by foreclosing the navy's discretion regarding women well beyond the legitimate demands of military preparedness and efficiency, it acted arbitrarily."[74] Sirica's ruling did not mandate that Navy officials immediately begin assigning women to all classes of ships; specific assignment policies were left to the discretion of Navy leaders. But the ruling did require "that executive authorities move forward in measured steps to approach these issues."[75]

In 1978 DOD narrowed the definition of Navy combat missions to "a mission of a unit, ship, aircraft or task organization which has as one of its primary objectives to seek out, reconnoiter or engage an enemy."[76]

On 20 October 1978 President Jimmy Carter signed into law the 1979 Defense Authorization Act including the Navy's amendment to section 6015 of Title 10 U.S.C. Three days later, the CNO announced the implementation of the "Women in Ships" program.[77] A team of naval architects had already been dispatched to the first ships slated to receive female crew to determine the modifications necessary to berthing spaces.[78]

The Women in Ships program commenced formally in November 1978. Fifty-six officers were scheduled for assignment to 14 ships, and 396 enlisted women were scheduled for assignment to 5 ships.[79] In keeping with prevailing legal restrictions, the vessels were various types of designated noncombatant vessels: material support ships of the Mobile Logistics Support Force (MLSF), destroyer tenders, repair ships, submarine tenders, auxiliary deep submergence support, and guided missile ships.[80]

Commanding officers of ships receiving female crew were directed to provide an initial short-term report followed by quarterly reports to monitor the Women at Sea program.[81] To facilitate the integration process, the Navy drew upon the experience of the *Sanctuary* pilot program and established formal Women in the Navy (WIN) workshops to anticipate and allay the fears and anxieties of the women going to sea for the first time and to address the concerns of their male shipmates and their spouses. A standardized format for the workshops evolved by adopting the best

practices of individual orientation programs developed by ship commanding officers, type commanders, fleet staffs, and the Navy's Human
Resource Management (HRM) centers. Junior enlisted (E1–E4) male
crewmembers on ships scheduled to receive female crew received at least
two half-day sessions of HRM training, which included an overview of
the history of women in the Navy and the reasons and plans for assigning
women to shipboard duty. Each of the HRM sessions was followed by a
discussion of personal/professional fears and assumptions, and concluded
with an exercise in team-building concepts. These same basic topics were
covered with all the higher-ranking groups, with additional topics added
to address their particular needs.

Petty officers (E5–E6) received additional training in the management
and leadership of integrated workforces and reviewed the special regulations and policies pertaining to women at sea. Chief petty officers and
officers (E7–O5) received additional training in supervisory concepts
and facilitated communications for integrated workforces. Spouses of
male crewmembers and prospective female crewmembers participated
in orientation programs that covered the basic topics presented to the
junior enlisted personnel and included a discussion of ways wives could
communicate concerns and help make the program work.

Women unrestricted line (URL) officers assigned to shipboard duty
first attended Surface Warfare Officer School (SWOS) and the required en
route technical training as well as a three-day HRM personal orientation
workshop. Female restricted line and staff corps officers were required
to attend the HRM workshop and received specific shipboard orientation
either before or after reporting on board.

Enlisted women received the most extensive orientation training, which
included the standard damage control and firefighting training required
of all ship's personnel, plus three days of HRM training and three to
five days of orientation to sea duty. While the initial workshops for ships
receiving female crew for the first time were sex-segregated, follow-on
workshops were integrated.[82]

A tally of the issues raised by junior enlisted personnel on USS
Samuel Gompers (AD 37) during workshop discussions of personal and

professional fears and assumptions provides an overview of the varying concerns of members of the soon-to-be-integrated crew. The most frequently raised issues included: How will sexual encounters be handled? What about women trading sexual favors for special treatment? What are the off-limits boundaries? Who will wake the women when it is their turn to stand watch? How will members of one sex get to their workspaces if they have to pass through berthing spaces occupied by the opposite sex? Other issues were seemingly more mundane but especially important to people who would be living and working together in confined spaces for an extended period. Heads (bathrooms) were a key issue. Male crewmembers complained that head facilities were already inadequate, and establishing separate heads for women would exacerbate the problem. Another frequently raised issue was sanitation and the disposal of female hygiene products. One common all-purpose complaint was the fear of "more bullshit rules."[83] A survey of enlisted women's attitudes from one workshop revealed that they hoped sea duty would provide more opportunity for advancement and make them true sailors. But they feared not being accepted and being given only simple jobs by the men supervising them.[84]

Following the disestablishment of the assistant chief of naval personnel for women billet in 1974, the Navy had relied on ad hoc advisory boards to address problems relating to women. But these efforts lacked consistency and effectiveness. Eventually, senior ranking Navy women proposed a new billet for a special assistant for women's policy, who would advise the chief of naval personnel on women's issues. The new billet, with the organizational designation of OP-01(W), was established in 1979.

Capt. Georgia Sadler was the special assistant to the chief of naval personnel for women's policy (PERS-00W) during the early years of the Women in Ships program.[85] As part of her duties she visited several of the ships that were being integrated and spoke with the officers and crew. Commanding officers of integrated ships came to Washington to debrief her at the end of their tours. Sadler concluded that there were three factors determining the success or failure of integrating a ship's crew: "Number one, leadership; number two, leadership; number three, leadership."[86]

The CO was the number one leader who set the tone and policies for the ship. Sadler noted that enlisted women were sometimes blamed and resented for what was perceived as favorable treatment because the CO and other leaders in the ship's hierarchy assigned women less demanding duties so they would not risk physical injury or have to take on especially dirty jobs. Successful COs assigned women throughout the ship, adjusting as necessary. One successful adjustment involved women working in the ship's galley. The women were having difficulty lifting the fifty-pound flour sacks to stow them on the shelves, and men had to do the job. When the men's grumbling reached the ears of the CO, he directed the ship's supply officer to order twenty-five-pound sacks instead. The women were able to lift the lighter sacks, the male crewmembers got fewer backaches, and there were more places to stow the flour. It was a simple, happy solution for all concerned. "That kind of attitude from the C.O. obviously made all the difference in the world on the ship."[87]

A recommendation that came from DACOWITS' fall 1975 conference called for developing nondiscriminatory physical standards that would match an individual's physical capabilities to specific job requirements.[88] This had never been done when the seagoing force was exclusively male, even though physical strength varied widely among men. Captain Sadler related an anecdote from her tenure. Navy officials set about creating tests to determine requirements for various ratings. The test for postal clerk involved a scale on a table and a forty-to-fifty-pound mailbag on the floor. The task was to weigh the bag. The first men who took the test hoisted the bag off the floor with varying degrees of difficulty and placed it on the scale. When the first woman entered the room, she studied the scenario briefly, then put the scale on the floor and rolled the sack of mail onto it. Sadler recalled it was a lightbulb moment for Navy officials: there could be more than one way to accomplish a task! "The study just sort of went away" after that, she said.[89]

The second key element of leadership Sadler described related to the male chief petty officers. Against all expectations, the chiefs proved to be among the strongest supporters of women on ships. The "salty" chiefs, who embodied naval tradition and whose leadership style often involved the liberal use of profanity and perhaps a little physical intimidation, had been predicted to be the most resistant to change. The chiefs' foremost concern was mission accomplishment. Because the women reporting on board were in general better educated than their male counterparts and caused fewer disciplinary problems, they won the chiefs to their side. The chiefs "learned new ways to interact with new and different subordinates."[90]

The third aspect of leadership concerned the petty officers, and it was their attitudes that presented the greatest challenge to the successful integration of women. The junior petty officers were the most negative. According to Sadler, this may have been because they were just learning the responsibilities of their higher rank, and the introduction of women into the shipboard environment brought the prospect of change and uncertainty. The fact that the women tended to be intelligent and were getting promoted quickly may have caused an additional measure of discomfort. Good COs recognized these issues and worked with the petty officers.[91]

Among the factors contributing to women's success on board ships was the higher quality of female recruits in terms of education levels and scores on the Armed Forces Vocational Aptitude Battery (ASVAB) test. This was in part because the Navy and the Marine Corps *required* higher minimum scores on the ASVAB for female recruits. In addition, women recruits required fewer waivers for law violations and drug and alcohol abuse.[92]

The number of women enlisting in the Navy rose dramatically between 1972 and 1982, outpacing all the other services. Slightly under 6,000 enlisted women were on active duty in the Navy in 1972. Ten years later, that number was 37,000.[93]

Based on the quarterly reports received from the COs of the integrated ships, the first year of the Women in Ships program was judged successful. The COs noted good morale among male and female crewmembers and said that the women were adapting well to their duties. Problem areas reflected the transitional nature of the program, such as a lack of senior women petty officers and mid-grade officers to serve as role models for junior women, and women's uniforms being unsuitable for the shipboard environment.[94]

The number of female officers assigned to seagoing billets was substantially smaller than the number of enlisted women assigned, and officers with warfare qualifications in the surface warfare, aviation, and special operations communities were a tiny fraction of them. The surface warfare and special operations communities were opened to women in 1976 following the Navy's initial amendment of section 6015. Surface warfare officers (SWOs), known colloquially as "ship drivers," are professionals trained in all aspects of running a ship. The special operations (SPECOPS) community is much smaller and should not be confused with special warfare—the elite Sea, Air, and Land (SEAL) combat forces that was only recently opened to women. SPECOPS officers are trained experts in diving, salvage, mine countermeasure, and explosive ordnance disposal. The career path of a SPECOP officer requires obtaining the surface warfare officer qualification as well.[95]

Like their surface Navy counterparts, female aviators were incrementally introduced into squadrons with noncombat missions. Aviation Officer Candidate School (AOCS) was opened to women in 1976, followed by the Naval Flight Officer (NFO) program in 1979. NFOs are the pilot's "back-seaters" who operate the plane's electronics and weapons. The types of squadrons to which women aviators and NFOs could be assigned included fleet composite, fleet logistics support, tactical electronic warfare, Antarctic development, oceanographic development, helicopter combat support, helicopter antisubmarine light, and training. A ceiling for annual accessions was established at twenty to thirty naval aviators and ten naval flight officers. In addition, nine special aviation skills were opened to enlisted women.[96] The number of enlisted women in aviation ground support ratings expanded significantly between 1972 and 1987 from 202 to 5,337. The Navy began assigning women to antisubmarine patrol (VP) squadrons in 1978. The successful performance of these women led Navy officials to begin detailing enlisted women to all operational VP squadrons by 1984, imposing a maximum ceiling of 25 percent on the number of enlisted women who could be assigned.[97]

Legal restrictions made it difficult for officers and enlisted women in naval aviation to fully exploit the limited professional opportunities the Navy provided. A long-term problem noted was that the restriction on the types of ships to which women could be assigned limited the number of qualifying billets for women SWOs. The limited billets were inadequate to accommodate the growing number of women entering the Navy officer corps via the Naval Academy, NROTC, and OCS. The lack of mid-grade officer billets impeded officers' abilities to remain operationally current and therefore competitive for promotion. The Secretary of the Navy drafted a letter to Congress in 1979 stating, "If the billet base is not expanded, the Navy must either access fewer than ten female surface officers annually or terminate upward mobility at the lieutenant level. Neither alternative is responsive to our personnel needs or to our equal opportunity commitments."[98]

Navy women could not serve as aircrew on VQ (fleet air reconnaissance squadron) aircraft, even though the aircraft played no active combat roles. They were excluded due to the "traditionally hazardous" history of the VQ community and the wording of Secretary of the Navy Instruction 1300.12, which reproduced the language of the amended section 6015 of Title 10 U.S.C. and included the word "reconnoiter" in the definition of a combat mission.[99] The policy reflected the danger of highly classified Navy Cold War reconnaissance missions conducted between 1950 and 1971. Ninety sailors lost their lives in shoot-downs, accidents, or unknown circumstances as they flew along the frontiers of communist nations to collect electronic intelligence (ELINT) about air defenses and industries.[100]

The incumbent CNO, Adm. Thomas Hayward, strongly objected to the proposal to open more MLSF ships to women. Hayward asserted that the underway replenishment ships operated regularly with combatants and were also performing combat missions. The Navy was therefore justified in excluding women from assignment to those vessels, which included ammunition, combat stores, fleet oilers, fast combat support ships, and replenishment oilers. Navy officials adhered to that interpretation in subsequent reviews of the policy between 1983 and 1985, taking the position that "the program would not be expanded until mandated by the American people through the Congress."[101]

These restrictions had a detrimental impact on the career aspirations of women in the warfare communities. Of the 269 women who entered the SWO community after 1978, 25 percent of those who were still on active duty changed back to nonwarfare designators due to a lack of a viable career path. The Navy tried to redress the shortcomings in women's career progression in 1983 by expanding opportunities for SWO women to be assigned temporary additional duty (TAD) to the Sixth and Seventh Fleets and MLSF detachments for women helicopter pilots and explosive ordnance disposal (EOD) officers.[102]

Congress considered the issue of women and combat in April 1979 during hearings debating the desirability of reinstating draft registration, which President Gerald R. Ford had ended in 1975. There was considerable debate among members of the House Armed Services Committee on the issue of whether women should be required to register for the draft. Representative Montgomery, who had opposed the admission of women to the service academies in 1976 because it was the academies' mission to train combat officers, now proposed legislation to require women to register. This was not due to any change of heart on the subject. It was an act of expediency, acknowledging the likelihood that any attempt to impose a male-only draft would be subject to a constitutional challenge in the federal courts. Requiring women to register would obviate the need for protracted court battles, and the precise terms of women's participation could be thrashed out later. Others in Congress believed that compelling women to register for the draft would expose them to the risk of combat assignments. Rep. David C. Treen (R-LA) opposed drafting women because he believed it would "inevitably lead to the abolition of the legal and traditional prohibitions against assigning women to combat jobs and units." If women were drafted and assigned exclusively to noncombatant positions, men would have legal standing to sue for equal treatment.[103] There would be no need for a slander campaign against military women to discourage them from joining the services and "free" men in noncombatant jobs to fight as there had been in World War II. Men now had recourse to the courts, and recent precedents indicated a significant prospect for success. What was sauce for the goose was sauce for the gander.

Carol Parr, who was the head of the National Coalition for Women in Defense (NCWD), an umbrella group of women's organizations that supported equal treatment for women in the military and favored the registration of women, took pains to point out that "combat and drafting [women] were two separate issues, like privacy and equal rights."[104]

Liberal and feminist organizations, traditionally supportive of women's rights issues, were troubled by conflicting motives. Although both the National Organization for Women (NOW) and the ACLU were members of the NCWD, their representatives were not anxious to be perceived as leading the charge for registering women for the draft. One women's rights advocate observed, "The whole issue of the draft has been used to help defeat the ERA. The lower the profile we take [on the draft issue] the better." Instead, NOW and the ACLU chose to focus their lobbying efforts on defeating the reinstatement of draft registration.[105]

The Soviet Union's invasion of Afghanistan in December 1979 only a month after American hostages were seized in Iran surprised the Carter administration and shocked the American public. In a show of resolve, President Jimmy Carter reversed his position opposing draft registration and proposed its reinstatement in his 1980 State of the Union Address. When the president submitted his registration plan to Congress in February 1980, he requested appropriations of $20.5 million so that women as well as men could be registered. Because previous selective service legislation had no provision for the registration of women, the president sought the consent of Congress through an additional appropriation.[106] Richard Danzig, Carter's principal deputy assistant secretary of defense for manpower, was a strong proponent of registering women. He argued that since women constituted only 9 percent of the total force, the services could be more selective in whom they accepted. "Every woman was a substitute for a man at the bottom of the pool." It cost less to recruit women, and they stayed in longer. It made sense for the services to raise their targets for female accessions above 10 percent.[107]

Carter's proposal to register women ignited a firestorm of political controversy that was skillfully exploited by cultural and political conservatives in the prelude to the 1980 presidential election. Previously, during Senate hearings on the ERA back in the spring of 1971, North Carolina senator Sam Ervin's unsuccessful efforts to modify the ERA's language to exempt women from combat and from the draft provided a major impetus to a grass-roots conservative effort to defeat the amendment. Phyllis Schlafly, a lawyer and conservative activist who founded the "pro-family" Eagle Forum and STOP ERA organizations in 1972, led the charge. The issue was perceived as relatively peripheral (at least by liberal feminist activists) since registration had been eliminated in 1975, but President Carter's proposal brought it back center stage just at the time that proponents of the ERA were struggling to get the last few states required for ratification before the extended deadline expired in 1982. Schlafly portrayed the president's proposal as part of a liberal feminist conspiracy to impose the draft on women and send them into combat. Carter handed the opposition more ammunition by submitting an ambivalently argued presidential message for inclusion in the testimony provided for congressional hearings held in February 1980. The president first argued that the universal registration requirement acknowledged the changing status of women in society and their greater participation in the workforce. While promising to exempt women from combat assignments, he also noted that military women have already been close to combat. In Kerber's words, "He raised the political stakes by linking women's registration to women's expanded willingness to meet 'the responsibilities of citizenship' and to the proposed Equal Rights Amendment."[108]

The public debate compelled supporters and opponents of the measure to articulate their positions, which revealed fault lines among the proponents of registration for women along political, racial, social, and gender lines. The issue was most problematic for feminists, whose support of professional equity for women conflicted with their antimilitary orientation. Ilene Rose Feinman observed that while feminists supported a woman's right to choose to join the military, their traditional ties to pacifist movements constrained them from openly encouraging it. ERA opponents on the right "regularly spoke to women's 'right' to be a homemaker, to be elevated on a pedestal, and to stand by her man."[109]

Despite their traditional hostility to the military, feminist organizations offered qualified support for the registration of women. Testifying on behalf of NOW, Judy Goldsmith focused on the equity argument, emphasizing the benefits that would accrue to women in a nonmilitary context, such as veteran's benefits and hiring preferences, as well as the better salaries and job opportunities provided to women in the military.

On the opposite side was the Coalition against Drafting Women, an umbrella organization created by the Eagle Forum encompassing several conservative groups. Sen. Jesse Helms (R-NC) and Rev. Jerry Falwell, founder of the conservative, fundamentalist Moral Majority movement, were among its more prominent leaders. Testifying on behalf of the Eagle Forum, Kathleen Teague, president of Virginia STOP ERA, dismissed NOW's position. "The purpose of the military of course, is the defense of our country. It is not to provide upward mobility or career opportunities for women." In an argument reminiscent of Madeleine Vinton Dahlgren's opposition to women suffrage based on the linkage of that civic right to the obligation to serve in the military, Teague argued passionately for the sanctity of True Womanhood. It was the duty of men "to be tough enough to defend us against any enemy," she insisted, and the responsibility of women to "transform them into good husbands, fathers, and citizens when they return from battle." What would women gain by "giving up their 'constitutional right to be treated like American ladies'"?[110]

The House and Senate subcommittees ultimately voted to exclude women from draft registration. But that did not put an end to the issue. Three days before America's nineteen- and twenty-year-old men were to start registering, a three-judge federal panel in Philadelphia ruled that the Selective Service Act of 1948 was unconstitutional because it did not include women. The suit was originally filed back in 1971 by a Philadelphia antiwar organization that had recruited three high school students to challenge the constitutionality of the law on a wide variety of grounds, including the fact that it discriminated against men by excluding women from the draft. One of the lawyers who originally filed the lawsuit observed that "no one initially took the sex discrimination change very seriously; it was one of the ironies of the case."[111] The case was dismissed by a federal judge in April 1972, but a decision of the Third District Court of Appeals a year later reinstated it, ruling that the only element of the appeal that was not unconvincing or moot was the claim of sex discrimination. The revival of draft registration resuscitated the long-dormant suit.

The timing of the ruling declaring the Selective Service Act unconstitutional could not have been worse from the perspective of the Carter administration, which immediately appealed to the Supreme Court. Justice William J. Brennan stayed the enforcement of the lower court's injunction preventing the government from proceeding with registration pending review by the full Court.[112]

As noted earlier, culturally and politically conservative women's organizations had collaborated with the intelligence services of the Army and Navy in the years between the world wars to forestall the agenda of progressive and pacifist women's organizations, in which the issue of civic rights for women figured prominently. The position of the opponents of women's suffrage argued that expanding civic rights demanded an equal measure of increased civic responsibility—mainly in the form of military service. That argument did not prevent suffrage, and the subsequent acceptance of women into the ranks of the military on a strictly voluntary basis to serve in carefully prescribed noncombatant roles had laid the argument to rest for several decades. In 1981, the Supreme Court case *Rostker v. Goldberg* became the battlefield for the latest phase in the ongoing struggle. Women were well on the way to achieving social, economic, and political equity, so why should they still be exempted from the civic obligation of military service?[113]

The prospect of combat duty for women significantly raised the stakes in the political debate. Margaret Chase Smith wrote in 1948, the year she helped win permanent status for women in the military, "Citizenship is without sex. . . . Since the granting of suffrage to women, the only differential between men and women as citizens has been the availability and acceptance of leadership."[114]

When Senator Ervin attempted to introduce language into the ERA exempting women from the draft and combat, Smith placed a statement from George Washington University's women's liberation organization into the *Congressional Record*. The statement, provided to Senator Smith by NOW, argued that exempting women from the draft diminished and marginalized them in the civic realm by precluding them from exercising self-determination and leadership. NOW did not, however, accept the concept that military service was a *prerequisite* for full citizenship. "Serving in the armed forces has never been a prerequisite to equality under the law. . . . If . . . both men and women will be subject to involuntary induction, we claim the right to answer for ourselves. . . . Whether to accept or resist induction is one of these issues. Where conscience dictates, and if it becomes necessary, we will resist the draft."[115]

Nine years later, NOW reversed course in an amicus curia brief to the Supreme Court arguing that "compulsory military service is central to the concept of citizenship to a democracy."[116] The Supreme Court issued its decision on *Rostker v. Goldberg* on 25 June 1981, holding in a six-to-three vote that the combat restrictions imposed on women were not an arbitrary or inadvertent product of ingrained cultural sexism. Women were therefore not "similarly situated" for the purposes of draft registration, and "the administrative and military problems that would be created by drafting women for noncombat[ant] roles were sufficient to justify the Military Selective Service Act [MSSA]."[117]

Vacillating legal tactics aside, it is doubtful that proponents of women's registration and the ERA would have been able to defuse the political time bomb that Phyllis Schlafly and the anti-ERA opposition had so carefully constructed. The anti-ERA activists drew no distinction between the draft and combat assignments for women, and the efforts of proponents of women's registration to parse the difference between being drafted and being sent into combat convinced neither their opponents nor the American public.

The intellectual and political provenance of the second feminist movement was problematic for both civilian feminists and military women. Feminists who honed their activist skills in civil rights and antiwar demonstrations characterized by civil disobedience and denunciations of militarism had little affinity for the armed forces, where deference to male authority was the institutional norm and the mission was to wage war. Many women in the military who had managed to maintain a tenuous toehold in their respective branches by not rocking the institutional boat were not convinced that feminist activism served their own best interests, though they may have sympathized with the objective of full equality. Beth Coye wrote, "Navy personnel generally . . . have dismissed this new movement as ridiculous or amusing, believing that the Navy is immune to implications of, and therefore can remain aloof from, the resurgent feminine movement."[118]

Women officers were more receptive to the second wave of feminism than were female enlisted personnel. This was congruent with the demographics of the second-wave feminists, who were mostly college-educated, middle-class, white women. For female Navy officers, feminism promised to widen their professional horizons through more varied assignments and promotions. While the same may have held true for enlisted women, full equality also carried with it the prospect of unwanted sea duty and gritty manual labor. There was a dramatic difference in the prospect of commanding on the bridge versus mucking the engine room bilges.

The defeat of the ERA and the federal court rulings upholding the constitutionality of male-only draft registration were bellwethers of a resurgent wave of conservatism sweeping the country. That changing political climate was a significant contributing factor to the stagnation of women's integration into the Navy. The new wave of political and cultural conservatism that elected Governor Ronald W. Reagan to the presidency in 1980 brought with it an ideological perspective that sought to halt or in some cases reverse the hard-won advances military women had so recently obtained. President Reagan brought with him a record of opposition to the ERA, and his new administration included very few women at the senior levels. During the 1980 campaign, Reagan asserted, "I do not want to see sex and sexual differences treated as casually and amorally as dogs and other beasts treat them. I believe this can happen under the ERA."[119]

Georgia Sadler wrote in 1983, "Navy and Marine Corps women began to sense a change in the atmosphere as they entered the 1980s. They became very concerned that, at a minimum, they were no longer marching forward and in fact might be forced to do an about face and march back."[120]

Navy women had made unprecedented progress in the 1970s, benefiting from the driving forces of the second feminist movement and judicial decisions that expanded the constitutional meaning of equal treatment under the law. In the decade between 1972 and 1982, the number of enlisted women had increased more than sixfold, from 6,000 to 37,000, while the officer corps nearly doubled from slightly over 3,000 to about 5,750. The number of enlisted women in nontraditional ratings rose from about 10 percent to 25 percent, and the number of ratings available to women expanded from about 25 percent to 86 percent. The officer corps had changed dramatically as well. Whereas nurses constituted 75 percent of female Navy officers in 1972, ten years later they numbered less than 50 percent, while the percentage of female unrestricted line officers rose to 45 percent.[121]

Once again, however, Navy women found their hard-won progress threatened by traditionalist attitudes that filtered down from the top levels as the Reagan administration sought to restrict and minimize their presence in the ranks. Women would be caught in the squalls generated by the collision of two attitudinal fronts: policies from the senior levels of the Navy that sought to roll back the progress made over the last decade, and personal hostility from the rank and file of Navy men in the form of sexual harassment. These squalls would culminate in a major tempest that would ultimately clear the way for the beginning of true integration for Navy women.

Secretary of the Navy and Mrs. Josephus Daniels, 1917 *Library of Congress*

Military and civilian personnel of the Supplies and Accounts Office in the Main Navy or Munitions Buildings, Washington, DC, circa 1918 *Naval History and Heritage Command*

American delegates to the International Congress of Women held at The Hague in 1915. Women involved in feminist, peace, labor, and social reform movements were regarded as subversive by some military and government officials. *Library of Congress*

Capt. Luke McNamee, director of Naval Intelligence, 1921–23, appealed to women's organizations to "renounce . . . the Delilahs of pacifism that would shear the Navy of its strength." *Naval History and Heritage Command*

The six women elected to the House of Representatives in 1940 increased pressure on the military to utilize women in the coming war. *Left to right*: Frances P. Bolton (R-OH), Clara McMillian (D-TN), Mary T. Norton (D-NJ), Edith N. Rogers (R-MA), Caroline O'Day (D-NY), and Jessie Sumner (R-IL). *Library of Congress*

Dr. Margaret "Mom" Chung (*third from left*) presenting the USS *Trigger* (SS 237) battle flag to the Naval Academy in 1946. Dr. Chung used her extensive social network to build political support to create the Women's Reserve. *Naval History and Heritage Command*

During World War II, WAVES made important contributions in disciplines supporting the production of operational intelligence.

An enlisted WAVE operates a Bombe machine to decrypt enciphered German radio communications. *National Security Agency*

An enlisted WAVE works on a chart in the Navy Hydrographic Office in 1944. *National Archives*

Left: Sen. Margaret Chase Smith ultimately prevailed in protracted legislative battles in the Senate Naval Affairs Committee to secure permanent status for Navy women. *Library of Congress*

Right: Capt. Joy Bright Hancock became the third director of the Women's Reserve in July 1946. She deftly maneuvered within the Navy bureaucracy to overcome institutional resistance to permanent status for women. She was among the first officers sworn into the Regular Navy in 1948. *NARA*

Cdr. Robin L. Quigley (*center left*) succeeded Capt. Rita Lenihan (*center right*) as WAVES director in 1971. Quigley clashed with Chief of Naval Operations Adm. Elmo R. Zumwalt Jr. (*left*) over his policies to integrate women into the Navy's operating forces. Secretary of the Navy John H. Chaffee is pictured at right. *NARA*

Seaman Apprentice Anneliese Knapp was among thirty-two women in nonmedical ratings assigned to sea duty in the hospital ship USS *Sanctuary* (AH 17) in 1972 to test the feasibility of expanding assignments for Navy women. *NARA*

Ens. Rosemary Conaster (later Mariner) was among the first women commissioned as naval aviators in 1975. She became the first woman to command an operational aviation squadron, VAQ-34, in 1990. *U.S. Navy*

Lt. Tammie J. Shults served under Cdr. Rosemary Mariner in VAQ-34 in the early 1990s. Shults became famous in 2018 as a commercial pilot when she safely landed a crippled airliner after its engine blew out in flight and killed a passenger. *U.S. Navy*

Left Following widespread reports of sexual harassment and discrimination against Navy women in 1987–88, Secretary of the Navy James H. Webb responded to public pressure. He approved assignments for women to logistics ships and narrowed the Navy's definition of what constituted a combat mission. *U.S. Department of Defense*

Right CNO Adm. Michael J. Boorda's unsuccessful efforts to mitigate the fallout from the 1991 Tailhook scandal antagonized the Navy's officer corps and resulted in unprecedented public criticism of his leadership. His subsequent suicide sent shock waves through the Navy. *U.S. Navy*

After the November 1993 repeal of the combat exclusion rule was implemented in 1994, women in naval aviation were rapidly integrated into the fleet. Lt. Shannon Workman was the first female combat pilot to pass fleet carrier qualifications in February 1994. *U.S. Navy*

During Operation Desert Fox in Iraq in 1998, Lt. Carol Watts (*left*) and Lt. Lyndsi Bates (*right*) of VFA-37 in USS *Enterprise* (CVN 65) were among the first women fighter pilots to fly into combat from a carrier. *U.S. Navy*

Adm. Michelle J. Howard was the first U.S. Navy woman promoted to the rank of admiral and became the thirty-eighth Vice Chief of Naval Operations in 2014. *U.S. Navy*

A sailor with a Female Engagement Team (FET) assigned to a Marine Corps unit in U.S. Central Command is briefed prior to military operations in urban terrain training. Such assignments increase exposure to direct ground combat. *U.S. Marine Corps*

Four female commanding officers of amphibious ships in January 2021: *(left to right)* Cdr. Kimberly Jones, USS *Tortuga* (LSD 46); Cdr. LaDonna Simpson, USS *Carter Hall* (LSD 50); Cdr. Kathryn Wijnaldum, *USS Oak Hill (LSD 51);* and Cdr. Kristel O'Canas, USS *Whidbey Island* (LSD 41) *U.S. Navy*

The enlisted women assigned to the blue crew of the *Ohio*-class ballistic missile submarine USS *Wyoming* (SSBN 742) were the first to complete a ballistic missile submarine deterrent patrol in 2022. *U.S. Navy*

Chief Operations Specialist Veronica Martinez receives her combination cover during a chief petty officer pinning ceremony on the flight deck of USS *Theodore Roosevelt* (CVN 71) in October 2022. *U.S. Navy*

Yeoman First Class Krystal Dawkins mans the helm of USS *Decatur* (DDG 73) during a replenishment at sea in the Philippine Sea in December 2022. *U.S. Navy*

= 6 =
FROM WAVES TO WARRIORS

Barriers based on sex are coming down in every part of our society. The armed forces should be no exception. Women should be allowed to play a full role in our national defense, free of any arbitrary and discriminatory restrictions. The only fair and proper test . . . is not gender but ability to do the job.
—Sen. Edward M. Kennedy, 1991[1]

I n the fifteen years that followed Z-gram 116, Navy women had expanded in numbers and were making incremental advances into uncharted territory. But it was a qualified success. In the general unrestricted line and staff corps communities, female officers had higher retention levels than their male counterparts, but female officers with warfare specialties found their careers stymied by the combat exclusion laws. The quality of women enlisted recruits surpassed that of the men.[2] On average, the enlisted women scored higher on the entry tests, and a higher percentage successfully completed high school. Women's long-term retention rates were about the same as men's, and women had far fewer disciplinary problems. Women recruits, however, still tended to gravitate toward traditional ratings in the administration and medical fields, which kept their numbers in technical seagoing ratings low.[3]

Women serving in areas that had traditionally been exclusively male faced a growing backlash from Navy men and from cultural and political conservatives in the government and civilian sectors. Despite claims from conservative polemicists decrying the "feminization" of the military and linking it with the perception of military weakness and disarray in the all-volunteer force, the growing presence of women in the ranks actually helped to save the AVF in its early years of transition in the post-Vietnam era.

The Navy came to rely increasingly on women to address the "Hollow Force" syndrome. In 1980, the Navy was forced to take a ship out of operational status due to shortages of essential personnel in technical ratings.[4] The aircraft carrier USS *John F. Kennedy* (CV 67) had to borrow fifty sailors from other ships in order to get under way for a Mediterranean cruise.[5] Navy officials announced a policy of "selective manning," effectively poaching crews from multiple ships to achieve an operationally ready status for one vessel. CNO Adm. Thomas Hayward told Congress that the Navy was suffering a "hemorrhage of talent," a situation military officials attributed primarily to low pay. "We are approaching the point where we may have no realistic alternative but to consider standing down some ships and aviation units," he warned.[6] *Fortune* magazine also reported on the pay problem, playing up the incorrect and widespread perception that the presence of women in shore billets was responsible for the extended deployments of male sailors at sea: "The typical sailor aboard could be said to have left two women behind—his wife and the blue skirt who has replaced him on shore."[7] In fact, male sailors' sea duty–shore duty rotation was not detrimentally affected by the presence of women in the Navy. If seven boiler technicians (BTs) are needed to get a ship under way and the crew only has two, then the answer is to recruit and train more BTs, male *and* female, not to discharge women. But the old "women are taking up all the shore billets" canard persisted nevertheless and provided a convenient vehicle for articulating the men's growing resentment of women in the ranks.

That resentment manifested itself in a particularly ugly fashion when the news broke of an investigation of female crewmembers for alleged lesbianism on USS *Norton Sound* (AVM 1) in the summer of 1980. The press accounts portrayed a command climate on the ship that was out of control, including allegations of drug dealing, loansharking, assaults related to gang activity, even murder.[8] But most of the stories in the national press centered on allegations of lesbian activity levied against sixteen female crewmembers—one-fourth of the women on board the ship. Initial reports stated the inquiry began after a list of women crewmembers was circulated and "female crewmembers checked the names of those they believed to be homosexual."[9] Navy officials denied that such a list had been circulated, countering that the investigation began after "a female crew member brought allegations of homosexuality through the chain of command." The attorney for the ACLU representing the accused women responded, "So many of the women have said this (that the roster was circulated) that it will just be a credibility battle." She labeled the investigation an "outrageous witch hunt."[10] Twenty-four women were initially accused. Eight women were immediately cleared, and the remaining sixteen were asked to submit to psychological testing. In the end, all but two women were cleared of the charges, but not before they had to undergo humiliating national scrutiny of the details of their sex lives. One female petty officer was found not guilty after a psychiatrist was called to testify that she denied being a lesbian under deep hypnosis and her former and current boyfriends took the stand to testify that they did not think she was a homosexual.[11] Navy officials lowered the curtain on this theater of the absurd by barring reporters from further hearings "after a complaint that the inquiry was 'being made into a circus.'"[12]

One of the two women ultimately found guilty and recommended for discharge stated that if the allegations were true, she should be discharged for "stupidity, not misconduct. . . . [I]t would have been stupid to try to conduct sexual activities . . . in an area crowded with sleeping women aboard a ship." Her Navy defense counsel observed, "The only ones who witnessed anything sexual had to be brought here from the psychiatric ward of the Navy Regional Medical Center."[13]

While this story was unfolding in the national press, a male petty officer from *Norton Sound* was convicted of nine counts of sexual harassment of female sailors, including exposing himself, making lewd remarks, and sexual assault. He was busted to the lowest enlisted rank and given a bad conduct discharge. The story in the *Navy Times* also related allegations of the murder of a female sailor who was lost overboard (a Navy investigation determined she committed suicide) and the existence of a group called the "Dirty Dozen" that purportedly engaged in loansharking, drug dealing, and assaulting other crewmembers. Given all the problems on *Norton Sound*, it would seem that Navy officials could have made better use of their time and resources than pursuing phantom predatory lesbians. Ebbert and Hall's characterization of the *Norton Sound* affair and an incident on USS *Yellowstone* (AD 41), in which eleven women were discharged from the Navy after admitting homosexuality (four later had the charges against them dropped after they requested a review of their cases for legal improprieties), is a masterpiece of understatement: "In retrospect, much more appears to have been made of the cases than the facts warranted."[14]

The trepidation with which some Navy women anticipated the conservative Reagan administration and the potentially detrimental impact its policies could have on their hard-won progress proved to be well founded. The administration's track record on appointing women, characterized by one correspondent as "the worst appointment record for getting women into good jobs since anybody started counting," was an early bellwether.[15] Initially, things looked promising when the administration nominated Helen Delich Bentley to be undersecretary of the Navy, with the endorsement of Secretary of the Navy John Lehman and Defense Secretary Caspar Weinberger. Bentley had served as head of the Federal Maritime Commission under two presidents—Richard Nixon and Gerald Ford—worked as a former maritime editor for the *Baltimore Sun*, and had been named GOP Woman of the Year in 1972. Her nomination ran aground due to the opposition of Sen. John Warner, who was rumored to have his own candidate in mind for the job. He questioned whether Bentley would be able to climb on and off ships at sea, saying he did not want her to humiliate the United States by falling overboard. "During the 25 years I was the *Sun* maritime editor, I probably climbed on and off ships practically every day, out in the middle of the Chesapeake Bay, ships underway, etc.," Bentley said, ". . . but it didn't change his attitude."[16] When asked by a *Wall Street Journal* reporter whether he told Bentley the Navy wasn't ready for a woman, Senator Warner responded, "Whether we like it or not, that is a man's world—one that is unlikely to change."[17] The public story was that her nomination was dropped because of residual debt and a lawsuit (which had been settled) from her unsuccessful congressional campaign and a business lawsuit that was in the process of being resolved. Critics pointed out that the administration had ardently defended male nominees for more senior positions who were carrying much heavier baggage, such as purported links to organized crime and "hanky panky with multinational corporations."[18] At the first sign of resistance, however, the administration dropped Bentley's nomination and made no attempt to defend her.[19]

In November 1980, two months before Reagan took office, Navy officials announced their intention to more than double the number of women assigned to shipboard duty in 1981. They planned to assign 1,502 enlisted women to 16 ships, up from 694 women assigned to 10 vessels. "The number of women officers would increase from 120 assigned to 27 ships to 158 aboard 29 vessels."[20] "This program is motivated not so much by equal opportunity or to blaze any new social trails," said Capt. James Kelly, who helped plan it, but "by a scarcity of skilled manpower."[21] Those plans were put on the back burner when the Reagan transition team took over the White House. Some military officials who remained opposed to integration and to adding more women in the services construed the ideology of the new administration as an invitation to stanch or even roll back the incursion of women into the ranks.

Before Reagan Defense Department officials could get settled in, they were confronted with a controversy precipitated by Army and Air Force leaders who, apparently in collusion with some conservative members of the Senate Armed Services Committee, sought to scrap the strength goals for women set by the Carter administration and hold the recruitment of women to a minimum while they assessed the impact of women's presence on military readiness. "There was no indication that the Navy or Marine Corps participated in this proposal," Jeanne Holm noted, "but, in response to press inquiries, they indicated that they shared some of their sister services' concerns."[22]

William D. Clark, the Army's acting assistant secretary for manpower and reserve affairs, and Lt. Gen. Robert G. Yerks, deputy chief of staff for personnel, testified before the Senate Armed Services Committee in February 1981 outlining their plans to cut back on the recruitment of enlisted women while they took "a new look at the entire issue of women soldiers." Clark testified that Army officials were finding it difficult to recruit women into "the wide range of skills available to them." Most preferred "to enlist in those traditional fields in which women work in civilian life."[23] Clark noted that the Army had been recruiting women who had not graduated high school to meet recruiting goals. Like their male counterparts who did not graduate high school, these women experienced higher attrition rates during their first enlistment. Clark also cited pregnancy and retention as ongoing problems. The gist of his testimony was that facing constrained resources, the Army did not want to expend any additional effort or resources on the recruitment and retention of higher-quality women.

Lieutenant General Yerks' testimony contradicted Secretary Clark's in one significant aspect. Yerks presented statistics on the distribution of female soldiers utilized in traditional and nontraditional skills. In fiscal year 1972, 90.1 percent of women were in the traditional skills category and 9.9 percent were in the nontraditional skill category. By fiscal year 1980, only 38.7 percent of women were in the traditional skills category while 61.3 percent were serving in nontraditional skills. Contrary to what Clark asserted in his testimony, the Army had in fact made significant progress in redistributing women into assignments utilizing nontraditional skills.

The proposal floated by the Army and Air Force, which the DOD dubbed "Womanpause," created a storm of controversy. "Its very name indicated the strong tinge of anti-woman feeling in the Defense Department and the unmistakable referencing to women's reproductive cycle, and indeed its marked endpoint in menopause," Feinman wrote.[24] Holm asserted that misogyny was not the sole motive for the proposal. Army officials hoped to undercut the AVF by reducing the number of women, who had been critical to its survival, and clear the way to reinstate the male-only draft.[25] Sen. William D. Proxmire (D-WI) called out Army officials on this hidden agenda. "Maybe what lies behind the Army's change of policy is the simple decision to restrict women recruits, accept the inevitable shortfalls in manpower levels, and then justify a return to the draft."[26]

When the final report was released in October 1981, its conclusions bolstered the hopes of service and other government officials opposed to increasing the number of women in the military. The report criticized the Office of the Secretary of Defense under the Carter administration for "setting . . . goals [that] had been based on equal opportunity considerations." Holm pointed out that the report had it backward. The Carter administration was trying to meet the manpower needs of the military without resorting to conscription or busting the budget to attract more men into the services. The administration employed the rhetoric of equal opportunity to provide additional political appeal within the context of the second feminist movement.[27]

The attempt by the service leaders to roll back the number of women in the military was checked by Secretary of Defense Weinberger. In January 1982 he issued a directive to all the service chiefs ordering them to "aggressively break down those remaining barriers that prevent us from making the fullest use of the capabilities of women." Deputy Defense Secretary Frank Carlucci ordered the service secretaries to analyze institutional barriers to the advancement of women, identify career paths that were closed or restricted by combat limitations, and quantify the impact of those limitations.[28] Furthermore, by 1983 Reagan administration officials were confronted with declining congressional support for funding their military buildup, especially for accessioning additional personnel, as well as with women voters' anger at the administration's policies. These realities compelled service leaders to make do with the man- and womanpower on hand, while civilian officials sought to avoid further antagonizing women voters.[29]

Although the opponents of women in the military did not appear to have the support of senior civilian officials in the Reagan administration, the failure of anyone in the senior echelons of the executive branch to actively disabuse them of these negative attitudes encouraged open hostility down the chain of command and fostered apathy toward redressing problems affecting women in the ranks.[30] Sexual harassment thrived in such an environment. In February 1980 the House Armed Services Committee held its first hearings on sexual harassment in the military. The Associated Press report carried in major newspapers emphasized a comment by Maj. Gen. Mary E. Clarke, commander of Fort McClellan in Alabama, that women were being harassed at "probably every installation." Other female military personnel testified that they were afraid to report sexual harassment because they would either be ignored or regarded as troublemakers.[31] The more significant point, not covered in the press report, was General Clarke's assertion that "the only solution to this problem is command concern and the involvement of each leader at every level of command."[32] Rear Adm. Fran McKee, assistant deputy chief of naval operations for human resource management (and the first female line officer to be promoted to flag rank), seconded Clarke's statement, noting that the Navy was a male-dominated hierarchical organization within which "sexism and sexual harassment could most easily occur in the absence of high-quality leadership and discipline based on sound equal opportunity tenets."[33] During questioning following her prepared statement, Rear Admiral McKee asserted, "I think that is the ultimate aim that we have in the Navy, that leaders at every level accept their responsibilities and learn to accept the management responsibilities of women in the workforce."[34]

At their spring 1980 conference, DACOWITS members issued a recommendation for the Departments of Defense, Transportation (which oversaw the Coast Guard in peacetime), and the armed services to expedite the promulgation of specific guidelines on sexual harassment.[35] The DOD adopted the guidelines on sexual harassment established by the Equal Opportunity Commission and developed an overall definition, and in August 1980 the Secretary of the Navy issued an instruction delineating the Navy's policy on sexual harassment.[36] Although DOD and Navy officials had officially acknowledged the problem, there was no effective process in place to ensure compliance and enforcement of the policy. Service newspapers such as *Navy Times* reported sporadically on incidents of sexual harassment, but such stories seldom reached the mainstream media.

The vestigial legacy of the WAVES still lingered into the 1980s in terms of the emphasis on double standards for the recruitment, discipline, and retention for Navy women. The elitist aspect of the service had been somewhat diluted by the expanding numbers of women entering the Navy after 1972, but the preoccupation with standards of proper "ladylike" conduct for Navy women persisted.

In contrast, no corresponding official efforts were made to provide for the "supervision and moral and spiritual guidance" of male sailors. On the contrary, the Navy tacitly condoned prostitution near military bases, especially in overseas ports such as Olongapo City in the Philippines, where a few dollars could purchase a wide array of sexual services from impoverished women and girls trapped in a cycle of exploitation. Sailors who availed themselves of such services considered it an entitlement for the arduous hours spent at sea. A Navy public affairs officer at Subic Bay, the major American naval base in the Philippines, conveyed the official attitude, stating, "It's not the Navy's job to 'baby-sit' or teach its men moral behavior. . . . [Y]ou can't tell them to keep their noses clean because we can't make moral judgments."[37]

The Navy's long-standing laissez-faire attitude toward its men's behavior was publicly challenged in August 1987 when DACOWITS members returned from an inspection tour of naval installations in the western Pacific with disturbing allegations of sexual harassment of female personnel and misconduct by senior male personnel. The most egregious case involved the CO and a senior petty officer from the salvage ship USS *Safeguard* (ARS 50), which had been handpicked by the base commander at Pearl Harbor to host a visit by the DACOWITS members because its mixed-gender crew had compiled an outstanding operational performance record.[38] In the course of interviewing female crewmembers, DACOWITS representatives learned that the women lived in a toxic command climate in which they were routinely subjected to offensive and derogatory comments and inappropriate behavior. The senior leadership was clearly part of the problem. During a training exercise, the CO allegedly broadcast an offer over the ship's VHF (Very High Frequency) radio to sell female crewmembers to a South Korean ship. During a port call in the Philippines, the CO and a leading petty officer publicly engaged in sex acts with local women in front of male and female subordinates.[39]

In the aftermath of the *Safeguard* scandal, Secretary of the Navy James Webb Jr. related an anecdote that he believed reflected the mentality prevalent among Navy men. Webb recalled talking to a "normal guy from Podunk, Iowa," while on a midshipman cruise who told Webb, "You know, I'm in the Navy for four years, and I want to do every gross thing I ever dreamed of doing. Then I am going back home and marry my girlfriend and be a farmer."[40]

In general, the prevailing attitude was that so long as the men performed their jobs at sea as required, their personal conduct ashore was their own business. Overseas deployments provided sailors with the opportunity to behave in ways that would not be tolerated by society back home, giving rise to the expression, "What happens on deployment stays on deployment." Compartmented morality was standard operating procedure. Now that women from Podunk, Iowa, were serving alongside these "normal" guys who were accustomed to living out the fantasy of "doing every gross thing they ever dreamed of doing," such attitudes were no longer tenable. But reforming a culture of masculine hedonism developed over two centuries would prove to be incredibly difficult.

The DACOWITS report led to an immediate investigation by local naval commanders. *Safeguard*'s CO was found guilty of ten charges and subjected to serious disciplinary action that effectively ended his military career. Excerpts of the DACOWITS report appeared in major newspapers around the country, excoriating the Navy and Marine Corps for the pernicious climate of sexual harassment they encouraged. The report described the "liberal and routine public use" of Philippine women at military clubs for noon burlesque shows and other "sexually oriented entertainment with the alleged participation of audience members . . . creating an environment in which females are regarded with little or no respect."[41]

The report also noted that COs continued to belittle Navy women, calling them "my girls," "honey," and "Navy gals." Women were shunted into jobs for which they were not trained and were then not promoted, and commanders ignored their complaints about sexual harassment and discrimination.[42] An editorial in the *Christian Science Monitor* depicted the growing gap between traditional Navy attitudes and public expectations: "An attitude that 'women deserve what they get, because they aren't supposed to be there' may linger in some quarters. This view never had much justification, and today it has even less, now that there are very few places indeed where 'women aren't supposed to be.'"[43]

The incident prompted Webb to authorize a thorough review of all Navy policies and to initiate a comprehensive study of Navy women. More than half the Navy women interviewed (1,400) in the study, which was conducted on ships and at naval installations worldwide, said they had been victims of sexual harassment, mostly in the form of verbal abuse.[44]

Many women in the Navy had low expectations that anything substantive would come from Webb's review. The April 1987 Senate confirmation hearings for his appointment as Secretary of the Navy had been contentious. A Naval Academy graduate and decorated former Marine Corps officer who served in Vietnam, Webb was an outspoken critic of policies with which he disagreed. In 1979 he published an article in *Washingtonian* magazine titled "Women Can't Fight." Eighteen years later one of Webb's critics would write that the article "initiated an assault that continues to the present day" and was "the single greatest purveyor of degradation and humiliation on the basis of gender that academy women have had to endure."[45] In his article Webb criticized the decision to admit women to the service academies, contending that it "sterilized the whole process of combat leadership training, and our military services are doomed to suffer the consequences."[46] Pressed on his position at his confirmation hearing, Webb responded by stating that he would not seek to "roll back the clock" to make the institution all male. "I believe the service academies no longer exist purely to train combat leaders. That used to be true. The mission changed once the law changed. I accept that."[47] Webb nevertheless portrayed women and combat as mutually exclusive. It was a view that held wide currency within and outside the service, and it remained codified in law.

Webb's measured responses to such challenges allowed him to weather the confirmation hearings, but they hardly reassured Navy women and their supporters that he would be receptive to their concerns. They were already up in arms over the actions of his predecessor in the post. The outgoing secretary, John F. Lehman Jr., left office under fire for reneging on an announcement he made in October 1986 to open more MLSF vessels to women. To avoid doing so, the Navy reclassified the underway replenishment logistics ships as "Combat Logistics Force" vessels. Official invocation of the word "combat" warded off the assignment of women. In addition, Lehman endorsed an effort by CNO Adm. Carlisle Trost to freeze the number of enlisted women in the Navy for five years despite the DOD's stated plan for a 10 percent increase by fiscal year 1991. Navy spokesmen justified the policy by arguing that "because women can't draw the same sea-going assignments as men, [the Navy] cannot afford to continue increasing the numbers of women filling shore-based job slots." The Navy had recently announced plans to build a six-hundred-ship fleet, but the combat exclusion law meant women could not be assigned to many of those ships.[48] It was the quintessential Catch-22: women were not allowed to go to sea in significant numbers due to the Navy's broad interpretation of what constituted "combat," and since they could not occupy enough seagoing billets, their numbers should be reduced. Defense Secretary Caspar Weinberger, angered because he was not consulted in advance regarding the change, overruled Lehman and Trost.[49] Rep. Don Edwards of California excoriated Lehman in an editorial parting shot and anticipated that James Webb would follow in his footsteps: "When sound personnel decisions are sacrificed so that a few macho leaders can indulge in nostalgia, we are in danger."[50]

The new Secretary of the Navy, however, surprised the skeptics with his actions. When the 1987 Women's Study Group completed its review of the progress of women in the Navy, it issued several recommendations that Webb quickly implemented. There was considerable pressure to act from other sources as well. A parallel effort was also under way at the

DOD level to evaluate the status of women in all the services. In addition, Rep. Beverly Byron (D-MD) introduced legislation to establish a two-year trial program opening a wider array of combat support jobs to women, while Sen. William Cohen (R-ME) and Sen. William Proxmire (D-WI) proposed amending the federal law in order to allow women in all the services to be permanently assigned to combat support billets.[51]

The Navy Women's Study Group released its findings shortly before the DOD Task Force on women in the military did, and each effort informed the other. The DOD report provided more explicit guidance in defining combat missions, stipulating, for example, that "risks of direct combat, exposure to hostile fire, or capture are proper criteria for closing non-combatant units to women, providing that the type, degree and duration of such risks are *equal to or greater than* the combat units with which they are normally associated."[52]

The report's authors questioned whether "changing war fighting doctrine, emerging technologies, and global strategies justify the use of risk or harm or capture alone as a primary criterion for identifying assignments precluded because of the combat exclusion." They noted that women were already "exposed to substantial risk of hostile fire or capture, depending on the specific wartime scenario." But they acknowledged that the legislative histories of the federal statutes that formed the basis of the combat exclusion law reflected congressional intent "to protect women from the most serious risks of harm or capture."[53]

Women had already proven they could meet the demands of sea duty. At the same time the Navy had closed the Combat Logistic Force ships to women, it opened assignment to Military Sealift Command (MSC) replenishment ships, vessels that in many cases performed missions similar to the CLF ships. The only difference was that MSC ships were commanded by civilian merchant mariners. The ship's crews were mostly civilians as well, with a small detachment of Navy personnel to provide communications and logistics support when operating in conjunction with the fleet.

These inconsistencies were difficult for the Navy to continue to defend against mounting scrutiny and outside pressure from the DOD,

Congress, and the public. In December 1987 Webb announced that the Navy had opened assignments to three of the five previously prohibited CLF ship types to women: oilers, ammunition, and combat stores ships. Furthermore, he approved the Women's Study Group's recommendation to modify the Navy's definition of combat. The change involved one small conjunction, substituting "and" for "or." Accordingly, the official Navy instruction defining combat was modified to read, "A combat mission is defined as one that has as one of its primary objectives to seek out, reconnoiter *and* engage the enemy."

This semantic revision opened up assignments for women as aircrew on board fleet air reconnaissance aircraft in two squadrons from which they had previously been excluded on the grounds of the "traditionally hazardous history" of the community and the word "reconnoiter" in the original combat definition.[54] For enlisted women, Webb approved recommendations to improve advancement opportunities for nonrated women recruits by revising recruitment and training policies to redistribute them into more technical ratings. The concentration of women in some traditional shore-based billets was beginning to adversely impact the sea-to-shore ratio for men in certain ratings.

The DOD task force implemented a department-wide survey to be periodically conducted in order to effectively assess and combat sexual harassment in all the services. Each service was tasked with developing a method to assist commanders with assessing their own command climate. A standardized definition of sexual harassment was promulgated, and each service was charged with developing regular programs to educate and train its personnel concerning sexual harassment and how to combat it. Each service was directed to review and modify its enforcement policies as needed to ensure that complaints and concerns would not go unheeded. Finally, the task force recommended changing the directive covering policies for on-base entertainment to "incorporate more explicit and well-defined standards of good taste."[55]

Reaction to the *Safeguard* scandal finally spurred Navy officials to create a framework of programs and policies intended to systematize and facilitate the integration of women into the Navy. Promulgating policy was only half the battle, however; implementing it effectively to overcome ingrained institutional resistance would be much more difficult.

By the end of the 1980s most Americans were accustomed to the fact that women were serving at sea and in dangerous regions of the world. While Navy officials continued to wrestle with integration policies, media coverage of naval operations in the Persian Gulf tanker war between Iraq and Iran focused national attention on the integrated crew of the destroyer tender USS *Acadia* (AD 42). The tender had been dispatched to the region to repair the frigate USS *Stark* (FFG 31) after it was struck by an Iraqi Exocet missile that killed thirty-seven sailors. Approximately 240 female officers and enlisted crewmembers were part of *Acadia*'s crew complement of 1,300. When the media and Congress raised questions about the wisdom of sending women into a potentially hostile area, Pentagon officials issued a statement that *Acadia* was not in a combat zone and that no attacks on U.S. ships in the southern Persian Gulf were anticipated. As a precaution, however, the Navy also detached the guided missile cruiser USS *Fox* (CG 33) from the *Constellation* carrier battle group to escort *Acadia*. A Navy official observed, "You can't have it both ways. If women are going to be allowed to go to sea on support ships, then they have to be available to go wherever that ship is needed."[56]

The media focus on Navy women serving at sea continued to erode public resistance to expanding their roles, but their continued concentration in selected shore-based billets was beginning to pose problems for maintaining equitable sea-to-shore rotation rates for male sailors in a few ratings. In September 1988 the Navy altered the promotion criteria for sixteen enlisted ratings, significantly lowering the qualifying scores for men, and only men, taking the exams to advance from E-3 to E-4. This discriminatory policy was justified as necessary because the combat exclusion laws that restricted women in these ratings to serving only on twenty-seven noncombatant ships reduced the number of men available for sea duty as well. The men who were serving at sea were facing longer tours because women were occupying shore billets, and male attrition was increasing. Unlike the Navy's previous efforts to use sea-to-shore rotation problems as an excuse to restrict or roll back the enlistment of women wholesale, this policy was selectively applied to address problems in specific ratings. Navy women reacted negatively nonetheless, and media coverage of the policy was critical. Instead of lowering the promotion standards for male sailors, critics suggested, perhaps the Navy should encourage them to study harder; likewise, the Navy should reconsider its policy of barring women from serving on combatant ships. In July 1989, Chief of Naval Personnel Vice Adm. Michael J. Boorda announced that the Navy had cut the number of ratings to which the new policy applied from sixteen to three because the right balance between male and female sailors had been achieved.[57]

As Navy women made headlines with their accomplishments, the public became acclimated to seeing them in nontraditional roles. In 1989 Cdr. Deborah Gernes became the first woman surface warfare officer to successfully screen for command of a ship, then took command of the fleet oiler USS *Cimarron* (AO 177) in 1991.[58] Lt. Cdr. Darlene Iskra, a special operations officer, was actually the first woman to assume command of a Navy ship in December 1990 when she relieved the CO of the salvage ship USS *Opportune* (ARS 41), who had fallen ill.[59] In July that same year Cdr. Rosemary Mariner, among the first group of women accepted for aviation training, became the first woman to assume command of a tactical electronic warfare aviation squadron.[60]

Accounts of the advances made by exceptional individuals in the early 1990s stood in sharp contrast to other media stories of continuing problems with integration. Over a three-month period in the summer of 1990, the press reported two incidents of rape of female crewmembers on board ships. One incident involved enlisted personnel; the second involved officers.[61] The public was further scandalized by an incident at the Naval Academy in which a female midshipman was chained to a urinal and photographed by her male classmates.[62] These reports were followed by the release of an inspector general's investigation at the Orlando Naval Training Center, where twenty-four rapes or sexual assaults had been reported over an eighteen-month period. The report noted that "the Navy's failure to take appropriate action against offenders . . . contributed to an atmosphere that makes women 'feel like they are second class members of the Navy.'"[63] The IG's investigation also found numerous violations of the rules against fraternization by male petty officers in supervisory roles over female recruits. Vice Adm. John S. Disher, chief of the Navy Education and Training Command, noted that the problems found at Orlando were "occurring throughout the entire Navy," and "much more needed to be done" to remedy the shortcomings.[64]

A decade after the initial clumsy attempts to purge alleged lesbians from the ranks of Navy women serving at sea, Vice Adm. Joseph S. Donnell, commander of the Surface Force Atlantic Fleet, issued a message to the officers in charge of nearly two hundred ships and forty shore installations directing them to scrupulously enforce the Pentagon's policy banning homosexuality, singling out lesbians. Donnell claimed that "lesbians are 'more aggressive than their male counterparts' and 'intimidating.'" Officers were not to be reluctant to pursue investigations merely "because lesbian sailors are generally 'hard-working, career-oriented, willing to put in long hours on the job and among the command's top performers.'"[65]

Donnell cited Navy statistics from 1985 to 1987 that he said showed lesbians were discharged at twice the rate of gay men. When asked why the admiral felt it necessary to step up enforcement of the rules against lesbians, his spokesman "said the reason was the increasing number of women in the Navy—about 6,000 in a total force of 600,000—and the fact that the officers 'maybe don't have as much experience with that side of the story.'"[66] A correspondent for the *San Francisco Chronicle* observed, "No evidence is produced to back up this claim, this is not social science, it is fear-driven chunky drivel."[67] The sophistry behind the vice admiral's directive was a throwback to attitudes of the 1940s and 1950s that portrayed military women as "abnormal." Sandra Lowe, a staff lawyer for the Lambda Legal Defense and Education Fund in New York, observed, "Women are always suspect who are competent. They don't want any of us here, and here is one group they can get rid of."[68]

These public relations woes were coupled with other high-profile debacles that marked a nadir in the Navy's public image. The investigation into the explosion in the gun turret of USS *Iowa* (BB 61) that killed forty-seven sailors initially placed the blame on a sailor who was purportedly part of a homosexual relationship gone awry. Following several months of intense and critical scrutiny, the Naval Investigative Service's original theory of the cause of the incident collapsed, and Navy officials were forced to apologize to the accused sailor's family.[69] All of these incidents illustrated the intractability of discriminatory attitudes within the service. This reality was confirmed by the results of a 1991 update to the 1987 *Navy Study on the Progress of Women in the Navy*, expedited in response to the recent spate of scandals. The study, based on 2,700 interviews and 4,000 written surveys of men and women from 160 commands worldwide, found that sexual assault and rape were rising even as they remained "seriously underreported." Three-fourths of the women and one-half of the men surveyed said sexual harassment was occurring within their commands. The rise was attributed "to alcohol, a breakdown of moral values and a belief by men that they have a 'right' to sexual relations."[70] The study also noted that Naval Investigative Service (NIS) agents could stand to benefit from new training programs after finding that "a majority of women and staff level advisers perceive that female and male NIS agents, in particular, are poorly trained to deal with victims of sexual assault and rape."[71] The panel that conducted the study cited "law and policy restricting the assignment of women, reinforcing the perception that women are not equal contributors and impacting women's career horizons negatively." The panel cited the performance of women in the Persian Gulf War as justification for liberalizing assignment policies for women, such as opening amphibious ships, mine countermeasures ships, and helicopter squadrons.[72]

When Iraq invaded Kuwait in August 1990, the media ran numerous stories focusing on women going off to war and leaving their families behind. Operation Desert Shield/Desert Storm raised military women's visibility and helped undermine outmoded myths and attitudes. Approximately 10 percent of the 37,000 American women who served in Desert Storm were Navy women.[73] Commander Mariner, one of the first women to qualify as a naval aviator in 1976, achieved another career milestone in July 1990 when she became the first woman to command an operational aviation squadron. Tactical warfare electronics squadron VAQ-34, based in Point Magu, California, was an electronic aggressor squadron that prepared pilots deploying for combat. VAQ-34 aircraft simulated enemy aircraft attacks against U.S. Navy aircraft or ships, mimicking the radars, rockets, and aircraft that those pilots and combatant ship commanders might encounter in theater. Tammie Jo Shults, a member of Mariner's squadron who became famous in 2018 for landing a crippled commercial airliner after its engine failed, recalled that "VAQ flying was not bad duty, but that was as close to combat tactical flying as we ladies could get."[74]

The favorable news coverage of the performance of American servicewomen provided momentum for further change.[75] In April 1991 DACOWITS recommended the repeal of the combat exclusion statutes to the secretary of defense.[76] Rep. Pat Schroeder of Colorado and Rep. Beverly Byron of Maryland introduced an amendment to the 1992 Defense Authorization Act targeting the ban on women in combat aviation. The amendment was easily adopted by a voice vote in May. William V. Roth (R-DE) and Edward M. Kennedy (D-MA) introduced a companion version of the amendment in the Senate.[77]

Many senior military officials in the Pentagon and conservative members of Congress reacted with alarm to the proposed amendment. In their view, the legislation was the first step down a steep and slippery slope that would end in removing all restrictions on women in combat. Although the proposed amendment was narrowly focused on women aviators, media coverage broadened the context of the debate to cover all combat roles. *Newsweek* published poll results indicating that 79 percent of Americans agreed that women should be eligible for combat, although 53 percent thought it should be on a voluntary basis.[78] In an effort to slow the momentum for change, Senate conservatives convened a public hearing to address the full range of combat assignments for women, not just aviation. All four members of the Joint Chiefs of Staff expressed their personal opposition to allowing women to fly combat missions but said they would carry out the will of Congress. Each service chief gave a brief statement that alluded in vague terms to "military effectiveness," but none provided any evidence to contradict the reports that women had performed well in the Persian Gulf War.[79]

Former Marine Corps commandant Robert Barrow's statement reprised the traditional arguments. He asserted that "the very nature of women" disqualifies them from ground combat. "Women give life, sustain life, they do not take it." He also stressed the importance of male bonding. Introducing women into combat aviation units would erode unit cohesiveness and damage the men's mutual respect and admiration for one another, which was based on their belief that "they and they alone are able to do what they have been asked."[80] Barrow's objection was based not on the ability of women to do the job but on men's *resentment* of that ability.

Two former fighter pilots, Sen. John McCain (R-AZ) and Sen. John Glenn (D-OH), led the Senate effort to kill the Kennedy-Roth proposal, with the backing of John Warner and Sen. Sam Nunn (D-GA). McCain and Warner had both come out publicly in favor of lifting the ban earlier but reversed their position under an onslaught of intense lobbying from retired military leaders and conservatives. Glenn and McCain proposed a substitute amendment to lift all combat exclusion laws temporarily; women could be assigned to combat units on a trial basis while a presidential commission examined the issue in depth.

In her detailed account of the debate that took place in the Senate Armed Services Committee, Jeanne Holm explained that while the Glenn-McCain amendment appeared to be an even better deal for all military women, the proposal to temporarily lift all combat exclusion laws was in fact a last-ditch effort to swing enough votes over to kill the Kennedy-Roth amendment. Unable to muster compelling evidence against the proposal to lift the combat ban for female aviators, opponents hoped that lifting exclusions against all military women would catalyze opposition, much in the way Phyllis Schlafly had invoked the prospect of the draft to defeat the Equal Rights Amendment. In fact, Schlafly was involved in this latest battle as well, assisted by Elaine Donnelly, who had served from 1984 to 1986 on the Defense Advisory Committee on Women in the Services during the Reagan administration. A staffer on the Senate Armed Services Committee noted that Schlafly and Donnelly engaged in a nonstop lobbying effort on Capitol Hill against lifting the combat ban: "They are covering this place like a blanket."[81]

Kennedy and Roth argued that their amendment was compatible with the Glenn-McCain amendment, and that members could vote for both, which is precisely what happened.[82] Opponents not only failed to forestall lifting the ban on women in combat aviation but inadvertently paved the way to lifting *all* legal restrictions against women in combat. The presidential commission now became their last line of defense.

Over the objections of Defense Secretary Richard B. Cheney, President George H. W. Bush dropped two of Cheney's proposed members and appointed staunch conservatives Kate Walsh O'Beirne of the Heritage Foundation and Elaine Donnelly of Phyllis Schafly's Eagle Forum to the Presidential Commission on the Assignment of Women in the Armed Forces.[83] Eight months of contentious debate ensued. "The commission's debates had a fractious tone, with members on each side of the issue contending their opponents viewed the evidence through ideological blinders."[84] At one point, five conservative commissioners staged a walkout, refusing to return unless the chairman of the commission allowed them to insert a chapter presenting their "Findings, facts, studies and information in support of the case against placing women in combat."[85]

The commission voted eight to seven to recommend reinstating the ban on assigning women to combat aircraft. They also voted initially against allowing women to serve on combatant ships but relented when the commission chairman admonished them that "our report will be ignored if it rejects any change in the *status quo*."[86] The two active-duty officers on the commission, Capt. Mary Finch, USA, and Brig. Gen. Thomas V. Draude, USMC, "accused what Finch called 'the moral majority here' of coming to the panel with their minds made up and said there were no comparable advocates on the other side."[87] Draude accused Elaine Donnelly of using "facts the way a drunk uses a lamppost, not for illumination but for support." Finch concluded, "If I was president, I would look at the makeup of the Commission and throw a lot of the recommendations out."[88]

While the commission deliberated and debated, the lurid details of another major Navy scandal were being revealed to the public. The Tailhook scandal would overshadow all subsequent debates on the issue of women in combat. By the time the commission promulgated its final report in

November 1992, its recommendations had been rendered moot. Commission member Charles Moskos observed that "Tailhook 'has cast a longer shadow' over the proceedings than even the performance of women in the Persian Gulf War."[89] As a frustrated Captain Finch had suggested it should, the incoming Clinton administration ignored the commission's findings.

The conservative members' attempt to predetermine the findings of the commission was thwarted by a number of factors. While they claimed to represent the views of a "silent majority" within the military and the American public, they could only do so by ignoring a growing mountain of evidence to the contrary. In addition to numerous public opinion polls that showed wide support for expanding roles for military women, internal Navy studies and DOD and GAO reports relating to gender integration since 1978 demonstrated that the integration of women into the military was working well. A 1990 GAO study of attrition and retention rates for women in the military concluded that while the overall attrition rate for enlisted women was 4.5 percent higher than for men, the basic pattern of attrition was similar. Most first-term losses for both sexes occurred within the first three months, when recruits go through basic training, and in the last three to six months, when they may leave the service early for reasons such as school attendance. In the intervening period, men and women left the services at relatively steady rates, with women's rates slightly higher than men's. Women officer losses were less than two percentage points higher than men's for the services as a whole. Career retention rates for enlisted and officer women between 1984 and 1988 averaged 5.54 percent lower than men's rates.[90]

A GAO report to the secretary of defense on the deployment of military women in the Persian Gulf War directly addressed the issues that had been repeatedly raised during debates over removing combat assignment restrictions for women. These included whether combat and noncombat role distinctions had any meaning in modern warfare; whether women could endure the hardships of long deployments and perform effectively; whether their presence had an adverse effect on unit cohesion and performance; and whether pregnancies had an adverse effect on a unit's deployment readiness.[91]

The GAO reported that women performed a wide range of duties throughout the deployment area and served in units that crossed the border into Iraq and Kuwait during the air and ground wars. Women received enemy fire, returned fire, and dealt with enemy prisoners. Perceptions of the women's performance were highly positive. Most of the commanders interviewed indicated that women performed as well as or better than men. In situations requiring physical strength, teamwork overcame individual limitations. There were few complaints that women were enjoying favoritism in terms of assignments or avoiding arduous tasks. However, rumors within some units that women would be removed or sent to rear areas because of combat restrictions undermined unit morale.[92] Men and women confronted the same arduous conditions during deployments and were perceived to deal with the accompanying stress equally. Focus group participants reported that gender homogeneity was not a requirement for effective unit cohesion during deployment. Instead, the general theme from the respondents was that "individuals who experience a crisis bond because of the crisis—not because they are women or men," and "the important factors are individual capabilities, personalities, training, and overall skill levels."[93] Responses to the pregnancy issue, which conservative opponents to the further integration of women into the military raised repeatedly, were the most interesting. "Although people readily identified pregnancy as a reason for not deploying, few recalled specific instances within their immediate unit or outside of it."[94]

All of these issues associated with the women-in-combat debate were relegated to the back burner as media reports detailing the egregious conduct of naval aviators during the 1991 Tailhook Symposium hit front pages around the country. Tailhook was the Navy's moral Pearl Harbor. Just as the Imperial Japanese Navy's surprise carrier strike against the U.S. Pacific Fleet forced the Navy to revise an outmoded doctrine centered on the primacy of the battleship, the fallout from the Tailhook scandal rained destruction on the precepts of a Navy culture that civil society could no longer condone or ignore. The seemingly unending litany of lurid revelations incensed the press, the public, and, most significantly, Congress.

The Tailhook Association, a private organization comprising active duty, Reserve, and retired Navy and Marine Corps aviators, defense contractors, and others, enjoyed official Navy support for its activities. Naval aviators were encouraged to attend the symposium as part of their professional development, and many flew to the meetings in Navy aircraft. The naval aviation community's senior leadership attended to discuss the state of the profession and impart their wisdom to the next generation. But there was another, seamier aspect to these conventions that was common knowledge within the ranks of the Navy. "For most of the association's thirty-five years," journalist William McMichael noted, "its conventions at the Las Vegas Hilton had been one of the Navy's dirty little secrets, like its officers' clubs and the X-rated after-hours action at Subic Bay, the Philippines."[95]

At the September 1991 Tailhook Symposium, a number of civilian and military women, including naval aviator Lt. Paula Coughlin, an admiral's aide, were accosted and assaulted by male aviators. Coughlin went public with the story of her assault at the hands of men who were purportedly her professional peers. The dirty little secret was out, and the ramifications would be profound. The scope of the misconduct and failure of leadership was outlined starkly in a memorandum for the secretary of defense from the deputy inspector general of the DOD that characterized the misconduct as "widespread." The memo cited ninety victims of indecent assault, multiple incidents of indecent exposure, and "other types of sexual misconduct." More than fifty Navy and Marine Corps officers made false statements during the investigation. Investigative files on "30 Navy flag officers, 2 Marine Corps general officers and 3 Navy Reserve flag officers" were forwarded to the acting Secretary of the Navy "to determine whether action is warranted with respect to the responsibility of each flag officer for the overall leadership failure that culminated in the events of Tailhook 91."[96]

An internal investigation conducted by the NIS stalled due to in-service stonewalling and a hostile attitude toward the victims expressed by the NIS commander, Rear Adm. Duvall M. "Mac" Williams. During a heated discussion with Assistant Secretary of the Navy for Manpower and Reserve

Affairs Barbara S. Pope on the role of women in the Navy, Williams was purported to have said, "What you don't understand Barbara, is that men in the Navy don't want women in the Navy." When Pope challenged this assertion, Williams responded, "Well, you know, a lot of female pilots are topless dancers and hookers."[97] Williams, along with Navy Inspector General Rear Adm. John E. "Ted" Gordon, would later be fired on the recommendation of the DOD inspector general for obstructing the investigation and withholding evidence pertaining to the involvement of senior officers.[98]

The protracted investigations and intense scrutiny from Congress and the media took a toll on the Navy's leadership. Secretary of the Navy H. Lawrence Garrett III and CNO Adm. Frank B. Kelso, both of whom had been present at Tailhook '91, eventually resigned. Assistant CNO (Air Warfare) Vice Adm. Richard Dunleavy, who initially lied to investigators about his level of involvement and knowledge of the Tailhook activities, received a letter of censure from the Secretary of the Navy and was demoted to the rank of rear admiral. Two of Dunleavy's deputies, Rear Adm. Riley Mixson and Rear Adm. Wilson Flagg, also received letters of censure. Thirty other flag officers received nonpunitive letters of caution.[99] The DOD investigators referred 119 Navy officers and 21 Marine Corps officers for possible disciplinary action on charges that included indecent exposure, indecent assault, conduct unbecoming an officer, and failure to act in a proper leadership capacity.[100] The IG's report noted that many officers fell back on "tradition" as an excuse for their conduct, equating the Tailhook convention to an overseas deployment. Officers felt entitled to "excessive drinking, indecent exposure and visits to prostitutes as common activities while on liberty" to compensate them for the hardships of sea duty.[101]

A female lieutenant commander who was interviewed for the DOD IG's report asserted that the atmosphere at Tailhook '91 was different from previous years. She felt that the Persian Gulf War, the subsequent force drawdown, and the contemporary congressional debate over expanding combat roles for women in aviation had engendered "an animosity in this Tailhook . . . that was telling the women that 'We don't have any respect for you now as humans.'" Men resented women for challenging their behavior and threatening their livelihood: "This was the woman that wanted to take your spot in that combat aircraft."[102] The IG's report concluded that the misconduct at Tailhook "so deviated from the standards of behavior the nation expects of its military officers that the repetition of this behavior year after year raises serious questions about the senior leadership of the Navy."[103]

Many naval officers complained that the Tailhook debacle was a political witch hunt that had unfairly ended many officers' careers and tarnished the reputation of the entire service. An unidentified male aviator lieutenant's reaction to Secretary of the Navy Garrett's resignation was typical: "Garret was destroyed by the news media who used Tailhook to further their 'feminist agenda.'"[104]

Tailhook demonstrated in stark terms the endemic nature of sexism and sexual harassment in the Navy, and it also exposed the moral bankruptcy of the Navy's leadership. Senior leaders lied and obstructed the investigations, justifying their actions in terms of protecting the institution when accountability, not obfuscation, would have served the best interests of the Navy. But the media and Congress were not to blame for the Navy's plight. Tailhook was a catastrophic failure of leadership at multiple levels, exacerbated by a refusal to recognize the bankruptcy of a behavioral culture cultivated over decades in an exclusively male environment.

As the institutional ship foundered in a storm of public recrimination, Navy leaders quickly redirected their energies from damage control to real reform. At a congressional hearing in July 1992, Rep. Beverly Byron laid out Congress' expectations. After recounting the litany of recent scandals across the services, she said, "I think this is the end of the line. We must be assured that sexual abuse and harassment will no longer be given lip service in the military and covered up."[105]

CNO Adm. Frank Kelso acknowledged that sexual harassment was endemic to the Navy culture. "Until Tailhook we dealt too often with sexual harassment at the local level, one case at a time, rather than understanding it as a cultural issue that had to be addressed throughout the Navy."[106]

While there was some debate about the extent to which the combat exclusion laws contributed to sexual harassment in the military, Congress took the view as articulated by Rep. Les Aspin that combat exclusion rules constituted an official policy of discrimination that contributed to unofficially endorsed discrimination in other ways.[107]

Within days of the public release of the final Tailhook report in April 1993, now–Secretary of Defense Les Aspin issued a memorandum on the assignment of women in the armed forces. The memo directed all the services to open more specialties and assignments to women. The provisions affecting the Navy included allowing "women to compete for assignments in aircraft, including aircraft engaged in combat missions" and "opening as many additional ships to women as is practicable within current law." Aspin specifically directed the Navy to draft legislation repealing the combat exclusion law and to "permit the assignment of women to ships that are engaged in combat missions."[108]

During House hearings in May 1993, Chief of Naval Personnel Vice Adm. Ronald J. Zlatoper urged Congress to repeal the combat exclusion laws. Noting that "the debate over whether women can do the job should have ended long ago," Zlatoper promised that the Navy would not compromise its standards to integrate women into combat assignments.[109] In the final version of the Defense Authorization Act of 1994, Congress repealed the combat exclusion law with three provisos:

1. Ninety days' notice of any change in policy barring women from ground combat in Army or Marine Corps Units
2. The establishment of specific gender-neutral physical requirements for any job specialty requiring strength, endurance, or cardiovascular capacity
3. Sixty days' notice of any change in qualifications for any job specialty expected to result in an increase or decrease of more than 10 percent of the number of women in that field.[110]

President William J. Clinton signed the bill into law on 30 November 1993 and it was implemented in 1994. With the new policy in place, the integration of women into the fleet accelerated. Within months of the repeal of the combat exclusion laws, Navy women fighter pilots began fly-ing combat sorties over the no-fly zone in Iraq. In October 1994 the aircraft carrier USS *Eisenhower* (CVN 69) deployed with women as permanent members of the crew.[111]

The repeal of the combat exclusion law vindicated Navy women's forty-five-year struggle to throw out gender stereotypes and be accepted on the basis of their demonstrated abilities. Although battered by tempests generated by colliding fronts of cultural change and ingrained traditions, the Navy weathered the storms and charted a new course, with women at the helm.

= Part IV =

INTEGRATION

= 7 =
HAZE GRAY AND UNDER WAY

After 20 years of women serving aboard ship—first support ships and, since 1994—combatants—it seems too many people in Washington and elsewhere are asking the wrong question. It's not "Can women serve at sea?" It's "Why are we still arguing about it?"
—*Navy Times* editorial, 23 November 1998, 31

Writing for *New Yorker* magazine in 1996, Peter J. Boyer observed that the fallout from Tailhook defined a new epoch for the U.S. Navy. "The scandal became the divide between the old Navy, flawed but secure in its verities, and the new, conceived in the heat of the nation's culture wars."[1]

Unlike the carefully planned phase-in of women onto surface ships in the 1970s and 1980s, female aviation warfare officers found themselves in the cockpits of fighter jets flying combat sorties within months of the repeal of the combat exclusion laws. This abrupt turn of events and the circumstances that made it possible exacerbated what would have been a tense situation under the best of circumstances.[2] The first wave of female naval aviators in combat assignments confronted virulent hostility from their male counterparts. This hostility was politicized and exploited by cultural conservatives in an effort to discredit the achievements of Navy women in warfare specialties and to blunt the momentum of change with which the old guard did not agree. The collateral damage from these skirmishes in the Navy's internal culture war would leave careers on both sides of the issue in ruins.

In October 1994, Lt. Kara Hultgreen, among the first women to carrier-qualify as an F-14 pilot, crashed when the left engine of her plane stalled on her landing approach to USS *Abraham Lincoln* (CVN 72).[3] The Navy did not treat this tragedy any differently than it had the deaths of ten male F-14 pilots who had died in the previous two years. Hultgreen was accorded the same military honors as any other fallen aviator. Subsequent to Hultgreen's death, however, in an unprecedented breach of military professionalism, excerpts from the flight-training records of another female F-14 pilot in the same air wing, Lt. Carey Lohrenz, were leaked to a conservative defense organization. The Center for Military Readiness (CMR) published a 125-page special report asserting that the Navy was rushing unqualified female pilots through the training pipeline. A CMR press release charged "that the Navy's integration of women into combat squadrons was part of a 'reckless race' with the Air Force that had been 'instigated by aggressive female officers, feminist advocates, and Navy Public Affairs Officers.'"[4] A Navy investigation determined the records had been leaked by a flight instructor, Lt. Patrick Jerome Burns, who claimed he had first tried to address his concerns unsuccessfully through the chain of command. His commanding officer and all the other flight instructors denied that Burns had ever discussed Lohrenz with them. The other instructors also testified that no undue pressure was ever put on them to pass women. It was standard procedure when training Navy pilots that individuals who were selected to make immediate cruises were designated "must pumps" and accelerated through training. Because Lohrenz was slated for assignment to *Abraham Lincoln*, which was scheduled to deploy to the Persian Gulf, she fell into this category, along with a number of male aviators.[5]

The media uproar prompted additional investigations by the Navy, which had initially ruled that Hultgreen's crash was caused by pilot error. When Hultgreen's plane was recovered after repeated attempts (her body was still strapped into the ejection seat), further analysis determined that mechanical failure, not pilot error, had caused the crash.[6] Nonetheless, Lieutenant Lohrenz's aviation career was damaged by the ostracism and hostility of her squadronmates. The stress of the media scrutiny and hostility of her male peers affected her performance in the cockpit, and she was grounded in 1995.[7] Two other female pilots who had been assigned to Carrier Air Wing 11 on *Abraham Lincoln* were also grounded, and one left following an illness to become a test pilot.[8] Lt. Missy Cummings, who qualified to fly the F/A-18 and was among the first women pilots sent to sea, recalled, "Any group of people who are at the vanguard of cultural change are generally not well accepted. We had a pretty rough time as female fighter pilots. The guys didn't want to share the treehouse." Although she loved flying, the endless hostility and isolation from her male shipmates made a career as a naval aviator unsustainable.[9] Cummings left the Navy and earned a PhD in systems engineering.

The Center for Military Readiness, the organization that made Lohrenz's stolen confidential training records public, was established by Elaine Donnelly in 1993, a year after Donnelly and the other conservatives appointed to the 1992 Presidential Commission on the Assignment of Women in the Armed Forces had tried unsuccessfully to stop the assignment of women to combat billets in aviation and on surface ships. Among the CMR's principles stated on its website was, "The armed forces should not be used for political purposes or social experiments that needlessly elevate risks, detract from readiness, or degrade American cultural values."[10] Some of the Navy's and Marine Corps' most senior retired officers sat on the CMR's Board of Advisors in 2006, including Gen. Robert Barrow, former commandant of the Marine Corps, who testified before the 1992 presidential commission that women should not be allowed to fill combat billets because it would diminish male aviators' self-esteem; and former CNO Adm. Carlisle Trost, whose attempt to reduce the numbers of women in the ranks of the Navy was overruled by Secretary of Defense Caspar Weinberger. The CMR's board also included a number of combat-decorated veterans of World War II, Korea, and Vietnam, many of whom retired from active service before the integration of women into seagoing billets and combat assignments became an issue, and who had no direct experience serving with women in those capacities.

Other Navy and Marine Corps board members and their dates of retirement included Rear Adm. John M. Barrett (1977), Gen. Robert H. Barrow (1983), Rear Adm. Jeremiah A. Denton (1977), Capt. Eugene B. "Red" McDaniel (1982), Vice Adm. David C. Richardson (1972), and astronaut Capt. Walter M. "Wally" Schirra Jr. (1969). Members of more recent vintage included Col. John W. Ripley, USMC (1992), and Cdr. Robert E. Stumpf, who retired from the Navy in 1996 after Congress refused to approve his promotion to captain because he had attended the 1991 Tailhook Symposium. Included among the more prominent civilians on the CMR Board of Advisors were David Horowitz, a disillusioned progressive who became a conservative writer; Beverly LeHaye, founder of Concerned Women for America; and Kate Walsh O'Beirne, Washington editor of *National Review* magazine.[11]

When the Navy inspector general's office declined to pursue an investigation of Lieutenant Burns' illegal disclosure of her confidential flight training records, Lieutenant Lohrenz filed a civil lawsuit against the Navy for violating the federal Privacy Act. The Navy settled the case out of court for $150,000 with no admission of wrongdoing, but Lohrenz had to resign from the service as part of the settlement.[12] Secretary of the Navy John Dalton blocked Lieutenant Burns' promotion to lieutenant commander with a written reprimand accusing him of acting dishonorably: "You violated federal law by releasing records of a shipmate knowing that such information would be used to humiliate the officer involved."[13] Lohrenz also filed a defamation action against Donnelly and the CMR as well as the *San Diego Union-Tribune*, the *Washington Times*, and "John Does 1–100" (retired officers of the Navy and other military services who allegedly assisted Donnelly and republished CMR's statements.[14]

The U.S. District Court in Washington, DC, issued a summary judgment that did not address the veracity of CMR's assertions that the Navy was rushing unqualified women through aviation training. It ruled only on the narrow issue of whether Lieutenant Lohrenz was a public figure, in which case the legal standard for proving libel is considerably higher. The court ruled that by virtue of choosing to fly a combat jet fighter while knowing of the public controversy surrounding women in combat, Lohrenz made herself a public figure, "and she must live with the consequences of that choice."[15]

The Federal Appeals Court further ruled that Lohrenz had failed to meet the burden of proof for libel, even though Navy officials had repeatedly contested Donnelly's version of the facts, because CMR's press releases reported the Navy's denials. "Reporting perspectives at odds with the publisher's own 'tend to rebut a claim of malice, not to establish one.'"[16]

The Supreme Court declined to hear a final appeal in the case.[17] Since the protracted court battle did not address the substantive issue of the accuracy of the reports and Donnelly's statements that women were the beneficiaries of a double standard, there was no definitive resolution to the argument. It is a historical irony that the case turned on the concept of Lohrenz's status as a public figure by virtue of choosing an unconventional career. While the reasoning behind the legal precedents in the appellate court decision have been questioned by the likes of conservative Supreme Court justice Antonin Scalia, there is ample historical precedent for the decision in that women who have chosen to make themselves conspicuous by entering previously forbidden territory in the public sphere have found themselves targets of vicious scandal and slander campaigns.[18] The experience of the WACs and WAVES in World War II and the services' preoccupation with protecting the moral reputation of their women members are prime examples.

A 1997 report by the Navy's IG on the integration of women into fighter jet squadrons was extremely critical of the process, citing a lack of direction from Navy officials in Washington to the wing commanders in the Atlantic and Pacific Fleets. But the experiences of the two carriers that first took on female pilots were dramatically different. While only four of the eight female pilots on board *Abraham Lincoln* in the Pacific Fleet successfully completed their tour, nine out of ten female pilots on *Eisenhower* in the Atlantic Fleet completed their tours, and "no significant gender-related issues were reported." *Eisenhower* returned from its deployment before *Lincoln* departed, and the IG's report faulted Navy officials for not having arranged to pass on lessons learned from "Ike's" deployment. The dramatic difference in the experiences on the two carriers strongly suggests the importance of establishing an appropriate command climate, which is an attribute that cannot be easily transferred from one commanding officer to another.

It is worth noting here that following Hultgreen's death, her squadron, Fighter Squadron 213, compiled the worst safety record among the Navy's F-14 squadrons, with three crashes. Lt. Cdr. John Stacy Bates was ruled responsible for two of those crashes. After he was found at fault in the first accident when he lost control of his plane during a banking maneuver, he received additional training and was cleared to fly again. In the second accident, Bates and his radar officer were killed, along with three civilians in Nashville, Tennessee, when their F-14 fully loaded with fuel crashed into a house shortly after attempting a steep takeoff at twice the normal angle of climb. The squadron's commanding officer was relieved of command a week after the third crash.[19]

In general terms, the IG's report cited the hostility within the tactical aviation community as rooted in male aviators' fear that their leaders would not manage gender integration fairly and female aviators' fear that they would be more harshly evaluated for any mistakes and lose their flight status while their male counterparts would be given opportunities to correct their problems. In its discussion of the Lohrenz case, the IG report concluded that the Navy had put excessive pressure on Lohrenz by publicizing her role as one of the Navy's first female combat pilots, which engendered resentment from the men. After Lieutenant Hultgreen was killed, the Navy failed to recognize the additional pressure that incident and the release of her training records to the media placed on Lohrenz, resulting in the deterioration of her performance as a pilot. The report criticized the incumbent commander of the Navy's Pacific air forces at the time, Vice Adm. Robert J. Spane, for announcing a firm "gender neutral" policy for all aviators under his command, which some of the commanding officers in Carrier Air Wing 11 interpreted as a directive to withhold extra instruction or encouragement to new carrier pilots for fear of being perceived as showing favoritism. The report concluded, "They became managers of their squadrons, they gave up being their leaders."[20]

While the first generation of female combat pilots were enduring the backlash from the Tailhook scandal, another controversy involving a female aviator in training was unfolding that would end the career of one of the Navy's most senior and revered leaders and set off a chain of events that culminated in the suicide of the Navy's senior uniformed officer.

In April 1994 President Clinton selected Adm. Jeremy Michael Boorda to serve as the twenty-fifth Chief of Naval Operations. Boorda was an unconventional choice for several reasons. He was the first CNO who was not a graduate of the Naval Academy. He worked his way up through the enlisted ranks. And he was a surface warfare officer, a warfare specialty that was not held in the same high esteem as aviation or submarine warfare. Boorda was selected for his reputation as a politically savvy "people person," someone from outside the ranks of the traditional old guard of Navy leaders tainted by Tailhook. Boorda made it clear from the outset that he was a strong advocate for expanding the roles of women in the Navy.[21]

Only five days after assuming office as CNO, Boorda was confronted with a controversy involving a female officer who had washed out of flight school. Lt. Rebecca Hansen filed a complaint that she was unfairly attrited in retaliation for filing a sexual harassment complaint against a flight instructor. Hansen's complaint worked its way through the chain of command and was reviewed in turn by her CO, a Navy review board, and the inspectors general for the Department of the Navy and the Department of Defense. At every level of review, Navy and DOD officials concurred that Hansen's performance in training was substandard and her attrition justified. She failed two of the most important courses in Aviation Officer Candidate School—navigation and engineering—requiring extra instruction before she passed. When she progressed to flight training, she repeatedly made the same mistakes and failed to accept responsibility for her poor performance. While she was in fact subjected to sexual harassment from one flight instructor, who was disciplined for his behavior, there was ample independent corroborating evidence from the other instructors that Hansen was not cut out to be an aviator. Hansen persisted in her complaint, however, enlisting the support of Sen. David Durenberger (R-MN).[22]

In an effort to put an end to the controversy, Secretary of the Navy John Dalton asked Vice CNO Adm. Stanley J. Arthur to review the Hansen case. Arthur was a Vietnam veteran of more than five hundred combat missions, the recipient of eleven Distinguished Flying Crosses, and former commander of U.S. Navy forces in the Persian Gulf War. He was highly regarded throughout the Navy. He had also supported integrating women into naval aviation and combat assignments. His impeccable professional credentials and reputation seemingly made him the ideal person to lay the Hansen case to rest. Admiral Arthur met with Hansen and Senator Durenberger and his staff prior to evaluating her case. Following his review, Arthur upheld the previous decisions and told Lieutenant Hansen that the record showed the Navy had done everything it could to help her succeed, but she had failed to meet standards. Senator Durenberger responded by placing a hold on Arthur's nomination to become commander in chief, Pacific Command, the Navy's most prestigious combatant command and a fitting capstone to a distinguished career. Senator Durenberger's chief of staff admitted that he "believed that Arthur was probably right about Hansen, but this wasn't a moment for taking the Navy's word for anything."[23] Durenberger refused to lift his hold on Arthur's nomination until the admiral answered all the senator's questions to his satisfaction.

Assistant Secretary of the Navy Frederick Pang met with Hansen and her lawyer to ascertain what it would take to get Hansen to accept her attrition from flight school. When this meeting failed to resolve the issue, another meeting was arranged between Hansen and Secretary of the Navy Dalton. Hansen wanted Dalton to offer her a position in his office working on women's policy issues. Dalton instead offered her a chance to become a naval flight officer, a "back-seater" to the pilot. She refused. In a second meeting with Assistant Secretary Pang, Hansen presented a list of demands that included "a written apology from Dalton, the excision of all negative evaluations from her record, return to flight school, time off to attend law school, time and money for civilian flight training, promotion, and when she finished law school, a job in the Navy working on women's issues."[24]

At this point Hansen should have been unceremoniously shown the door, and the wheels of the Navy bureaucracy were turning to make that happen. Admiral Boorda intervened, however, telling Admiral Arthur to persevere while Boorda worked with Congress. Sen. Sam Nunn, chairman of the Senate Armed Services Committee, assured Boorda that he could get Arthur confirmed to the Pacific Command assignment, but when Boorda reported back to Arthur, the CNO emphasized that the chairman of the Joint Chiefs of Staff, Gen. John Shalikashvili, was growing impatient with the delay and implied that continued delay might result in the Navy losing the coveted position to a senior officer of another service branch. Arthur submitted his request for retirement in the interest of preserving the CINCPAC position for the Navy.[25]

Boorda's failure to defend Arthur's nomination stunned the Navy's officer corps and incited tremendous animosity toward him. This animosity was further exacerbated when Boorda agreed to meet with Lieutenant Hansen during an official visit to the Great Lakes Naval Training Center. During that meeting, Boorda offered Hansen any other opportunity in the Navy she wanted aside from flight training, and even invited her to come and work for him directly. Secretary of the Navy Dalton had already decided to discharge Hansen, and Boorda's offer unilaterally undermined the entire official review process that had played out so painstakingly up to that point. "In the eyes of the institution," Boyer wrote in his *New Yorker* article, "Boorda had just traded Stan Arthur for Rebecca Hansen, sacrificing the Navy ideal for the perfect symbol of the Navy's post-Tailhook torment."[26]

Boorda's first major decision as CNO permanently tainted his tenure in office and subjected him to open ridicule from the ranks of current and former Navy officers in the pages of the Naval Institute's *Proceedings* and the *Navy Times*. The August 1995 issue of *Proceedings* included a satirical essay on the post-Tailhook Navy, where aircraft carriers came equipped with nurseries and sensitivity training took precedence over mission readiness. The article caused an uproar. Over the next year, letters to the *Proceedings* editors appeared regularly either praising or excoriating both the essay and its author. Some described the satirical scenario as "more truth than spoof," while others expressed their disgust with the essay, its author, and *Proceedings* for publishing it. Rear Adm. John J. Natter, a Reservist, called it "professional pornography."[27]

In April 1996 former Secretary of the Navy James Webb delivered a speech at the annual meeting of the U.S. Naval Institute at the Naval Academy denouncing leaders "guilty of the ultimate disloyalty: to save or advance their careers, they abandoned the very ideals of their profession to curry favor with politicians."[28] Where were these people, Webb asked, when "certain political elements" tried to use the Tailhook incident to discredit the Navy? He criticized the "Acting Secretary of the Navy, who had never spent a day in uniform," for describing the Tailhook scandal at a press conference as a cultural problem—which, of course, was *exactly* what it was. The many officers who were questioned during the investigation cited "tradition" as the rationale for their behavior. "How," Webb asked, "could the Chief of Naval Operations . . . fail to defend the way of life he had spent a career helping to shape?"[29] Webb also mentioned the Hansen case and Admiral Arthur's retirement, asking "where is the outrage?"[30] The audience of active-duty and retired Navy personnel and midshipmen gave Webb a standing ovation.[31]

In May, the *Navy Times* published a vitriolic anonymous letter to the editor calling on Admiral Boorda to resign, charging he had lost the respect of every officer in the Navy. "Behind his back," the writer sneered, "admirals often refer to the CNO as 'Little Mikey Boorda.'"[32]

In yet another loose end from the Tailhook debacle, the Senate Armed Services Committee placed a hold on the promotion of Cdr. Robert E. Stumpf, an F-18 pilot and commander of the Blue Angels flight demonstration team. Stumpf had been invited to the 1991 Tailhook Symposium to receive an award for leading the best fighter squadron in the Navy. While at the convention he attended a party organized by his subordinates that featured nude exotic dancers, one of whom performed a sex act on one of the pilots. Stumpf was not in the room when this event occurred, and an investigation by a Navy court of inquiry acquitted him. Members of the Senate Armed Services Committee, however, were angered because they had only recently been informed of Stumpf's presence at Tailhook, despite their directive that the records of all the officers eligible for promotion who had attended the symposium be flagged for the committee's review. The committee refused to approve Stumpf's promotion. Boorda, still smarting from the hostility and ridicule precipitated by his failure to defend Admiral Arthur, promised Stumpf he would support his promotion even if he had to lay his stars on the table, as Webb said Boorda should have done on behalf of Admiral Arthur.[33]

Before Boorda could follow through on his pledge, he learned that he himself was the subject of an investigation by journalists for *Newsweek* magazine for having worn medal devices denoting valor in combat that he technically was not authorized to wear. The day he learned of the investigation, Boorda drove from the Pentagon to his residence in the Washington Navy Yard at lunchtime and shot himself.[34]

That dramatic act of self-destruction can only be fully understood within the context of the culture war that was being waged within the Navy at the time. Boorda, the leader who was going to fix all the ills of the post-Tailhook Navy, was instead consumed by them. His reluctance to stand up to Congress and defend his subordinates who were being unfairly penalized cost him his credibility and respect within the Navy, both the rank and file and the leadership. Boorda knew full well the magnitude of the contempt, derision, and humiliation he would suffer were he to be exposed for wearing combat decorations to which he may not have been entitled. Boorda had enlisted in the Navy to escape an unhappy home life, and he had risen to its highest rank. "He deeply believed the Navy had saved his life. He evidently concluded he could save its life . . . by sinking himself and his mistake."[35]

Shortly after Boorda's suicide, former CNO Admiral Zumwalt, who had commanded Naval Forces Vietnam from 1968 to 1970, submitted a memorandum to incumbent Secretary of the Navy John Dalton asserting that Zumwalt had verbally directed that sailors who received decorations while serving on ships in the combat zone were authorized to wear the "V" device. Secretary Dalton subsequently placed a memorandum along with Zumwalt's memo and a revised transcript of service in Admiral Boorda's official personnel file. In September 1996, Boorda's son formally petitioned the Board for Correction of Naval Records to authorize the combat V for his father. The Awards Division of the OPNAV staff submitted a memorandum recommending against the petitioner's request, noting that the CNO did not have the authority to authorize award of the combat V. At the time Boorda was awarded the Navy Achievement Medal, V devices were not authorized to be worn on that award. Eligibility to wear the combat V on the Navy Commendation Medal required specific authorizing language in the award citation. The governing Navy directive stipulated the device was to be authorized for personnel who had directly participated in combat operations and been "exposed to personal hazard due to hostile action." Although Boorda's award citation stated that his ship was involved in combat operations, he was not exposed to personal hazard. Furthermore, when he was recommended for the award, there was a box on the form to specifically designate if the individual was recommended for the V device. That block was not checked. Therefore, the board found "no error or injustice warranting corrective action."[36]

In her memorandum acknowledging the board's final determination, Assistant Secretary of the Navy Carolyn H. Becraft noted that "the rules governing the award of the combat V have been far from clear." She did not think it unreasonable for someone "to believe in good faith that wearing a combat V device was justified."[37] Boorda's suicide marked the nadir of the Navy's post-Tailhook travails.

The passions released during these controversies and the personal and professional destruction they caused attested to the tenacious hold of custom and tradition on those involved. Many in the Navy were unable or unwilling to distinguish between the high ideals of naval service and leadership and the loutish behavior of the seagoing subculture. Although Webb was unwilling to concede the point, the magnitude and persistence of this behavior made clear that it was endemic to the Navy's culture.

Webb's criticism in response to Boorda's actions in the Hansen case were legitimate, but Webb's well-known vocal opposition to women in the Navy and his insistence on rationalizing the worst aspects of the male "warrior culture" as a means to keep women in their place ensured his message would be perceived in many quarters as just another act of defiance and obtuseness on the part of the Navy's leadership.

Following the death of Admiral Boorda, the intensity of the culture war within the Navy abated, as its leaders began to sort through the wreckage and salvage the worthwhile values inherent in the Navy's traditions and discard those aspects of the hypermasculine hedonistic sea-going subculture that were no longer acceptable in an integrated service. The shock of Boorda's suicide tempered the passions of the Navy's most vocal critics in Congress as well, and as passions on both sides moderated, it became possible to pick up the pieces and move forward.[38]

The Navy leadership resolved to execute the orders from its civilian bosses swiftly. Debate would continue in the pages of the *Proceedings* for years afterward. While Navy leaders and fleet operators gave interviews and wrote articles about the progress being made, critics countered with charges that the leadership was ignoring or glossing over significant problems and stifling opposing views to enforce politically correct social engineering policies that would degrade the Navy's fighting capabilities.[39]

Women serving in the surface warfare community certainly had their own challenges to overcome, but their experiences did not achieve the level of high drama that surrounded the integration of women into combat aviation. One reason was that the Navy already had an established track record and process for integrating women into ships, a process which by nature required an incremental approach. Furthermore, the surface warfare specialty in the Navy has long been regarded as the least prestigious, lacking the glamour of the submarine and aviation warfare communities. The lack of an elite status probably helped mitigate the level of resentment toward women. As Congress was still debating lifting the combat exclusion rule in 1992, the Navy was already testing the waters by assigning small groups of women volunteers to temporary duty on combatant ships performing training missions.[40]

When the aircraft carrier *Eisenhower* deployed for the Persian Gulf in April 1994 with 415 women on board as ship's crew, news stories followed the traditional pattern of focusing on the few women who got pregnant and the few sailors removed from the ship for having sexual relations. In a reprise of the sensational headlines that accompanied the return from deployment of *Acadia* during the Persian Gulf War, headlines referred to *Eisenhower* as the "Love Boat."[41] These types of stories served as evidence to cultural conservatives that the presence of women in the Navy undermined its readiness and effectiveness. When the incidents covered by the press stories were put into context, the reality was far less scandalous. Thirty-eight women reported pregnancies. Twenty-four became pregnant before the ship deployed to the Mediterranean, and fourteen reported pregnancies after the ship deployed. Fifteen pregnant women had to be sent home from deployment; another seventeen women were reassigned for other medical reasons; and eight were reassigned for nonmedical reasons. In all, about 9 percent of the female crewmembers were reassigned for various reasons. In comparison, 171 men were reassigned for medical reasons and 221 were reassigned for nonmedical reasons, constituting about 8.6 percent of the male crewmembers. From a mission accomplishment perspective, *Eisenhower*'s deployment was accident- and mishap-free.[42]

In 1989 the Navy revised its pregnancy policy from granting separation upon request of the member to retaining the member on active duty unless she could prove extenuating circumstances and show an overriding and compelling need to be released from her service obligation. Following the elimination of the combat exclusion law in 1993, Navy officials reviewed the policy in order to develop clear department-wide guidance. Women are now allowed to serve at sea up to their twentieth week of pregnancy, provided their ship can access emergency medical care within six hours. Women are deferred from sea duty and travel away from their home area for four months to allow them time to recover and to arrange childcare. If they leave sea duty within six months of the end of their sea tour, the sea duty is considered completed. Otherwise, they report back to their ship to complete their prescribed sea tour. According to the official Navy instruction, "Pregnancy and parenthood are natural events that may occur in Service members' lives and can be compatible with successful naval service."[43] In response to the spate of critical news stories concerning the pregnancies of crewmembers on *Eisenhower*, Navy officials reiterated their support for women who become pregnant while serving, while also acknowledging the need to educate sailors to minimize unplanned pregnancies.[44]

In 2000, *Eisenhower's* CO, confronted with a shortage of men to fill out his crew, rearranged the berthing spaces on the ship to accommodate more women and increased the female crew complement to 610. The skipper noted that in the past year, approximately sixty female sailors had been removed from the ship for pregnancy, but "a large and disproportionate number of men had to be kicked off for disciplinary problems." While most of the women would remain in the Navy, and some would return to the ship, men removed for reasons of discipline were usually discharged from the Navy.[45]

Over the next two decades, the integration of women would accelerate, shaped by the same social, political, economic, and technological imperatives that had driven change in the past and the exigent need to exploit their talents for a rapidly transforming Navy.

= 8 =
SITREP

*The doors that women pushed open, many of them were
unlocked by men—proving we have always worked best
when we work together.*
                                    —Tammie Jo Shults, 2020[1]

During the first decade after Congress lifted the combat exclusion laws, women in the Navy made significant progress integrating into the operational forces, which opened doors to other opportunities. In addition to aircraft carriers, the Navy opened nearly all combatant ship types to the assignment of women, including cruisers, destroyers, frigates, amphibious warfare ships, and mine countermeasure command and control ships. Assignment to patrol craft as commanding officers was opened to women in 2005. The women who persevered through decades of cultural and institutional discrimination and obstruction were finally earning opportunities to lead and fully contribute to the Navy's mission "at the pointy end of the spear."

The reaction to the Tailhook debacle was not the only force driving this change. The collapse of the Soviet Union and the retreat of its navy from the world's oceans did not diminish the demands on the U.S. Navy's operational forces. In his annual review of the state of the U.S. Navy in 1998 for the U.S. Naval Institute *Proceedings*, Scott Truver noted the significant increase in "peacetime, crisis-response and combat missions." During the Cold War the Navy and Marine Corps conducted on average one crisis response every eleven weeks. In the 1990s the tempo increased to one operation every four weeks, while at the same time the services faced diminishing resources as America's political leaders and taxpayers sought to realize a "peace dividend."[2]

The Navy's struggle to meet global commitments with limited resources took a toll on ships and personnel. Retention was still a problem, and a strong American economy with low unemployment made it difficult to compete with the private sector to attract the highly skilled men and women needed as the Navy sought to leverage technology to reduce manning for at-sea billets. Secretary of the Navy Richard Danzig called it "a 'war' for people."[3] The Navy could not execute its missions effectively unless it fully exploited the talents of its women officers and enlisted sailors.

In July 1996 Vice Adm. Patricia Tracey became the first woman in the U.S. armed forces to achieve three-star rank as chief of naval education and training. She subsequently served as director, Navy Staff executing the priorities established by the CNO. Her extensive portfolio included coordinating with Navy leadership the realignment of training, maintenance, and manning policies for new ships designed for smaller, mixed-gender crews.[4]

In 1998, five women career surface warfare officers were selected to command combatant ships. Four of the ships were "amphibs" designed to transport Marines and their equipment to execute amphibious operations. Cdr. Maureen Farren took command of USS *Mount Vernon* (LSD 39) in June, followed by Cdr. Anne O'Connor in USS *La Moure County* (LST 1194) in September. Cdr. Michelle Howard took the helm of USS *Rushmore* (LSD 47) in December, followed by Cdr. Grace Mehl, who took command of USS *Gunston Hall* (LSD 44) in January 1999. The crew of *Mount Vernon* had other women officers on board but no enlisted women. The other three amphib crews were integrated. Cdr. Kathleen McGrath, selected for command of the frigate USS *Jarrett* (FFG 33) in December 1998, took over a ship that had no other women assigned to its crew. Her executive officer told a reporter, "She's not in command because she's a woman. She's in command because she's better than everyone else who's not in command." No major modifications were made to the ship to accommodate its first female CO. "Among the only major changes aboard was the removal of a spring-loaded toilet seat that was always in the up position." A sixth woman, Cdr. Pam Markiewicz, was selected to command USS *Carter Hall* (LSD 50) in November 1998.[5]

The ships participated successfully in fleet, joint, and international exercises and operations and in humanitarian missions; enforced UN-imposed sanctions against Iraq; and supported Operation Allied Force against the Federal Republic of Yugoslavia to stop the ethnic cleansing in Kosovo. Commander Howard's ship, *Rushmore*, was also used as a test platform for the "Smart Ship" program to determine if new technologies and manning procedures could be used to reduce crew numbers and workload for the LPD 17–class amphibious ships still in the design phase.[6] All of the women COs were seasoned ship operators who stepped up to address the challenges confronting the Navy at the turn of the twenty-first century.

Commander Mehl distinguished herself in command while supporting Operations Allied Force and Joint Guardian, and Joint Task Forces Noble Anvil and Shining Hope. Her Bronze Star citation noted, "She was the catalyst behind a flawless amphibious landing that delivered the combat power of the entire 26th MEU [Marine Expeditionary Unit] ashore in only 34 hours, facilitating the Unit's initial operational capability for peacekeeping operations in a total of 42 hours from first craft touchdown."[7]

Asked in a 2015 interview how this first cohort of women combatant COs had adapted so quickly, Adm. Michelle Howard observed that while there was some initial uncertainty because the women's operational experience, while extensive, had been limited to logistics ships due to gender restrictions, "the driving of the ship is actually very similar. What's different is the movement of Marines." She and the other women skippers found that their experience on logistics ships provided a solid foundation as they developed new skill sets. "On logistic ships, you spend so much time resupplying other ships, you do some of the most vulnerable high-risk maneuvering as an officer of the deck that you can do."[8]

In December 1998 coalition forces executed Operation Desert Fox in Iraq to retaliate against President Saddam Hussein's ongoing obstruction of UN arms inspection teams searching for evidence of weapons of mass destruction. During four days of air and missile strikes, women sailors on board USS *Enterprise* (CVN 65) were the first to engage in combat operations. Lt. Lyndsi N. Bates and Lt. Carol E. Watts of VFA-37 and Lt. Kendra Williams of VFA-105 were among the first Navy female fighter/strike pilots to fly combat missions.[9]

The women who deployed forward shared the same danger and took the same risks as their male shipmates. When al Qaeda terrorists attacked USS *Cole* (DDG 67) in Aden, Yemen, in October 2000, two of the seventeen crewmembers killed were enlisted women—Seaman Recruit Lakiba Nicole Palmer and Mess Management Specialist Seaman Lakeina Monique Francis.[10] Ship's engineer Lt. Cdr. Deborah Courtney and navigator Lt. Anne Chamberlain played critical roles in damage control and crew rescue efforts. Cdr. Kirk Lippold, *Cole*'s CO, recounted how Lieutenant Courtney led the effort to stabilize the ship and prevent it from sinking. Lieutenant Chamberlain initiated the triage and evacuation of the wounded, then returned to the ship to help with damage control operations. "From a commanding officer's perspective," Lippold said, "it is exactly that type of leadership and responsible decision making that make us the greatest Navy in the world."[11]

In April 2001 a Chinese F-8 fighter harassed and collided with a Navy EP-3 electronic surveillance aircraft over the South China Sea. The damaged American plane made an emergency landing on Hainan Island, and its twenty-four-member crew was detained and interrogated for eleven days by the Chinese military. Among the Navy crewmembers held were Lt. (j.g.) Regina Kauffman, Lt. Marcia Sonon, and Aviation Machinist Mate Second Class Wendy Westbrook.[12]

When al Qaeda terrorists attacked the American homeland in September 2001, Yeoman Third Class Melissa Rose Barnes, Storekeeper Third

Class Jamie L. Fallon, and Information Technician First Class Marsha D. Ratchford were among the 184 people killed at the Pentagon.[13] Capt. Deborah Loewer, a career surface warfare officer who was then serving as director of the White House Situation Room, was traveling with President George W. Bush in Florida on the day of the attacks. She reported the grim news to Chief of Staff Andrew Card, who whispered it to the president as he read a story to schoolchildren.[14]

The scale of the 9/11 attacks and the barbarity of employing hijacked civilian airliners against both civilian and military targets made it abundantly clear that principles of noncombatant immunity and clearly defined zones of conflict were quaint concepts of the past. After NATO authorized military operations under the treaty's article 5 providing for collective defense, coalition forces launched air strikes and cruise missile attacks on several cities in Afghanistan in retaliation for the Taliban regime's sheltering al Qaeda and its leader, Osama bin Laden.

The outrage following the attacks kindled a patriotic fervor that temporarily boosted recruiting and retention numbers for the Navy. At the end of 2002, recruiters had met their goals for sixteen months straight and attrition rates had dropped by 23 percent. At-sea manning shortfalls were also substantially reduced. CNO Adm. Vern Clark stated: "We are growing a more senior force to lead and manage the increasingly technical 21st-century Navy."[15]

Women continued volunteering to serve despite, or perhaps because of, the increasing likelihood of combat against regimes and terrorist organizations that brutally oppressed women. When the carrier *Abraham Lincoln* made a port call in Hobart, Australia, in 2001 following a six-month deployment in the Arabian Gulf, a local newspaper noted that one thousand of the ship's five-thousand-member crew were women, a fact the paper predicted was sure to delight local merchants hoping to benefit from shopping sprees. A reporter for an Atlanta newspaper noted that women were so thoroughly integrated that few Americans seemed to notice that they were performing combat missions. Women were flying off carriers and patrolling the no-fly zone over southern Iraq, dropping bombs in Bosnia, and participating in air strikes against the Taliban.[16]

Despite these advances, American military women nevertheless found themselves fighting their own leaders' efforts to impose Islamic Sharia law on them. Ostensibly to avoid offending the Saudi Arabians hosting U.S. forces stationed there to enforce the no-fly zones over Iraq, commanders directed several hundred American servicewomen, mostly Air Force personnel, to wear the abaya (a dress or cloak that conceals the entire body) and a headscarf when going out in public off duty. The servicewomen were also told to always be accompanied by a man when they went outside and to ride in the backseat when in a vehicle. The DOD actually went so far as to requisition and issue abayas to female servicewomen.[17] Following several unsuccessful attempts to get the DOD to eliminate the policy, Lt. Col. Martha McSally, at the time the highest-ranking female pilot in the Air Force and the first woman military pilot to fly in combat during a tour of duty in Kuwait in 1995–96, took her case to federal court. McSally's suit contended that the policy violated her religious freedom as a Christian and discriminated against women because male servicemembers were not required to grow beards to conform to Islamic religious standards. In fact, the men were expressly prohibited from wearing traditional Muslim clothing while off base. Female State Department personnel serving in-country were under no similar requirement, nor were the spouses of military personnel. The fact that the requirement was U.S. government policy, not Saudi government policy, made it all the more inexplicable and indefensible. Whatever the source of the policy, American servicewomen were furious. One news story related an incident where "a female mechanic whose legs were whipped by an enraged religious fanatic pulled a Colt .45 pistol and told him if he touched her again, she would blow his head off."[18]

Secretary of Defense Donald Rumsfeld defended the abaya policy as reasonable because "the Saudis allow us the use of [their] bases. It is more in our country's interests to be there and to recognize that we have to live with some of their laws and rules and customs."[19] Public opinion did not agree. An editorial in the *Norfolk Virginian-Pilot* pointed out, "Just because a practice is deemed customary does not automatically make it acceptable." The U.S. government advocating that Afghan women be free from their burkas while the American military "has been busily forcing its female members into them" was sheer hypocrisy.[20]

Congress intervened, inserting language into the National Defense Authorization Act (NDAA) of 2003 that prohibited military commanders from requiring female personnel to wear the abaya. But McSally paid a price for challenging senior leadership. Until she filed the lawsuit she had enjoyed a successful career and been deep-selected for promotion ahead of her peers. After contesting the abaya policy in court, she received performance reviews that labeled her "unprofessional, disloyal and unfit to be a leader." The *Arizona Daily Star* characterized the Air Force's retaliation against McSally "for defending a principle fundamental to American life" as "reprehensible."[21] In 2004 McSally was slated to take an assignment at the U.S. Air Force Academy. Such assignments are usually considered "sunset tours" for officers expecting to retire soon. Instead, however, she was selected to command the 354th Fighter Squadron and became the Air Force's first female fighter squadron commander.[22] It was a rare happy ending for an officer who dared to challenge the system, and a tacit acknowledgment that she had been wronged.

Navy women were demonstrating their command abilities as well. Saddam Hussein's continued refusal to allow UN inspectors to determine whether Iraq was stockpiling or importing weapons of mass destruction led to military action in March 2003 to depose his regime. The U.S. Navy forward-deployed seven carrier strike groups, nine expeditionary strike groups, thirty-three attack submarines, and some six hundred Navy and Marine Corps tactical aircraft to support Operation Iraqi Freedom. The amphibious assault ship USS *Saipan* (LHA 2) under the command of Capt. Norma Lee Hackney spent a record 148 consecutive days at sea conducting more than 2,440 aircraft sorties and 3,600 flight hours, mishap-free, while providing maintenance and logistic support to Marines ashore in Iraq.[23]

Women were also serving with the ground forces in Iraq, although by law they were prohibited from serving in units below the brigade level that engaged in direct combat. The nature of the insurgency, however, eradicated any distinction between frontline and supporting units. After initial combat operations transitioned into stabilization operations, Iraqis began using women to commit suicide bombing attacks at checkpoints, knowing the male coalition troops would not antagonize the local population by searching them. The coalition countered by recruiting female troops as volunteers to search women at checkpoints. The Marine Corps led the effort with the "Lioness" program. Women stationed in Iraq from all branches of the services volunteered to participate. They were provided one week of training in "weapons systems, language and cultural norms, Marine Corps Martial Arts Program tactics, and combat lifesaving techniques" and then temporarily attached to checkpoint units.[24] By attaching the women volunteers to units temporarily, local commanders avoided violating official policy prohibiting women from being assigned to units likely to be involved in direct combat. The women assumed the same risks as their male counterparts, but without the same level of training, and did not receive equal recognition. Without official documentation of their combat assignments, their service would not count toward promotion, and if wounded in the line of duty they would not be eligible to receive the same veteran's benefits.[25]

In July 2005 a military convoy in Fallujah, Iraq, was attacked by a suicide bomber with a vehicle-borne improvised explosive device. Six troops were killed, including three women, and eleven of the thirteen wounded were women. One reporter called it "the worst attack of the Iraq war involving female U.S. troops and the deadliest for American women in uniform since a Japanese kamikaze slammed into the USS *Comfort* in 1945 during World War II, killing six nurses aboard."[26] Among those killed was Navy Culinary Specialist First Class Regina R. Clark, a Reservist deployed with the 30th Naval Construction Regiment. Clark was a veteran of Operation Desert Storm who was mobilized one week after the 9/11 terrorist attacks.[27]

The Lioness concept was expanded and applied in Afghanistan as Female Engagement Teams (FETs). In addition to performing searches, FET members visited Afghan women in their homes and provided humanitarian aid to cultivate trust and goodwill. In 2009 the commander of NATO's International Security Assistance Forces (ISAF) directed all deploying units to create all-female teams. The Army and Marine Corps

Special Operations Commands and the Navy Special Warfare Command further expanded the concept in 2010, creating Cultural Support Teams (CSTs). "CSTs were designed to provide persistent presence and engagement—a key tenet of population-focused operations conducted by SOF [Special Operations Forces]."[28] The CSTs and predecessor organizations received mixed reviews regarding their effectiveness. The ad hoc assignment of personnel and their limited training made integration into the units they supported difficult. Although women accepted for CST duty were subjected to much more rigorous physical training and mental screening to operate with SOFs, some SOFs concluded that the risks outweighed the benefits of including them in certain situations.[29] What the experiences in Iraq and Afghanistan did prove was that women were willing to accept and perform assignments that exposed them to direct ground combat.

The disconnect between DOD and service assignment policies concerning women and the actual practices in the theater of operations was partially the result of a failure to confront the nature of warfare in Afghanistan and Iraq, where there were no clearly defined front lines. Although Army policy prohibited women from serving in units that had a "routine mission" of engaging in direct combat, which it defined as "repelling the enemy's assault by fire, close combat, or counterattack,"[30] women performed essential missions as military police, truck drivers, and in logistics and supply that routinely exposed them to combat. The Army awarded more than 1,500 women the Combat Action Badge, created in 2005 to "provide special recognition to Soldiers who personally engaged, or are engaged by, the enemy."[31] Whether combat was incidental or integral to the mission of the unit was a thin distinction once bullets started to fly and bombs to explode. Concerns over the exposure to combat of women serving in support units led Congress in 2005 to insert language into the NDAA for fiscal year 2006 requiring the secretary of defense to give Congress thirty legislative days to respond to any proposed change to ground combat policies involving women.[32] What this meant in effect was that Congress let itself off the hook from making a politically controversial decision about combat policies through inertia.

A 2005 briefing by the Navy Office for Women's Policy noted that twelve female surface warfare officers had commanded combatant ships, including amphibious ships, destroyers, and frigates. Four women surface warfare officers held major operational commands, including Mine Warfare Command, Amphibious Squadron Seven, Amphibious Squadron Two, and commander, Task Force 53. Seven female aviators held commands of naval air stations, air wings, and helicopter squadrons; one commanded an amphibious ship, the traditional training pipeline to aircraft carrier command—the premier combatant in the U.S. Navy.[33]

The first two decades of the twenty-first century saw symbolic, sartorial, and significant changes for women in the Navy. The Naval Academy class of 2004 and those that followed sang revised gender-neutral lyrics to the school song, "The Navy Blue and Gold," at graduation, and that same year the Navy revised its uniform regulations to make skirts optional. In 2016 the distinctively female "bucket" cover that had been part of the prescribed women's uniform since 1942 was phased out in favor of the men's/alternative combination cover.[34]

Old animosities resurfaced in 2006 when former Navy secretary James Webb announced his candidacy as a Democrat for a U.S. Senate seat in Virginia. The key issue motivating his candidacy was opposition to the war in Iraq, which had become increasingly unpopular after the premise on which it was waged—the threat of Iraqi weapons of mass destruction—proved to be false. Webb's incumbent Republican opponent, Sen. George Allen, who supported the war, held a press conference with five female Naval Academy graduates who denounced Webb for writing the article "Women Can't Fight" thirty-seven years earlier. Other military women offered support for his candidacy, calling him a "man of integrity." Webb countered that he had opened more billets to women than any of his predecessors as Navy secretary, which was true, and expressed regret for any difficulties that article may have caused for women at the Naval Academy and in the armed forces, although without repudiating the views the article expressed. He narrowly defeated Allen, who had his own problems with much more recent racist comments and expressed admiration for the Confederacy.[35] Webb served a single term in the Senate, then declined to run for reelection. He subsequently made a short-lived bid for the 2016 Democratic presidential nomination.

In 2017 the Naval Academy Alumni Association selected Webb to receive its Distinguished Graduate Award despite a petition and letter-writing campaign opposing his nomination by some women graduates, who pointed out that he had never repudiated the views he expressed in the 1979 *Washingtonian* article. Capt. Barb Geraghty, USN (Ret.), a member of the first class of women to graduate in 1980, told the *Washington Post* that Webb's article was deliberately provocative and destroyed unit cohesion in the brigade of midshipmen at the Naval Academy. "I have lost track of how many times men thrust that article in my face and used it as a reason for why I didn't belong," she said. Capt. Wendy B. Lawrence, USN (Ret.), class of 1981, who served as a helicopter pilot and became the first female academy graduate to become an astronaut, said Webb's article inflicted lasting damage on Naval Academy women: "Here it is 38 years later, and we are still talking about it." The controversy was unfolding within the context of yet another sex scandal, this time in the Marine Corps, where hundreds of Marines were being investigated for sharing nude photos of female Marines online without permission.[36] Webb ultimately declined to accept the award, saying, "Clearly, if I had been a more mature individual, there are things that I would not have said in that magazine article. To the extent that this article subjected women at the Academy or the armed forces to undue hardship, I remain profoundly sorry."[37]

Several policy changes made during the administration of President Barack Obama had a significant effect on the integration and advancement of Navy women. In 2010, in accordance with the provisions of the 2006 NDAA, Secretary of Defense Robert S. Gates notified Congress with a letter of intent to repeal the policy prohibiting women from serving in submarines. Vice Adm. John J. Donnelly, commander of the submarine force, stated the case for the policy change. Women were earning "about half of all science and engineering bachelor's degrees. . . . Maintaining the best Submarine Force in the world requires us to recruit from the largest possible talent pool."[38] Absent congressional action, the repeal went into effect in April 2010. That action marked the culmination of a ten-year effort to integrate women into one of the few remaining male bastions in the U.S. Navy.

In a speech to the Naval Submarine League in the summer of 1999, incumbent Navy Secretary Richard Danzig had fired a rhetorical shot across the bow of the submarine community with a warning that it "risked becoming dangerously out of touch with society if it did not adapt to include women, as well as more minority submariners." He admonished the community for its "Narcissus-like" preoccupation with sustaining its image as a "white male preserve."[39]

In June 1999, the Navy authorized brief (forty-eight hours) assignments of female NROTC midshipmen to five submarines. A Navy spokesman claimed the timing of the assignment of women to the submarines on the heels of Danzig's remarks was coincidental. The assignment was intended to "provide the ROTC midshipmen with the 'full impact' of submarine life. Though they don't serve aboard subs, . . . women who are destined to become naval officers should still be familiar with them."[40]

The Navy was then in the process of building the new *Virginia* class of submarines, and DACOWITS recommended that given the Navy's difficulty with recruiting enough qualified men for the submarine service, the new generation of submarines should be designed to accommodate mixed-gender crews, especially since the new submarines had an antici-pated service life of forty years. The incumbent CNO, Adm. Jay L. Johnson, dismissed the idea, stating, "For us, for me as chief of naval operations, I do not intend to change."[41]

Secretary Danzig's speech and the DACOWITS recommendation prompted a spirited debate in the pages of the Naval Institute's *Proceed-ings*. Former CNO Adm. Carlisle Trost, who had attempted to circumvent policy and freeze the number of enlisted women in the Navy in 1991 but was overruled by Secretary of Defense Caspar Weinberger, made a rather strange argument against changing policy in an essay titled "Not in Our Submarines." While acknowledging that women were capable of serving in submarines, he insisted that removing operational equipment during modifications to accommodate mixed-gender crews would degrade the boats' combat capability. Further, Trost argued that "the impact on crew morale, motivation, and retention stemming from the views of submariners' wives . . . matter—big time!" In closing, Admiral Trost urged the Navy to remain focused on maintaining combat readiness—"not on the attainment of fantasy-driven social-engineering goals or political expediency."[42]

Capt. Lory Manning, USN (Ret.), director of the Women in the Military Project for the nonprofit Women's Research and Education Institute (WREI), responded, "I have heard nothing . . . about removing operational equipment from submarines to attain a 'fantasy-driven social-engineering experiment.'" Manning pointed out that the stringent requirements to sustain the operational readiness and nuclear safety of the submarine force required the Navy to recruit the "best and the brightest" people. While Navy enlistment was down, women now constituted 18 percent of the force. Therefore, "it makes sense to investigate seriously the possibility of women serving aboard submarines."[43]

Capt. K. H. Wieschoff, USN (Ret.), who commanded an aviation training squadron in the 1970s when women were first being integrated into that warfare community, called Admiral Trost's claim of social engineering specious. Wieschoff derided Trost's essay for "absence of any argumentation to support its position that the 'voices of experienced military leaders are being overridden by faulty social philosophy.'"[44]

Master Chief Petty Officer (MCPO) James McLain, who served on both attack and ballistic missile submarines, responded to Trost's claim that wives would object to having women serve on board with, "I don't feel that what my wife thinks of my serving on submarines with women should have much bearing on their placement."[45]

In 2009 the Navy formed the Women in Submarines (WIS) Task Force "to provide flag officer level oversight for the planning and execution of the Women in Submarines integration based on the proposed timeline approved by the Chief of Naval Operations."[46] In 2010 the first nineteen women were assigned to four *Ohio*-class ballistic and guided missile submarines. After ten years, five of the women signed contracts for a department head tour, a retention rate comparable to that of their male counterparts—26 percent for the women and 27 percent for men. In 2015 the Navy began assigning enlisted women to submarines. For the most part, the integration of women into submarines lacked the drama of previous integration efforts in other warfare communities, with the exception of an incident on USS *Wyoming* (SSBN 742) when male enlisted crewmembers secretly videotaped women officers and trainees while they undressed.[47] The incident made the national news on the eve of the planned release of the Defense Department's sexual assault report. One unidentified male submarine officer told a Military.com correspondent, "It sucks. It was bound to happen."[48] Twelve sailors were initially investigated by the NCIS; seven were ultimately charged, and six were found guilty. The sailor who made the tapes received the stiffest sentence: two years' confinement, forfeiture of pay, reduction in rank, and a dishonorable discharge. The lightest sentence went to a sailor who initially denied any knowledge of the videos, then subsequently told investigators what he knew. He was fined and sentenced to thirty days' confinement with a reduction in rank. One of the officers victimized decided to leave the Navy; another testified that she "had worked too hard to have someone take that opportunity away by betraying her trust." Other women officers said the incident made it impossible for them to return to the boat for its next deployment.[49]

When the second cohort of eighteen women was selected for submarine service in 2011, Secretary of the Navy Ray Mabus said the Navy was not going to make a big announcement about putting women on submarines, assign a few women to submarine crews, and then forget about it. "We're going to do the same thing we did with surface ships, which is fully integrate women into the crews of all classes."[50]

Another major milestone for women in the surface warfare community came in 2010, when Rear Adm. Nora Tyson pinned on a second star and took command of Carrier Strike Group 2, comprising thirteen ships, eighty combatant aircraft, and roughly nine thousand personnel. Throughout her thirty-eight-year career, Tyson was reluctant to discuss her achievements in the context of gender. One reporter noted, "Her stock line, when pressed about being a trailblazer: 'I am the beneficiary of some really good timing.'"[51] Tyson joined the Navy in 1979 as a general unrestricted line officer, which at the time destined women for administrative billets and was for many a dead-end career path. Tyson took advantage of the recent opening of naval aviation to women, qualified as a naval flight officer in 1983, and served with an air reconnaissance squadron.

The only ship to which female aviators could be assigned at the time was USS *Lexington* (CVT 16), a training carrier. Tyson served a tour as assistant operations officer in *Lexington* until 1991. When the combat exclusion law was lifted in 1994, her experience on that ship enabled her to take an assignment on board *Enterprise*, an operational carrier, as navigator. She subsequently screened for command of the amphibious assault ship USS *Bataan* (LHD 5), leading disaster relief efforts in the aftermath of Hurricane Katrina and then deploying twice to the Persian Gulf to support the war in Iraq.

When she was promoted to assume command of CSG-2 on the newly commissioned carrier flagship USS *George H. W. Bush* (CVN 77) the former president himself administered the oath of office to her via video teleconference from his home in Kennebunkport, Maine. The carrier strike group's first deployment involved combat operations supporting Operations Enduring Freedom (Afghanistan) and New Dawn (Iraq). In 2015 Tyson assumed command of Third Fleet and became the first woman to command an operational numbered fleet. In her typical self-effacing manner, she stated in her remarks during her retirement from the Navy at the end of that tour that "while she was proud to have been the first woman to command a carrier strike group and command an operational numbered fleet, she was most proud of being a part of a Navy that had moved past those milestones."[52] While the timing of her career was indeed fortuitous, it opened a pathway for her prodigious talent to benefit the U.S. Navy and chart a course for future generations of women to follow.

Adm. Michelle J. Howard's storied thirty-five-year career as a surface warfare officer began with her graduation from the U.S. Naval Academy in 1982. Her initial sea tours were on two ships well past their prime, the submarine salvage vessel USS *Hunley* (AS 31), commissioned in 1959, and the training carrier *Lexington*, commissioned in 1943. Her subsequent seagoing assignments included two ammunition ships—USS *Mount Hood* (AE 29), where she served as chief engineering officer deployed to support Operation Desert Shield/Desert Storm, and later USS *Flint* (AE 32), where she served as first lieutenant (a position responsible for overseeing the Deck Department). In 1996 she became executive officer of the amphibious ship USS *Tortuga* (LSD 46) deployed to the Adriatic to support peacekeeping operations in the former Republic of Yugoslavia. When she took command of another amphibious ship, USS *Rushmore* (LSD 47), in 1999, she became the first African American woman to command a ship. She subsequently commanded Amphibious Squadron 7 and Expeditionary Strike Group 2. In 2009, three days into her new assignment as commander, Combined Task Force (CTF) 151, a multinational counterpiracy effort, she was tasked with rescuing the crew of the merchant ship *Maersk Alabama* from Somali pirates. The successful operation was later depicted in the 2013 film *Captain Phillips*. In 2010, she was the maritime task force commander for Baltic Operations under U.S. Sixth Fleet.

Her shore duty tours included high-level assignments on the staff of the CNO and the Joint Chiefs of Staff. In July 2014 Howard was appointed the thirty-eighth Vice Chief of Naval Operations (VCNO), the second-highest-ranking position in the U.S. Navy. When she pinned on the four stars of an admiral, she became the first woman to achieve that rank.

As she rose through the ranks, Howard was often called to take on extra assignments relating to gender integration. When she complained to her mother about her extra duties, her mother "told me that I needed to embrace the role I was in or quit the Navy. She said, 'you are where you are historically and until you quit, there's not going to be anybody ahead of you.' She was absolutely right."[53] Howard developed expertise on diversity and gender issues and became a sought-after speaker. In a 2014 interview for the Forbes Women's Summit, Howard recalled how she realized that taking command of *Rushmore* was much more than a personal achievement. Civilians across the country and from all walks of life told her how inspirational her success was for them. "To me there is an obligation to this public, not only a warfighting obligation that I signed up for, but there became a greater obligation of role model."[54]

Capt. Rosemary Mariner was another beneficiary of good timing when as a recent OCS graduate in 1973 she was selected to be one of the first women to attend flight school. After graduating as a naval aviator in 1974 she became the first woman to fly an attack aircraft, and she screened for command of an electronic warfare squadron, another first. Throughout her career she actively and publicly advocated for the integration of women. In a 1993 appearance on the *MacNeil/Lehrer NewsHour* discussing the Tailhook scandal and the debate on removing restrictions on women serving in combat, she observed, "When you segregate people, you institutionally make them inferior, and it's an issue of equal responsibility, equal risk, and in order to be respected in this profession I think it has been a fundamental first step."[55] She played an important role in helping to get those restrictions for women in aviation repealed in 1994. After retiring from the Navy, Mariner taught military history at the University of Knoxville in her home state of Tennessee.[56] In 2017 Mariner observed, "There have been remarkable changes in the military. . . . What I'm still concerned about are these reports of sexual assault and sexism and criminal activity that still go on."[57]

Mariner's death from ovarian cancer at the age of sixty-five in January 2019 prompted an outpouring of tributes. The most poignant and fitting salute took place during her graveside service in Maynardsville, Tennessee, when four F/A-18 aircraft piloted by women performed the Navy's first all-female Missing Man formation in her honor. A Navy spokesman explained, "The maneuver features four aircraft flying above the funeral service in formation as one of the aircraft leaves the formation and climbs vertically into the heavens."[58]

Despite the remarkable progress made by women in the twenty-first century, long-lasting cultural change within the Navy as an institution remains a work in progress. Success will require sustained commitment to accountability for improper conduct and reform of policies that have repeatedly been proven as inadequate to ensuring that accountability, particularly the military justice system.

In its 2004 report, DACOWITS investigated the issue of sexual assault, "a command issue that negatively affects unit cohesion, morale, performance, readiness and, most importantly, mission accomplishment." This was in response to reports of sexual assault of servicemembers both in the United States and overseas. In September 2003 a civilian commission appointed by Secretary of Defense Rumsfeld to investigate allegations of frequent and unpunished incidents of sexual assault at the U.S. Air Force Academy released a scathing report. Since 1993, the report stated, Air Force officials had ignored and failed to act upon repeated warnings from the Air Force surgeon general, the service's Office of Special Investigations, and the Senate Armed Services Committee of serious sexual misconduct problems at the academy. The Air Force general counsel insisted that she found "no systemic acceptance of sexual assault at the academy" or "institutional avoidance of responsibility."[59] In February 2004, after the Pentagon released survey results revealing that large numbers of women serving in the central command area of operations in the Middle East since 11 September 2001 reported being sexually assaulted during their tours of duty, the secretary of defense announced the establishment of the Care for Victims of Sexual Assault Task Force. The Pentagon's revelation led to a storm of outrage in editorial pages across the country. "Women join the U.S. military for the same reasons men do," one editorial noted, "to serve their country, to learn job skills, to earn money for college. They don't sign up to be raped, beaten and then abused by a system that ought to be protecting them."[60]

The DACOWITS report stated that servicemembers were aware of the extent of the problem and the resources available to victims, but they did not trust the system to punish offenders and feared negative repercussions for reporting an assault. DACOWITS recommended that the Uniform Code of Military Justice (UCMJ) "be revised to clarify and be consistent with the official definition of sexual assault, ensuring a clear and consistent legal standard, distinct from sexual harassment and other sex-related offenses."[61]

The DOD task force found that military departments and services were primarily managing sexual assault regulations and programs independently with no central oversight. Definitions, policies, and processes for sexual assault prevention and reporting across services were inconsistent and incomplete. The task force recommended creating a single defense-wide point of accountability. The Joint Task Force for Sexual Assault

Prevention and Response, which stood up in October 2004, created a new DOD-wide sexual assault policy in January 2005 and then transitioned into the Sexual Assault Prevention and Response Office (SAPRO) under the Office of the Secretary of Defense. Between 2004 and 2019, ten selected military sexual assault task forces, committees, and panels were established to address the issue, and Congress "enacted over 100 provisions intended to address different aspects of the problem as part of the annual National Defense Authorization Act and as stand-alone legislation affecting veterans and civilians."[62]

Sexual harassment and sexual assault in all branches of the military have been mired in an endless cycle: scandal followed by public and media outrage, proclamations by military leaders that such behavior is unacceptable, and pledges to address it. While actions to redress earlier notorious incidents, such as Tailhook, played a significant role in advancing the integration of women into the Navy and other service branches, the intractability of the endemic problem led Congress to call for major reform of the military judicial process to ensure prosecution and accountability of offenders. In 2006 Congress amended the UCMJ, abolishing the time limit on all rape charges. In 2018, however, the U.S. Court of Appeals for the Armed Forces (CAAF) set aside the rape convictions of three Air Force men. Their defense team asserted that although the UCMJ provided that rape was punishable by death and was not subject to a statute of limitations, a 1977 Supreme Court ruling determined in a civilian criminal case that imposition of the death penalty for rape of an adult woman was excessive and violated the Eighth Amendment prohibition against cruel and unusual punishment. If the rapists could not be punished by death, their attorneys asserted, the UCMJ statute of limitations for their crimes should have expired five years after they were committed, and they should never have been charged or prosecuted. The Court ruled unanimously against the defendants, noting in its opinion, "Respondents contend that the UCMJ phrase 'punishable by death' means capable of punishment by death *when all applicable law is taken into account* [emphasis in original]. By contrast, the Government sees the phrase as something of a term of art, meaning capable of punishment by death *under the penalty provisions of the UCMJ* [emphasis in original]."[63] The ultimate effect of this ruling was not that the military would start executing convicted rapists, but that there was no statute of limitations on bringing charges.

Sexual harassment and assault remained endemic in the services at least partly because rape victims, female or male, were reluctant to bring charges against the perpetrators. At the heart of that reluctance was the structure of the military justice system that gave military command-ers—most of them males—total control over the process in their role as the convening authority for courts-martial.

In November 2012, Lt. Col. James Wilkerson, USAF, an F-16 pilot who was serving as inspector general for the 31st Fighter Wing in Aviano, Italy, was convicted by an all-male military court-martial of aggravated sexual assault of a woman staying at his home. He was sentenced to a year in prison and dismissal from the Air Force. After Wilkerson served three months in jail, Lt. Gen. Craig Franklin, commander of the Third Air Force, overturned the conviction and reinstated him. Franklin also tried to get Wilkerson promoted and returned to flight status. The press and members of Congress excoriated Franklin's actions, but because he was acting within his discretion as the convening authority for courts-martial under the UCMJ, senior DOD officials could not overrule his decision. Wilkerson ultimately retired as a major.[64] Lieutenant General Franklin subsequently retired in January 2014 at the rank of major general, a lower pay grade, "'for the good of this command and the Air Force' because of persistent doubts about his impartiality in overseeing sex-abuse investigations."[65]

In May 2013, Lt. Col. Jeffrey Krusinski, chief of the Air Force Sexual Assault Prevention and Response branch at the Pentagon, was arrested and charged with sexual battery after he assaulted a woman in a parking lot. An exasperated Rep. Jackie Speier of California told a reporter for *USA Today*, "When I saw this it made me literally sick to my stomach. How many more reasons do we need to take cases of rape and sexual assault out of the chain of command?"[66]

In 2013, Sen. Kirsten Gillibrand (D-NY) introduced the Military Justice Improvement Act (MJIA), which would remove the decision to prosecute sexual assault and serious crimes from the chain of command and put it in the hands of independent, trained, professional military prosecutors. Military leaders and some members of Congress strongly opposed the measure, arguing that it would undermine the military commander's accountability for the good order and discipline of his or her personnel, a key tenet of command. The MJIA was introduced as an amendment to the 2013 NDAA, but the provision did not receive a vote and was omitted from the final authorization act. An attempt to introduce the MJIA as a stand-alone bill in 2014 was filibustered. Gillibrand persisted, introducing the bill as an amendment to every subsequent NDAA through 2020 and as a stand-alone bill in 2017 and 2019, without success.[67]

In October 2017, the #MeToo movement, a social movement against sexual violence originally founded as a program to help young women of color who survived sexual abuse, assault, and exploitation, seared the national conscience after the New York Times reported multiple accusations of sexual harassment and assault by film director Harvey Weinstein, one of the most powerful men in the film industry.[68] Women from all walks of life began using #MeToo on Twitter to report their own personal experiences, unleashing a torrent of public accusations and personal anecdotes from women and men that illustrated how pernicious and widespread the problem was. Several prominent men in the media, business, and government were publicly accused and disgraced for inappropriate and criminal conduct.[69] The movement created a major shift in the cultural climate, making it difficult to continue to minimize or ignore incidents when people used positions of power to abuse others and avoid the consequences.

Support for the proposed reforms of the military justice system gained ground in 2021 following the gruesome murder of Army Specialist Vanessa Guillén at Fort Hood, Texas. An investigation revealed she had reported being sexually harassed by a superior (not the person who killed her) on two different occasions, and no action was taken. Her accused murderer, a fellow soldier, escaped detention and killed himself.[70] It was just the latest in a series of highly publicized violent incidents on the base. An official investigation found that the command's Sexual Harassment/Assault Response and Prevention Program (SHARP) was ineffective due to under-resourcing and inadequately trained personnel. The inadequacy of the program resulted in a "pervasive lack of confidence" in it and a climate conducive to sexual assault and harassment. Furthermore, commanders failed to take proactive action to address known crime issues on and off base. More than a dozen Army officials were fired or disciplined as a result of the investigation.[71]

In April 2021 Senator Gillibrand held a bipartisan press conference to introduce the Military Justice Improvement and Increasing Prevention Act (MJIIPA) with Republican senator Joni Ernst, a combat veteran and sexual assault survivor, as a lead co-sponsor.[72] By May, sixty-two senators had announced their support for the legislation. Gillibrand asked for unanimous consent to advance the bill to a floor vote from the full Senate, noting that previous legislation to protect victims of sexual assault had been stripped out of past NDAAs in conference. That motion was blocked, as were the next twenty attempts to move the bill to the Senate floor. The principal opponents of the reforms were Sen. Jack Reed (D-RI), chair of the Senate Armed Services Committee, and Sen. James Inhofe (R-OK), the committee's ranking Republican member. Senator Gillibrand attributed their obstruction of the will of the filibuster-proof majority of their Senate colleagues at least partially to their background as Army veterans, noting, "They have such a deep respect for the chain of command that they are often overly deferential to it."[73] A *New York Times* editorial agreed, noting, "In the Senate, process is often the murder weapon of choice. Reform advocates are accusing Mr. Reed and Mr. Inhofe of being too deferential to the military and trying to delay and dilute the bill, if not derail it altogether."[74] Rep. Jackie Speier, chair of the House Armed Services Military Personnel Subcommittee, and Rep. Michael R. Turner, the ranking Republican member of the House Armed Services Strategic Forces Subcommittee, introduced a companion bill named the *Vanessa Guillén Military Justice Improvement and Increasing Prevention Act (H.R. 4104)*.[75]

In June 2021 Secretary of Defense Lloyd Austin accepted all the recommendations of an independent joint commission he appointed to conduct a ninety-day review of sexual assault and harassment in the military. The most consequential proposed change mirrored the key provision of the

Senate and House legislation, directing the DOD to work with Congress to change the UCMJ to shift responsibility from military commanders for prosecuting sexual assaults and related crimes as well as domestic violence, child abuse, and retaliation. Each military service would stand up a dedicated office to handle prosecution of such offenses.

Other policies that the defense secretary has authority to implement include standardizing nonjudicial punishments across all the services and establishing a separation process for servicemembers with substantiated claims of sexual harassment; creating professional career paths within the services' legal communities for both lawyers and investigators to specialize in the handling of sexual assault cases; and eliminating collateral duty sexual assault coordinators and victim's advocates in favor of independent advocates outside the command structure—although whether/how that last recommendation could be implemented in a shipboard environment remains to be determined.[76]

In September 2021 Secretary of Defense Austin announced an implementation roadmap that envisioned a gradual phase-in of policies and programs between 2027 and 2030.[77] The delayed and attenuated timeline drew bipartisan criticism in Congress. Eight senators—four Democrats and four Republicans, including three members of the Senate Armed Services Committee—sent a letter expressing their "disappointment and concern" with the Pentagon's "vague approach and lax timeline," insisting that "a problem of this magnitude demands an immediate, proportionate response."[78]

The final version of the 2022 NDAA included provisions for military lawyers to prosecute sexual assault, rape, murder, stalking, and domestic violence offenses, and took charging decisions away from commanding officers. However, military commanders retained power as convening authority for courts-martial as well as the ability to select panel members (the equivalent of a civilian jury), approve witnesses, and manage the trial. Senator Gillibrand was scathingly critical of this outcome: "Committee leadership has ignored the will of a filibuster-proof majority in the Senate and a majority of the House in order to do the bidding of the Pentagon."[79]

Given the history of all the armed services on this issue, the next inevitable high-profile sexual assault or harassment case will be intensely scrutinized to determine whether the compromise policies can in fact truly effect a sea change in military culture. If the military is serious about attracting and retaining the high-caliber personnel it needs to wage warfare in the twenty-first century, its leaders cannot afford to backslide on this issue.

Another proposed amendment to the 2022 NDAA that did not receive as much media attention concerned requiring women to register with Selective Service, as men have had to do since 1980. The prospect of drafting women for combat was an effective bogeyman for conservative activist Phyllis Schlafly in her successful effort to derail the Equal Rights Amendment in 1982, and the Supreme Court upheld the constitutionality of the male-only draft in 1981. Changes in the assignment policies of military women over subsequent decades invite reevaluation of the issue, although neither the Supreme Court nor Congress has shown much enthusiasm for addressing a political and cultural hand grenade that no one wants to be caught holding.

The 1981 *Rostker v. Goldberg* Supreme Court decision ruled that women were not "similarly situated" (a legal term used in class-action lawsuits that stipulates that the facts and legal issues of the plaintiff and the defendant must be the same) as men for Selective Service, because its purpose is to procure combat troops. The prevailing restrictions against women serving in combat meant a male-only draft was not unconstitutional. Despite the partial repeal of the combat exclusion rule in 1994, women remained banned from ground combat by policy. Two more challenges to the law in 2003 and 2009 on the grounds that the Selective Service law violated the equal protection rights of the plaintiffs were dismissed by the Supreme Court, which ruled that "there has not been a sufficient change in the material circumstances . . . to justify relitigation of the issue at this time in this case."[80]

In February 2013, after the DOD eliminated the rule excluding women from direct ground combat assignments, Rep. Charles B. Rangel (D-NY) introduced the All-American Selective Service Act, which would have required women to register. A decorated combat veteran of the Korean War, Rangel had long believed that a policy of universal conscription would induce political leaders to more carefully consider the consequences of committing American military men and women to battle.[81] "Reinstating the draft and requiring women to register to the Selective Service would compel the American public to have a stake in the wars we fight as a nation. We must question why and how we go to war, and who decides to send our men and women in harm's way." Cornell University professor Beth Livingston commented on Rangel's proposed legislation: "I think it would start a conversation about how our gender stereotypes aren't necessarily true and aren't necessarily based in reality. I think it would start a conversation that included men and how unrealistic expectations toward masculinity can affect men."[82] Rangel's bill never made it out of committee. He introduced similar legislation in the next Congress that would require reinstatement of the draft whenever an authorization on the use of military force or declaration of war is in effect and also provided for the registration of women with the Selective Service System. That bill met the same fate.

The Senate-passed version of the NDAA for fiscal year 2017 also would have required women to register with Selective Service. The Senate Armed Services Committee report on the bill noted that "the ban of females serving in ground combat units has been lifted by the Department of Defense, and as such, there is no further justification to apply the selective service act to males only." The provision failed to make it into the final version of the NDAA, but the legislation did create a National Commission on Military, National, and Public Service to further consider the issue. The commission's final report, issued in March 2020, recommended that women be required to register and be included in any future draft. The report noted that "the current disparate treatment of women unacceptably excludes women from a fundamental civic obligation and reinforces gender stereotypes about the role of women, undermining national security." Further, expanding registration would enable the president "to leverage the full range of talent and skills available during a national mobilization."[83]

While the commission was deliberating, the issue was also being relitigated in the courts. In 2019, federal district courts in Texas and New Jersey issued rulings that found that because of recent policy changes allowing women to serve in combat roles, the rationale that underpinned the *Rostker v. Goldberg* decision was open to review. In the Texas case, brought by the National Coalition for Men, the district court held that the all-male registration requirement violated the Constitution and ruled for the plaintiffs. The government appealed the decision, and the Fifth Circuit Court subsequently reversed the ruling. While it acknowledged that the facts underpinning *Rostker* had changed, the Fifth Circuit held that only the U.S. Supreme Court could overrule its own precedent.[84] In the New Jersey case, the plaintiff, Elizabeth Kyle Labelle, filed a class-action suit that argued that her inability to register with Selective Service violated her equal protection and substantive due process rights under the Constitution: "This archaic exclusionary policy sends a message to all U.S. citizens and institutions that women are not capable of shouldering the responsibilities of citizenship to the same extent as men." In her decision, District Court judge Esther Salas dismissed the due process claim, noting "after all, joining the military is not a personal right, and by inference neither is registration for the draft." On the issue of equal protection, however, she ruled in favor of the plaintiff, explaining, "men and women are similarly situated for purposes of the MSSA because they can both serve in combat roles. . . . Defendants cannot show that the classification drawn is substantially related to achieving the MSSA's objectives."[85]

Represented by the ACLU, in January 2021 the National Coalition for Men and two men who were required to register with Selective Service petitioned the U.S. Supreme Court to review the issue and overrule *Rostker*. Ten prominent military general and flag officers, led by the retired former head of the National Security Agency (NSA), four-star Air Force general Michael Hayden, filed a friend-of-the-court brief in favor of the petition. The brief argued that exempting women "from the selective service is inimical to the Nation's security interests. . . . Whatever the rationale's merit in 1981, it is no longer true."[86]

An amicus brief filed by the Modern Military Association of America asserted that the changing nature of modern warfare and the historical performance of women in the services had convinced military and civilian leaders that "women are essential to all aspects of American military operations."[87] The National Organization for Women (NOW) Foundation, with a coalition of women's rights organizations, filed a brief supporting the petition that argued "requiring men to register but not women—reflects a familiar stereotyping of sex roles." The policy made no sense in the new legal and social context.[88]

A coalition of conservative organizations including the Center for Military Readiness, Eagle Forum, and Concerned Women for America along with five military general and flag officers filed an amicus brief opposing the petition, arguing that the "petitioners misperceive *Rostker*'s fundamental premise, ignore the role, authority, and responsibility of Congress in raising and supporting armies." The brief also argued that because of the physiological differences between the sexes, women were not similarly situated to serve as replacements for male combat casualties. Finally, the brief asserted the petitioners were attempting to "short-circuit the on-going legislative process."[89]

The Biden administration weighed in as well, but without taking a position on either side of the debate. Acting solicitor general Elizabeth B. Prelogar filed a brief opposing the petition on the grounds that Congress was already actively deliberating the issue. Supreme Court justices Sonia Sotomayor, Stephen Breyer, and Brett Kavanaugh declined to refer the case for review by the Court. Justice Sotomayor explained, "the Court's longstanding deference to Congress on matters of national defense and military affairs cautions against granting review while Congress actively weighs the issue."[90]

Despite bipartisan support for a provision that required women to register with Selective Service in both the House and Senate versions of the NDAA, the language was excised from the final compromise version after a small group of conservative lawmakers threatened to vote against the NDAA if the provision remained.[91] The political and cultural hand grenade was deftly lobbed back in the direction of the Supreme Court.

This protracted back-and-forth between the legislative and judicial branches of government attests to the fact that although the legal context has changed irrevocably in terms of women's role in the military, extending the obligation of registration for Selective Service to women remains likely to catalyze significant resistance from conservatives who defend traditional cultural values, as well as progressives who support gender equality but oppose militarism. One possible outcome should the Supreme Court review and overturn *Rotsker* is that Congress might abolish draft registration altogether to avoid political punishment at the polls. Rep. Vicki Hartzler (R-MO), arguing that mass conscription has outlived its usefulness, introduced legislation to end mandatory registration and place the Selective Service System into deep standby mode, with a two-thirds majority vote in both houses of Congress required to reactivate it. "Given the strength of our nation's Armed Forces and the apparent lack or purpose of the Selective Service's use," she insisted, "it is wholly unnecessary to burden American citizens with registering for the draft."[92]

Historically, the all-volunteer force has depended heavily on the integration of women for its success. As we enter the third decade of the twenty-first century, technological change will continue to expand women's participation in warfighting as traditional concepts of what constitutes combat have been transformed by warfare in the cyber domain. The armed forces of this century require men and women who are well educated and able to adapt to rapidly evolving technology. All the services in recent years have recognized the need to overhaul industrial-era personnel policies and practices in order to recruit and retain the talented people they need. As they have in the past, women will play an important role in charting the U.S. Navy's course into the future.

———

The integration of women into the Navy and the fleet succeeded despite the formidable challenges posed by cultural friction. The process featured short periods of revolutionary changes in prevailing cultural norms catalyzed by the exigency of war in the first half of the twentieth century, and public condemnation of institutional scandals in the latter half. The evolution of social, economic, technological, and political conditions also shaped the process from the initial militarization of women during World War I to their achievement of regular status after World War II, and then qualifying for sea-going and combat assignments.

During World War I, a few perceptive men in leadership positions transcended the mental and emotional constraints of culturally dictated gender roles to recognize the changing role of women in society and the need to harness women's potential to contribute to the national defense. The War Department's opposition to the precedent of militarizing women established by Secretary of the Navy Josephus Daniels and the quick reaction of Congress to eradicate that precedent reflected the strength of the cultural resistance to be overcome. New technology provided women an entry into the military, but it also limited their duties primarily to tasks that had not been previously gendered as male. Women both within and outside the Navy assumed traditional archetypal roles to support the war effort: Yeomanette viragos marched with rifles in parades to promote recruiting and war bond drives, and civilian women staged patriotic pageants and formed recruiting corps to instigate public support.

Suffrage expanded the role of women in the public sphere and made them a force to be reckoned with in the realm of civil-military relations. Ambivalence over the changing role of women in society was expressed in the alliance formed between the intelligence organizations of the Army and Navy and conservative women's patriotic organizations, who worked together to oppose the perceived threat progressive women's organizations posed to deeply held American cultural values. Civil and military leaders addressed that ambivalence by honoring the traditional roles performed by women, evoking the comfortable values of domesticity and motherhood to reassure a dubious public that the militarization of women would not destroy the underpinnings of American society. Dr. "Mom" Chung built her social and political network by skillfully practicing domestic values to achieve political and personal objectives. The Civilian Advisory Council established in World War II to oversee the creation of the women's services and the Defense Advisory Committee on Women in the Services in the postwar era employed the same strategy to serve their objectives.

The total mobilization effort demanded by World War II brought women into the military in unprecedented numbers—more than 80,000 into the Navy alone. The influx of women into an exclusively masculine domain provoked a range of responses. It made converts out of military leaders who had previously opposed utilizing women such as Gen. George C. Marshall and Adm. Chester Nimitz, who learned to value the important contributions women made to the war effort. In the lower ranks, however, the militarization of women stoked resentment as women occupied the safe billets ashore and outside the combat zones, increasing the likelihood that men would be sent into harm's way. Whether they engaged in combat or not, men were also deprived of the symbolic value of the military uniform as an exclusive badge of masculinity. The large-scale participation of women in the military fueled fears in the civilian sphere that women's presumed innate moral propriety would be compromised. These resentments and perceptions combined in the malicious slander campaign directed at the WAC and the WAVES during World War II and also contributed to the services' postwar preoccupation with promoting and preserving a proper ladylike image of military women once they achieved regular status.

The concept of separate spheres for men and women enjoyed a resurgence in the post–World War II era, marginalizing military women for the ensuing three decades. Their overall numbers and ranks were capped, and the number of ratings available to Navy enlisted women was reduced. The fact that an ambitious recruiting campaign failed to substantially increase the number of women enlisting to meet the already low 2 percent ceiling testified to the fact that absent the exigency of a hot war, when patriotism helped mitigate social disapproval, most women were content to resume their prewar lives and social status rather than risk ostracism for pursuing an unconventional career choice.

President Richard Nixon's initiation of the all-volunteer force in 1973 revitalized and accelerated the integration of women into the services. Although this was an unanticipated development—Nixon was no champion of feminism—and was unwelcome among a number of leaders in the military establishment, that bell could not be unrung. Like Secretary of the Navy Josephus Daniels before him, CNO Adm. Elmo Zumwalt Jr.

charted a new course for Navy women by expanding opportunities and further enhancing their value to the Navy. As women moved into seagoing assignments, the possibility of exposure to combat became the next focal point of the institutional and cultural debate. The debate intensified within the context of the political clash over the ratification of the Equal Rights Amendment. Cultural conservatives rallied opposition to the ERA by reviving an old argument equating political and economic equality with the civic obligation to bear arms, linking the ERA to the draft. Civic equality predicated on reciprocal military obligation has never been a part of conscription in this country, but the argument was emotionally charged enough to effectively kill the ERA. The debate also exposed the fissures between feminist activists and military women. Feminists' rejection of all things associated with the military rendered them unable to respond effectively to the arguments of the cultural conservatives and distanced them from military women, who as a distinct minority in a male-dominated hierarchy were more pragmatic than political in their approach to issues of equality.

The debate over draft registration for women that prevented the ratification of the ERA was the high-water mark for cultural conservatives' resistance to expanding the participation of women in the military. Once women started going to sea in significant numbers after 1978 and proved themselves capable, arguments for their continued marginalization became increasingly untenable. The scandals of the 1980s and 1990s were the inevitable consequence of the clash of a male sea-going subculture infused with misogyny, homophobia, and hypermasculine hedonism and the values and expectations of newly arrived female shipmates seeking to be treated as professional equals who embraced the goals, if not the politics, of the second feminist movement.

The pernicious sexist male sea-going subculture was perpetuated by the repeated failure of Navy leaders to acknowledge its inappropriateness and to take unambivalent and substantive action to eradicate the behavior in which it manifested. Not until several of the Navy's most senior leaders were compelled to walk the metaphorical plank, prodded over the side by congressional and public opprobrium, did the message begin to penetrate their collective conscience. The fallout from the Tailhook scandal resulted in an intense cultural war within and outside the Navy that claimed casualties on both sides. As the struggle ebbed, a path was cleared for a more systematic and rational integration process.

The preoccupation with issues of sex and sexuality on the part of the military, the public, and the media obscures the true nature of the fundamental human dynamic underlying the history of the integration of women into the Navy and the fleet. That dynamic is respect. Sex, sexuality, and gender are all proxy issues exploited by both sides for their power to incite emotional reactions to advance particular agendas. When women first ventured beyond the well-defined confines of the domestic sphere, they had to earn respect by disproving prevailing assumptions based on their traditional sex and gender roles. The fear that women would relinquish their accepted and respected role in society as the homemakers and moral mentors of subsequent generations in exchange for the uncertainties of some nebulous future underpinned the tenacious cultural resistance.

The continued use of the term "social experimentation" by contemporary cultural conservatives when discussing issues pertaining to expanding the roles of women in the military evokes a commitment to preserving an outmoded conception of cultural norms. Perceiving a decline in public respect for women's traditional roles, these people carry on the struggle by attacking the women who blaze new trails and the men who support them. The only way to negotiate a cease-fire in the culture war surrounding women in the military is for both sides to accept that it is not a zero-sum equation. The fact that some women choose to pursue a military career does not diminish the contributions of the women who choose to stay home and raise families. Some exceptional women manage to do both, and policies continue to evolve to help Navy women and men maintain a sustainable career/life balance.

The success of military women does not diminish the status of military men unless they choose to perceive it that way. Demonstrated ability to accomplish the mission should remain the overriding standard as the integration process continues. Navy women volunteered to go into harm's way to fight regimes and terrorist organizations that brutally oppress women, and some paid the ultimate price. Today women are forward-deployed around the globe and take the same risks that men take. On 19 August 2021, Capt. Amy Bauernschmidt took command of the Nimitz-class nuclear aircraft carrier Abraham Lincoln, the penultimate seagoing command in the U.S. Navy.

It must not be forgotten that the advancement of military women was achieved with the support of men. Male Navy leaders on both sides of the integration fight claimed to be promoting the best interests of the institution. The true leaders were the men who recognized and accepted that the integration of women was a necessary condition for the success of the Navy as an institution and worked to implement it. Some conservative politicians still pay lip service to outmoded cultural views of appropriate roles for military women—but the historical record shows that they cannot turn back the clock.

September 2021 marked the fiftieth anniversary of the all-volunteer force. Women have contributed significantly to the AVF's success, and they constitute 20 percent of today's Navy. In December 2015, when Secretary of Defense Ashton Carter announced the abolition of all restrictions on women's military assignments and occupations in all the services, he observed, "Our force of the future must continue to benefit from the best people America has to offer. . . . This includes women, because they make up over 50 percent of the American population."[93]

Let us conclude with a return to the scene that opened this book, the 1997 commissioning of the destroyer Hopper—a combatant ship named for a woman and partially crewed by women—that was witnessed by generations of Navy women who proudly served in uniform from 1917 to that day. Such an event will never happen again. The World War I generation has slipped away, and the ranks of the World War II generation are rapidly dwindling. Most of those women present that day in 1997 had probably believed such an event to be impossible in their lifetimes, but collectively they contributed to its realization through their patriotism, perseverance, persistence, and professionalism. It has been a long voyage, with more than its fair share of squalls and tempests, but in the words of English historian Edward Gibbon, "The winds and waves are always on the side of the ablest navigators."[94]

— NOTES —

ABBREVIATIONS

ACNP	Assistant Chief of Naval Personnel
ACoS	Assistant Chief of Staff
AWC	Army War College
MCSL	Margaret Chase Smith Library
MID	Military Intelligence Division
NA	National Archives
NARA	National Archives and Records Administration
ONRL	Office of Naval Records and Library
PUL	Princeton University Library
RG	Record Group

INTRODUCTION

1. "USS *Hopper* Commissioning (1997), part 1," YouTube video, 9:25, posted by Navy History and Heritage Command, 5 March 2010, https://www.youtube .com/watch?v=_qD5HC_PxfM.
2. Commander, Naval Information Forces (NAVIFOR), https://www.navifor .usff.navy.mil/About-Us/History/.
3. The term "militarize" as used here refers to the formal incorporation of women into the Navy with military rank and subject to military discipline, consistent with the definitions "to give a military character to" and "to adapt to military use" in the *Merriam-Webster Online Dictionary*, http://www.m-w .com/dictionary/militarize.
4. Mike Ives, "First Woman Completes Training for Elite U.S. Navy Program," *New York Times*, 16 July 2021, https://www.nytimes.com/2021/07/16/us/navy -woman-warfare-program.html.
5. Department of Defense, *2020 Demographics Profile of the Military Community*, https://download.militaryonesource.mil/12038/MOS/Reports/2020 -demographics-report.pdf.

6. See Susan H. Godson, *Serving Proudly: A History of Women in the U.S. Navy* (Annapolis: Naval Institute Press, 2001), 49, 73, 132; Jean Ebbert and Marie-Beth Hall, *Crossed Currents: Navy Women from World War I to Tailhook* (Washington, DC: Brassey's, 1993), 341; Janann Sherman, *No Place for a Woman: A Life of Senator Margaret Chase Smith* (New Brunswick, NJ: Rutgers University Press, 2000), 68.

CHAPTER I. WRESTLING WITH WOMEN

1. Josephus Daniels, *The Wilson Era: Years of War and After, 1917–1923* (Chapel Hill: University of North Carolina Press, 1946), 211.
2. Peter Karsten, *The Naval Aristocracy: The Golden Age of Annapolis and the Emergence of Modern American Navalism* (New York: Free Press, 1972), xiv.
3. Maurine Weiner Greenwald, *Women, War and Work: The Impact of World War I on Women Workers in the United States*, Contributions in Women's Studies 12 (Westport, CT: Greenwood Press, 1980), 38.
4. Committee on Public Information, Division on Women's War Work, Press Release No. 12, 18 June 1917, RG 45, Naval Records Collection of the Office of Naval Records and Library, Subject File [hereafter ONRL Subject File] 1911–1927, NA-3 "Enlisted Personnel, General Info.," box 355, folder 6, National Archives [hereafter NA].
5. Josephus Daniels, *The Cabinet Diaries of Josephus Daniels, 1913–1921*, ed. E. David Cronon (Lincoln: University of Nebraska Press, 1963), 521.
6. Jonathan Daniels, *The End of Innocence*, Franklin D. Roosevelt and the Era of the New Deal Series, Frank Freidel, gen. ed. (New York: De Capo Press, 1972), 93–94.
7. Elmo R. Zumwalt Jr., *On Watch: A Memoir* (New York: Quadrangle, 1976), 66.
8. Karsten, *The Naval Aristocracy*, 128.
9. Madeleine Vinton Dahlgren, *Thoughts on Female Suffrage and in Vindication of Women's True Rights* (Washington, DC: Blanchard and Mahoun, 1871), 4, Rare Books Collection, Library of Congress. The italics are Dahlgren's.
10. See Linda K. Kerber, *Women of the Republic: Intellect and Ideology in Revolutionary America* (Chapel Hill: University of North Carolina Press, 1980); and Barbara Welter, "The Cult of True Womanhood: 1820–1860," *American Quarterly* 18, no. 2, pt. 1 (1966): 152.
11. Kerber, *Women of the Republic*, 11–12.
12. Welter, "The Cult of True Womanhood," 152.
13. Karsten, *The Naval Aristocracy*, 132–33.

14. "Women's Presidents to Aid Navy League, Heads of Ten Organizations with 500,000 Members Will Act on National Committee," *New York Times*, 16 August 1915, 9.

15. Armin Rappaport, *The Navy League of the United States* (Detroit: Wayne State University Press, 1962), 49–50.

16. LaRae Umfleet, Wilmington Race Riot, Wilmington, NC, 1898, North Carolina Office of Archives and History Research Branch, https://digital .ncdcr.gov/digital/collection/p249901coll22/id/5842, 31 May 2006, 5.

17. *Congressional Record*, 65th Cong., 2nd sess., 1918, vol. 56, 442.

18. *Congressional Record*, 1918, 545–56; and U.S. House of Representatives, *Biographical Directory of the United States Congress, 1774–Present*, https:// bioguide.congress.gov/search/bio/H000934.

19. F. D. Lochridge, Acting Chief of War College Division, to Chief of Staff, 22 December 1917, RG 165, Records of the War Department, General and Special Staffs, War College Division, Army War College, General Correspondence [hereafter AWC General Correspondence], 1903–1919, box 532, folder 10730–1 to 26, NA.

20. Secretary of War to Chairman, Committee on Military Affairs, U.S. Senate, 22 December 1917, AWC General Correspondence, 1903–1919, box 532, folder 10730–1 to 26, RG 165, NA.

21. See Archibald Douglas Turnbull, "Seven Years of Daniels," *North American Review* 212 (1920): 606–17, for a critique of Daniels' tenure as Secretary of the Navy. According to Turnbull, Daniels saw the Navy as "a wonderfully organized machine for vote-getting." From his office emanated "a flood of orders, all more or less impossible of enforcement, all more or less subversive of discipline." There is no specific mention of the enlistment of women, probably since by the time this article was published Congress had disposed of that threat.

22. Maj. B. Wells, General Staff, to Chief of Staff, 23 June 1917, AWC General Correspondence, 1903–1919, box 270, folder 8196–1–18, RG 165, NA.

23. Bureau of Navigation, Nav-641-MGH, "Enlisted Personnel Furnished by Each State during the World War," ONRL Subject File 1911–1927, NA3, Enlisted Personnel, box 354, folder 10, RG 45, NA.

24. Joy Bright Hancock, *Lady in the Navy: A Personal Reminiscence* (Annapolis: Naval Institute Press, 1972), 28.

25. Linda Grant DePauw, *Battle Cries and Lullabies: Women in War from Prehistory to the Present* (Norman: University of Oklahoma Press, 1998), 18–23.

26. "Columbia Calls: Y.W.C.A. Girls Entertain the Camp with Patriotic Pageant," *Periscope* 1, no. 1 (19 July 1918): 2, ONRL, ZPN-13, Thirteenth Naval District, box 982, folder 4, "The Periscope Newspaper," RG 45, NA. *Periscope* was a publication of the Naval Training Camp at Puget Sound.

27. Woman's Navy Recruiting Service, insert in flyer, "Join the Navy," ONRL Subject File, 1911–27, NA-1-Navy Personnel: Regulars and Reserves, box 354, folder 6, RG 45, NA.

28. DePauw, *Battle Cries and Lullabies*, 21.

29. "Spokane Shows the Yeomanettes a Royal Time," *Periscope* 1, no. 9 (11 October 1918): 4, ONRL, ZPN-13, Thirteenth Naval District, box 982, folder 4, "The Periscope Newspaper," RG 45 NA.

30. Lettie Gavin, *American Women in World War I: They Also Served* (Niwot: University Press of Colorado, 1997), 6, 9, 20–21.

31. Linda K. Kerber, *No Constitutional Right to Be Ladies* (New York: Hill and Wang), 261; DePauw, *Battle Cries and Lullabies*, 20.

32. Gavin, *American Women in World War I*, 10.

33. U.S. Department of Labor, Women's Bureau, *The Occupational Progress of Women: An Interpretation of Census Statistics of Women in Gainful Occupations*, Bulletin of the Women's Bureau 27 (Washington DC: GPO, 1922), 2.

34. Margery W. Davies, *Woman's Place Is at the Typewriter: Office Work and Office Workers, 1870–1930* (Philadelphia: Temple University Press, 1982), 58.

35. Greenwald, *Women, War and Work*, 10–11.

36. Eunice C. Dessez, *The First Enlisted Women, 1917–1918* (Philadelphia: Dorrance, 1955), 60–62.

37. Gavin, *American Women in World War I*, 3.

38. Gavin, 77–95.

39. Cdr. G. P. Dyer, Supply Corps, U.S. Navy, "Navy Supply Department in War Time," U.S. Naval Institute *Proceedings* [hereafter *Proceedings*] 46, no. 3 (March 1920): 379, 382.

40. Dyer, 391–92.

41. Kelly Miller, *Kelly Miller's History of the World War for Human Rights* (Washington, DC: Austin Jenkins, 1919), 597.

42. Cara Moore Lebonick, "Mustering Out: The Navy's First Black Yeowomen," *Rediscovering Black History* (blog), National Archives and Records Administration [hereafter NARA], 9 November 2020, https://rediscovering-black-history.blogs.archives.gov/2020/11/09/golden-14/.

43. Dahlgren, *Thoughts on Female Suffrage*, 6.

44. Hancock, *Lady in the Navy*, 48.

45. *U.S. Statutes at Large*, 41 (May 1919–March 1921): 138.

46. Josephus Daniels to Bureau of Navigation, Washington, 21 October 1919, General Correspondence, 1913–25, file 9875, box 620, folder (3035–3078), RG 2, NA. Emphasis added.

47. "Suffrage Wins in Senate; Now Goes to States," *New York Times,* 5 June 1919, 1, 4.

48. Nancy Woloch, "Feminist Movement," in Eric Foner and John A. Garraty, eds., *The Reader's Companion to American History* (Boston: Houghton Mifflin, 1991), 394.

49. The Yeomen (F) managed to win the support of Sen. Tasker Oddie of Nevada, who proposed striking the word "male" from the act. He received no support from his Senate colleagues and withdrew the proposal. Bureau of Naval Personnel Administrative History, World War II, box 3, folder "Women's Reserve" [hereafter Women's Reserve Official History], RG 24, NA.

50. Memorandum, Navy Department Historical Section, 19 April 1923, 2, ONRL Subject File 1911–1927, NA-3 Enlisted Personnel, box 355, folder 4, RG 45, NA.

51. Gavin, *American Women in World War I,* 5.

52. Greenwald, *Women, War and Work,* 47–58.

53. Greenwald, 60.

54. Hancock, *Lady in the Navy,* 50.

55. Col. T. F. Dwyer, CAC, "Conservation by Utilization of Women in the Military Service," 10 March 1922, Course at the Army War College, 1921–22, G-1, War Department General Staff, G-1 Personnel Numerical File [hereafter G-1 Numerical File], 1921–42, box 10, folder 7000–1, RG 165, NA.

56. Memorandum, Maj. E. S. Hughes to Assistant Chief of Staff, 21 September 1928, Subject: Participation of Women in War [hereafter Hughes memorandum], 11, G-1 Numerical File 1921–42, box 55, folder 9835, "Participation of Women in War," RG 165, NA.

57. Extracts from Studies Made by Officers of the 1924–1925 Class at the Army War College G-1 Course, Subject: Utilization of Women in the Military Service during War, 13, War Department General Staff, G-1 (Personnel) Numerical File, 1941–42, box 10, folder 7000–1 [hereafter AWC Women in War Studies Extracts], RG 165, NA.

58. AWC Women in War Studies Extracts, 16.

59. AWC Women in War Studies Extracts, 16. Emphasis added.

60. AWC Women in War Studies Extracts, 1.

61. AWC Women in War Studies Extracts, 26.

62. AWC Women in War Studies Extracts, 23.

63. Memorandum, Anita Phipps, Director of Women's Relations, to Assistant Chief of Staff, G-1, 1 July 1929, 1, War Dept. General Staff G-1 (Personnel) Numerical File, 1921–42, box 55, folder 9835, RG 165, NA [hereafter Phipps memorandum].

64. Mattie E. Treadwell, *The Women's Army Corps,* The United States Army in World War II, Special Studies (Washington, DC: Office of the Chief of Military History, Department of the Army, 1954), 10–15.
65. Phipps memorandum, 3, 5.
66. Hughes memorandum, 4.
67. Treadwell, *Women's Army Corps,* 14.
68. Treadwell, 14, n. 43.
69. John Whiteclay Chambers, *To Raise an Army: The Draft Comes to Modern America* (New York: Free Press, 1987), 75, 81. Chambers described the defining characteristics of the leading figures of the pro-conscription organizations of the era: "Most were Old Guard Republicans . . . all were men; women were consciously excluded"; John A. Holabird to Maj. Gen. Charles P. Summerall, 22 March 1929, G-1 Numerical File, 1921–42, box 55, folder 9835, NA; Secretary of War to the Honorable Jed Johnson, House of Representatives, (n.d.), G-1 Numerical File, 1921–42, box 55, folder 9835, NA; Secretary of War to Mrs. John F. Sippel, (n.d.), G-1 Numerical File, 1921–42, box 55, folder 9835, NA.
70. Secretary of War to Mrs. John F. Sippel.
71. Memorandum for A.C. of S., G-1, Subject: Status of Director of Women's Relations, 6 March 1931, G-1 Numerical File, 1921–42, box 55, folder 9835, RG 165, NA.
72. Phipps memorandum, 5.
73. See Jeffery M. Dorwart, *Conflict of Duty: The U.S. Navy's Intelligence Dilemma, 1919–1945* (Annapolis: Naval Institute Press, 1983), 12, 71–85.
74. Name Index Cards to the Correspondence of the Military Intelligence Division of the War Department General Staff, 1917–1941, Microfilm Publication M1194 (Washington, DC: National Archives and Records Service, General Services Administration, 1981) [hereafter MID Name Index]. Cards describing information maintained on individuals or organizations are filed alphabetically. For MID inquiries on sharing information, see "National Committee of Patriotic and Defense Societies" and "National League for Women's Service" in the archives' correspondence files.
75. Notations identifying correspondence from individuals and organizations offering such information can be found on individual cards throughout the Name Index File.
76. Letter, W. D. Puleston, Director of Naval Intelligence, to Mr. Percy M. Hansen, 17 September 1936, encouraging him to contact the local chapter of the American Legion and Mrs. George Sartell, regent of the Jamestown Chapter of the Daughters of the American Revolution, for more information. ONI Day File, 1929–1942, box D30, folder "Sept 1936," NA. W. D. Puleston

to Father Edmund B. Walsh, 20 February 1937, refers Father Walsh to the American Coalition of Patriotic Societies and the Committee on National Defense through Patriotic Education, Daughters of the American Revolution, for more information on "the general subject of radical activities," ONI Day File, 1929–1942, box D32, folder "Feb 1937," RG 38.4, NA.

77. MID Name Index, roll 2, "Jane Addams."
78. MID Name Index, roll 42, "Carrie Chapman Catt," and roll 201, "Margaret Sanger."
79. MID Name Index, roll 229, "Ida Tarbell."
80. MID Name Index, roll 104, "International Ladies' Garment Workers Union."
81. Capt. Luke McNamee, U.S. Navy, "Keep Our Navy Strong," *Proceedings* 49, no. 5 (May 1923): 810.

CHAPTER 2. FROM EXIGENT TO EXPENDABLE

1. Hancock, *Lady in the Navy*, 61.
2. Capt. W. B. Palmer, memorandum for the Assistant Chief of Staff, 2 October 1939, Subj: Women with the Army (emergency) [hereafter Palmer memo for ACoS], (War Dept General Staff) G-1 Personnel Numerical File 1921–42, box, 183, folder 15839 (Adjutant General's Office), RG 165, NA.
3. Palmer memo for ACoS.
4. Treadwell, *Women's Army Corps*, 15–17.
5. Office of the Clerk, U.S. House of Representatives, *Women in Congress: Congresswomen's Biographies*, http://bioguide.congress.gov/congresswomen /index.asp, 17 June 2006.
6. Treadwell, *Women's Army Corps*, 17.
7. Brig. Gen. Wade H. Haislip, G-1, memorandum for Chief of Staff, 29 April 1941, G-1/15839–10, cited in Treadwell, 17, n. 54.
8. Treadwell, 20–22, 29.
9. Treadwell, 24.
10. Bureau of Naval Personnel Administrative History, World War II, "Women's Reserve," 3, box 3, RG 24, NA [hereafter Women's Reserve Official History].
11. Women's Reserve Official History, 3–4.
12. Women's Reserve Official History, 4.
13. Hancock, *Lady in the Navy*, 51.
14. Women's Reserve Official History, 6.
15. Hancock, *Lady in the Navy*, 52.
16. Hancock, 36–37, 40, 49, 264–65.
17. U.S. Department of Labor, Women's Bureau, *The New Position of Women in American Industry*, Bulletin 12 (Washington, DC: GPO, 1920), 74.

18. Treadwell, *Women's Army Corps*, 16.
19. Clark G. Reynolds, *Admiral John H. Towers: The Struggle for Naval Air Supremacy* (Annapolis: Naval Institute Press, 1991), 359, 380–81.
20. Doris Weatherford, *American Women and World War II*, History of Women in America (New York: Facts on File, 1990), 44–45.
21. Women's Reserve Official History, 6–7.
22. Hancock, *Lady in the Navy*, 52–53.
23. Women's Reserve Official History, 8–9. The Bureau of Navigation was reorganized and renamed the Bureau of Personnel in May 1942.
24. Women's Reserve Official History, 9.
25. Women's Reserve Official History.
26. Judy Tzu-Chun Wu, "Mom Chung of the Fair-Haired Bastards: A Thematic Biography of Doctor Margaret Chung (1889–1959)" (PhD diss., Stanford University, 1998), 116–18; published as *Doctor Mom Chung of the Fair-Haired Bastards: The Life of a Wartime Celebrity* (Berkeley: University of California Press, 2005).
27. Wu, "Mom Chung of the Fair-Haired Bastards," 116, 119.
28. Wu, 116.
29. Wu, 140.
30. Wu, 175.
31. Wu, 178–79; Hancock, *Lady in the Navy*, 55; U.S. House of Representatives, Office of the Clerk, *Biographical Directory of the United States Congress, 1774–Present*, "Maas, Melvin Joseph, 1894–1964," http://bioguide.congress.gov/scripts/biodisplay.pl?index=M000001, 3 April 2001; "Melvin Joseph Maas, Major General, United States Marine Corps," http://www.arlingtoncemetery.com/mjmaas.htm, 6 June 2001. Chung referred to McQuiston alternately as admiral and captain. Hancock's memoir stated that McQuiston was a lieutenant commander at the time. Given that Hancock had served in the Navy and was employed by BuAer at that time, her recollection is probably accurate.
32. Wu, "Mom Chung of the Fair-Haired Bastards," 180; Hancock, *Lady in the Navy*, 54.
33. Women's Reserve Official History, 10; Godson, *Serving Proudly*, 110.
34. U.S. Congress, *Proceedings and Debates*, 77th Cong., 2nd sess., vol. 88, part 2, 23 February 1942–25 March 1942 (Washington, DC: GPO, 1942), 2592–93.
35. *Proceedings and Debates*, 2606.
36. *Proceedings and Debates*, 2607.
37. Treadwell, *Women's Army Corps*, 25.
38. Women's Reserve Official History, 20. In 1943 the Army reversed its position against giving women military status as a result of bureaucratic confusion

and inequities concerning administration, training, discipline, and benefits arising from the WAAC's auxiliary status—just as Major Hughes' 1928 study and Navy officials had predicted. Representative Rogers introduced remedial legislation to make the WAAC part of the Army. It became law in September 1943, and the name of the organization was changed to the Women's Army Corps (WAC). See Treadwell, *Women's Army Corps*, 219–30.

39. Women's Reserve Official History, 22.
40. Women's Reserve Official History, 12.
41. Hancock, *Lady in the Navy*, 60.
42. Women's Reserve Official History, 12–13.
43. Women's Reserve Official History, 13.
44. Wu, *Doctor Mom Chung of the Fair-Haired Bastards*, 167.
45. Ann M. Simmons, "Susan Ann Cuddy Dies at 100: Pioneering Korean American in U.S. Military," *Los Angeles Times*, 1 July 2015, https://www.latimes.com/local/obituaries/la-me-susan-ahn-cuddy-20150701-story.html.
46. U.S. Congress, Senate, "Establishing a Women's Auxiliary Reserve in the Navy," Report No. 1511, CIS U.S. Serial Set, Miscellaneous Senate Reports, 77th Cong., 2nd sess., S. Rpts. 4, no. 1415–1631, microfiche.
47. Women's Reserve Official History, 20, 26.
48. Women's Reserve Official History, 15.
49. Women's Reserve Official History, 15–16, 19.
50. Hancock, *Lady in the Navy*, 61.
51. Hancock, 59–61, 210.
52. Susan Godson, "The WAVES in World War II," *Proceedings* 107, no. 12 (1981): 48.
53. Women's Reserve Official History, 74.
54. Women's Reserve Official History, 78; Chief of Naval Personnel, Procurement Directive No. 1–44, 8 January 1944, Enclosure (A), Records of the Bureau of Naval Personnel, Regulations Governing Women Accepted for Volunteer Emergency Service ("WAVES"), July 1942–Nov 1945, box 1, RG 24, NA.
55. Treadwell, *Women's Army Corps*, 200–203.
56. John O'Donnell, "Capitol Stuff," *Washington Times-Herald*, 9 June 1943, editorial section.
57. Treadwell, *Women's Army Corps*, 206.
58. Treadwell.
59. Treadwell, 218.
60. Women's Reserve Official History, 114.
61. Jeanne Holm, *Women in the Military: An Unfinished Revolution*, rev. ed. (Novato, CA: Presidio Press, 1992), 69.

62. D'Ann Campbell, "Servicewomen of World War II," *Armed Forces and Society* 16, no. 2 (1990): 254–55.
63. Women's Reserve Official History, 74.
64. Campbell, "Servicewomen of World War II," 255.
65. Women's Reserve Official History, 72.
66. Women's Reserve Official History, 24, 105; Treadwell, *Women's Army Corps*, 544.
67. Women's Reserve Official History, 110.
68. Women's Reserve Official History, 80.
69. Women's Reserve Official History, 110.
70. Women's Reserve Official History, 112.
71. Women's Reserve Official History, Supplement, 7–8.
72. Women's Reserve Official History, Supp., 12.
73. Women's Reserve Official History, Supp., 17–18.
74. D'Ann Campbell, "Fighting with the Navy: The WAVES in World War II," in *New Interpretations in Naval History: Selected Papers from the Tenth Naval History Symposium*, ed. Jack Sweetman (Annapolis: Naval Institute Press, 1993), 356.
75. Women's Reserve Official History, Supp., 6.
76. Navy Department, July 21, 1945, "Eighty-Six Thousand WAVES on Third Anniversary," ACNP Records, Series I, Subject Files, 1940–1970, microfilm, roll 1, frames 65–68 [hereafter ACNP Records].
77. ACNP Records, roll 1, frames 65–68.
78. ACNP Records.
79. Edwin T. Layton, *And I Was There: Pearl Harbor and Midway—Breaking the Secrets* (New York: William Morrow, 1985), 33.
80. John Prados, *Combined Fleet Decoded: The Secret History of American Intelligence and the Japanese Navy in World War II* (Annapolis: Naval Institute Press, 1995), 78–80.
81. Liza Mundy, *Code Girls: The Untold Story of the American Women Code Breakers of World War II* (New York: Hachette Books, 2017), 3–6.
82. Mundy, 138.
83. Jennifer Wilcox, *Sharing the Burden: Women in Cryptology during World War II* (Fort George M. Meade, MD: Center for Cryptologic History, National Security Agency, 1998), http://www.nsa.gov/publications/publi00014.cfm, 20 June 2006.
84. Capt. Henri H. Smith-Hutton, USN (Ret.), oral history interview by Paul B. Ryan, U.S. Naval Institute, Annapolis, MD, 1976, 396–97.
85. W. J. Holmes, *Double-Edged Secrets: U.S. Naval Intelligence Operations in the Pacific during World War II* (Annapolis: Naval Institute Press, 1998), 210–11.

86. Kathleen Broome Williams, *Improbable Warriors: Women Scientists and the U.S. Navy in World War II* (Annapolis: Naval Institute Press, 2001), 39–47.
87. Williams, 46.
88. Williams, 47, 65.
89. Hancock, *Lady in the Navy*, 213–16.

CHAPTER 3. READY ABOUT

1. Ferdinand Eberstadt, *Report to the Commission on the National Security Organization*, vol. 3, chap. 12, "Personnel Administration, Policies and Practices," sect. 14 (1948), "Women in the National Security Establishment," 191, Ferdinand Eberstadt Papers, box 82, Seeley G. Mudd Manuscript Library, Princeton University Department of Rare Books and Special Collections [hereafter Eberstadt Papers, PUL].
2. *Congressional Record*, House, 12 May 1948–2 June 1948, Proceedings and Debates of the 80th Congress, 2nd ses., Women's Armed Services Act of 1948, 6969.
3. Lt. Cdr. Winifred R. Quick, memorandum to Capt. Joy B. Hancock, 16 April 1947, Subject: Guidance and personnel convention, notes on, Records of the Assistant Chief of Naval Personnel for Women (Wilmington, Del.: Scholarly Resources, 1991), series I, folder "Future Planning (1943–1947)," microfilm, roll 3, frames 2861–62 [hereafter ACNP Records].
4. Hancock, *Lady in the Navy*, 213.
5. Hancock, 214.
6. Mildred A. Horton, memorandum to Chief of Naval Personnel, 17 September 1945, Subject: Women in the peace-time Navy, problems related to, ACNP Records, microfilm, roll 4, frames 4141–42. Following her marriage to the Reverend Dr. Douglas Horton in August 1945, Captain McAfee took the name of her husband. Naval History and Heritage Command, Naval Historical Center Online Library of Selected Images, https://www.history .navy.mil/content/history/nhhc/our-collections/photography/us-people/m /mcafee-mildred-h-horton.html.
7. Pers-107-MN, Lt. Cdr. G. J. Grimm, USNR, memorandum to Capt. L. N. Miller, USN, Subject: A proposed plan for the incorporation of women into the permanent U.S. Naval Reserve, 8 January 1944, ACNP Records, microfilm, roll 3, frames 2920–22.
8. Although no author is attributed to the official history of the Women's Reserve, the writing style and observations correlate closely with Joy Bright Hancock's memoir, *Lady in the Navy*. Hancock was intimately involved in laying the groundwork for bringing women back into the Navy prior to World War II. Her experience as a Navy insider earned the respect of senior

male leaders in BuPers. While she recognized the need to acknowledge the concerns of the public about the propriety of military women, that was not her overriding concern. She focused on the best way to utilize women to accomplish the Navy's mission.

9. Proposed Codification of Regulations on Women's Reserve, ACNP Files, microfilm, roll 4, frames 4284–96.

10. Pers-10B-SP, Memorandum for Captain Hopwood from Lt. Christopher S. Sargent, USNR, Subject: Proposed reorganization of the Waves, 7 March 1944, ACNP Records, series I, folder "Historical Data—Women's Reserve (June 1943–December 1946)," microfilm, roll 4, frames 4282–83.

11. Pers-170-MEK, memorandum from Cdr. Tova P. Wiley, USNR, to Planning and Control, 21 February 1945, Subject: Proposed statement in BuPers Information Bulletin concerning enrollment of WAVES in Regular Navy after the war, ACNP Records, "Historical Data," frame 4159.

12. Statement of Vice Adm. L. E. Denfeld, USN, 3 April 1946, concerning the Women's Reserve legislation H.R. 5915, "To amend the Naval Reserve Act of 1938, as amended, so as to establish the Women's Reserve on a permanent basis, and for other purposes," ACNP Records, "Historical Data," frame 4013.

13. U.S. House of Representatives, 79th Cong., 2nd sess., Naval Affairs Committee, Hearings on H.R. 5915, "To establish the Women's Reserves on a permanent basis," 9 May 1946, 3319–39.

14. Sherman, *No Place for A Woman*, 58–59.

15. Sherman, "'They Either Need These Women or They Do Not': Margaret Chase Smith and the Fight for Regular Status for Women in the Military," *Journal of Military History* 54 (January 1990): 59.

16. *Congressional Record*, House, 21 May 1946, Hearings on H.R. 5915, "To amend the Naval Reserve Act of 1938, as amended, so as to establish the Women's Reserves on a permanent basis," 3328.

17. Chief of Naval Operations, memorandum to Chief of Naval Personnel, 19 April 1946, Subject: WAVE enlisted personnel—report on, ACNP Records, series I, folder "Historical Data—Women's Reserve (June 1943–December 1946)," microfilm, roll 4, frames 4048–49.

18. Capt. Jean T. Palmer, memorandum to Director, Planning and Control Division, 7 May 1946, ACNP Records, roll 4, frame 4044.

19. *Congressional Record*, House, May 21, 1946, Hearings on H.R. 5915 "To amend the Naval Reserve Act of 1938, as amended," 3334.

20. Sherman, "Either They Need These Women or They Do Not," 65–66.

21. Hancock, *Lady in the Navy*, 226–27.

22. Hancock, 231–32.
23. Hancock, 230.
24. U.S. House of Representatives, 80th Cong., 2nd sess., Committee on Armed Services, Subcommittee No. 3, Organization and Mobilization, Hearings on S. 1641, "To establish the Women's Army Corps in the Regular Army, to authorize the enlistment and appointment of women in the Regular Navy and Marine Corps and the Naval and Marine Corps Reserve, and for other purposes," 18, 23, 25, 27 February, 2, 3 March 1948: [hereafter Committee on Armed Services, Subcommittee No. 3], 5563–5747.
25. Committee on Armed Services, Subcommittee No. 3, 5585.
26. Committee on Armed Services, Subcommittee No. 3, 5570.
27. Committee on Armed Services, Subcommittee No. 3, 5573.
28. Committee on Armed Services, Subcommittee No. 3, 5565–66.
29. U.S. Congress, *Statements and Speeches*, 80th Cong., 1948, vol. 5, 6 April 6 1948: 159, MCSL; Sherman, "Either They Need These Women or They Do Not," 73–74.
30. Sherman, "Either They Need These Women or They Do Not," 75–76.
31. Margaret Chase Smith to James V. Forrestal, 22 April 1948, MCSL.
32. Sherman, "Either They Need These Women or They Do Not," 71.
33. *Congressional Record*, 2 June 1948, 7052–57; Sherman, "Either They Need These Women or They Do Not," 76.
34. "Margaret Smith Referred to as Mother [of the] WAVES," *Independent Reporter* (Skowhegan, ME), 14 December 1944, press folder, MCSL.
35. Memorandum, 17 February 1988, Folder: Armed Services Committee, Women in the Armed Forces, Subfolder: Smith Legislation on Women in the Armed Services, MCSL. Inconsistencies in the spelling of the organization's acronym are in the original text.
36. Notes on the Conference of District and Air Command Directors (W), 24 August 1948, 2–4, ACNP Records, microfilm, roll 2, frames 2172–2225.
37. Committee on Armed Services, Subcommittee No. 3, 5689.
38. House Subcommittee No. 3, 5711.
39. Notes on the Conference of District and Air Command Directors (W), 24 August 1948, 6, ACNP Records, microfilm, roll 2, frame 2227.
40. Notes on Conference of District and Air Command Directors, ACNP Records, 16–18; *United States Navy Regulations* (1920; reprint, Washington, DC: GPO, 1941), chap. 3, art. 150, 54.
41. Notes on Conference of District and Air Command Directors (W), 23–25, ACNP Records, microfilm, roll 2, frames 2172–2225; Lori Lyn Bogle and

Joel L. Hewitt, "The Best Quote Jones Never Wrote," *Naval History* (April 2004): 18–23.

42. *Congressional Record*, House, 12 May 1948–2 June 1948, Proceedings and Debates of the 80th Cong., 2nd sess., Women's Armed Services Act of 1948, 6969.

43. Capt. Joy Bright Hancock, memorandum to Admiral Sprague, 14 September 1948, Subject: Conference with Mr. Radom of the Eberstadt Committee, ACNP Records, microfilm, roll 3, frames 2847–48.

44. Ferdinand Eberstadt, *Report to the Commission on the National Security Organization*, vol. 3, chap. 12, sect. 14, "Women in the National Security Establishment," 186, Eberstadt Papers, PUL.

45. Eberstadt, 187.

46. Eberstadt, 188.

47. Eberstadt, 190–91.

48. Bureau of Naval Personnel, A Statistical Survey of WAVE Distributions and Rating Group Assignments, October 1951, ACNP Records, series I, folder "Subject Files (1940–1970)," microfilm, roll 1, frames 398–404.

49. Bureau of Naval Personnel, Statistical Survey of WAVE Distributions.

50. Notes on the Conference of District and Air Command Directors, 23–25, ACNP Records, series I, folder "District Directors Conference, 1948," microfilm, roll 2, frames 2186–87.

51. *Congressional Record*, House, 12 May 1948–2 June 1948), Proceedings and Debates of the 80th Cong., 2nd sess., Women's Armed Services Act of 1948, 5577.

CHAPTER 4. BECALMED IN THE DOLDRUMS OF DOMESTICITY

1. Assistant Chief for Women to Director, Plans and Policy Control Division, 28 December 1953, memorandum, Report of Ad Hoc Committee on Increasing the Attractiveness of Military Service as a Career, ACNP Records, Series I, Subject Files (1940–1970), folder "Ad Hoc Committee Report (December 1953)," microfilm, roll 1, frame 23.

2. Godson, *Serving Proudly*, 182–83.

3. Godson, 43.

4. Lt. Josephine Chenault to Capt. Joy B. Hancock, 17 May 1951, ACNP Records, Series I, Subject Files (1949–1970), folder "Chief of Naval Air Technical Training Command," microfilm, roll 1, frames 667–68.

5. Capt. Joy B. Hancock to Lt. Josephine Chenault, 23 May 1951, ACNP Records, Series I, Subject Files (1949–1970), folder "Chief of Naval Air Technical Training Command," microfilm, roll 1, frame 669.

6. "Services: Women Wanted," *Newsweek*, 29 October 1951, 26; "Services: Luring the Ladies," *Newsweek*, 5 November 1951, 27–28.

7. Two weeks after he signed the Women's Armed Services Integration Act, President Truman signed Executive Order 9981 desegregating the armed services: "Establishing the President's Committee on the Equality of Treatment and Opportunity in the Armed Services," Code of Federal Regulations: Title 3—The President, 1943–1948 compilation (Washington, DC: Federal Register Division, NARA, 1957). See Anna Kasten Nelson, "Anna M. Rosenberg, an 'Honorary Man,'" *Journal of Military History* 68 (January 2004): 133–62.

8. "George C. Marshall, September 21, 1950–September 12, 1951, 3rd Secretary of Defense, Truman Administration," Department of Defense, Secretaries of Defense Biographies, https://history.defense.gov/DesktopModules /ArticleCS/Print.aspx?PortalId=70&ModuleId=18327&Article=571266; "Women Wanted," *Newsweek*, 26.

9. Nelson, "Anna M. Rosenberg," 158.

10. Douglas T. Miller and Marion Nowak, "The Happy Home Corporation and Baby Factory," chapter 14 in *The Fifties: The Way We Really Were* (Garden City, NY: Doubleday, 1977), 147, 155: "In 1950 . . . men's average marriage age was 22.0 and women's 20.3, a significant drop from the 1940 figures of 24.3 and 21.5 respectively."

11. Functionalism was a concept developed by social scientists to introduce objectivity into the analysis of other cultures as opposed to judging them by Western standards. Behavior and artifacts were assessed in terms of the function they performed within a specific culture without imposing personal judgments. As misapplied in the American progressive education system, functionalism lost its intended purpose as a tool for objectivity and was instead bent to serve a nonobjective purpose—to train a child for a preplanned future extrapolated from his or her social position in society. Miller and Nowak, "The Happy Home Corporation," 150–51.

12. Laura McEnaney, "Atomic Age Motherhood: Maternalism and Militarism in the 1950s," in Linda K. Kerber and Jane Sherron De Hart, eds., *Women's America: Refocusing the Past*, 5th ed. (New York: Oxford University Press, 2000), 449.

13. Committee on Armed Services, Subcommittee No. 3, 5564.

14. Miller and Nowak, "The Happy Home Corporation," 162–63.

15. Dorothy C. Stratton, "Our Great Unused Resource—Womanpower," *New York Times Magazine* 1 October 1950, 30.

16. Stratton.

17. Nelson, "Anna M. Rosenberg," 159.

18. Marietta Henderson, Coordinator, Family Life Education Council, to the Reverend Martin Vick, President, North Carolina Family Life Council, 13 January 1951, ACNP Records, Series I, Subject Files, 1940–1970, folder "Assistants (W) Miscellaneous, (1948–1965)," microfilm, roll 8, frames 468–74.

19. ACNP Records, Series I, Subject Files, 1940–1970, Folder "Assistants (W) Miscellaneous, (1948–1965)," microfilm, roll 8, frames 475–76.

20. See "Opportunities for Women," *Parents* magazine (April 1952): 123; "The Last Frontier," *Independent Woman* (January 1953): 8–10; "Role in Defense Described to Advisory Council," *Independent Woman* (January 1953): 25; "Skirting the Military," *Independent Woman* (October 1953): 348.

21. Mary Morris, "What's behind the Girls behind the Men?" *Mademoiselle* (July 1951): 56–62, 106–107; ACNP Records, Series II, Publicity Files (1942–1972), Folder "Publicity Press Clippings (1951–1952)," microfilm, roll 14, frames 858–67.

22. Kate Holliday, "Are Women in Uniform Immoral?" *Woman's Home Companion* (August 1952): 32–33, 47–48; ACNP Records, Series II, Publicity Files (1942–1972), Folder "Publicity Press Clippings (1951–1952)," microfilm, roll 14, frames 868–71.

23. Holliday, "Are Women in Uniform Immoral?," 48; ACNP Records, "Publicity Press Clippings," frame 871.

24. Guy Richards, "Waves Find Stricter Moral Code in Boot Camp Than in Own Homes," *New York Journal American* (June 1962); ACNP Records, microfilm, Series II, Publicity Files (1942–1972), roll 14, frames 780–83.

25. Holm, *Women in the Military* 151–56.

26. Jean Ebbert and Marie-Beth Hall, *Crossed Currents: Navy Women in a Century of Change*, 3rd rev. ed. (Washington, London: Brassey's, Batsford Brassey, 1999), 147; Godson, *Serving Proudly*, 199.

27. Holm, *Women in the Military*, 156.

28. Press release, WAVES STRENGTH, n.d., ACNP Records, Series I, microfilm, roll 4, frames 3831–32.

29. Conference of District and Air Command Assistants (W), 16–18 May 1956, Bureau of Naval Personnel, Washington, DC, ACNP Records, Series I, Subject Files, 1940–1970, Assistants (W) Misc., 1948–65, p. 5, microfilm, roll 1, frame 189; Tom Compere, ed., *The Navy Blue Book*, vol. 1 (New York: Published for Military Publishing Institute by Bobbs-Merrill, 1960), 283.

30. Ebbert and Hall, *Crossed Currents*, 156.

31. Conference of District and Air Command Assistants (W), 16–18 May 1956, ACNP Records, pp. 5–6, microfilm, roll 1, frames 189–90.
32. Milton Lehman, "Why Are They Quitting?" *Saturday Evening Post*, 30 July 1955, 34; "Navy Fishes for Volunteers—Drafts, Too," *Business Week*, 24 September 1955, 30; "The Draft: Reluctant Call-up," *Newsweek*, 26 September 1955, 37–38.
33. Memo for the Record, September 8, 1952, "Utilization of Enlisted Women," file 9, OP-01(W) Files, Bureau of Naval Personnel, Navy Department, cited in Ebbert and Hall, *Crossed Currents*, 143.
34. Assistant Chief for Women to Director, Plans and Policy Control Division, memorandum, 6 June 1951, Detention of Women Personnel of the Armed Forces, ACNP Records, series I, Subject Files (1940–1970), microfilm, roll 2, frames 1150–51.
35. "WHAT . . . is a WAVE?" Excerpts from minutes of Conference of District and Air Command Assistants (W), 16–18 May 1956, ACNP Records, Series II, Publicity Files, folder "Miscellaneous Publicity (1945–1966)," microfilm, p. A-1, roll 14, frame 675.
36. Chief, Naval Air Reserve Training Command, to Commanding Officers of all Naval Air Stations and Naval Air Reserve Training Units This Command, 20 June 1951, CNART Instruction 133.17, Designation of Wave Representative, ACNP Records, Series I, Subject Files (1940–1970), folder "Chief of Naval Air Reserve Training Command (1943–1952)," microfilm, roll 1, frame 551 [hereafter, CNART Instruction 133.17].
37. Conference of District and Air Command Assistants (W), 16–18 May 1956, ACNP Records, Series I, Subject Files (1940–1970), folder, "Assistants (W) Miscellaneous (1948–1965)," microfilm, pp. 40, 46, roll 1, frames 224, 230.
38. CNART Instruction 133.17. This understanding was stated in Hancock's handwritten marginal notes on the instruction.
39. "Four Waves Assigned to Duty on Transports," *Navy Times*, 12 September 1953, 3.
40. Commanding Officer, USS *Thomas Jefferson* (APA 30) to Chief, Naval Transportation Service, 24 September 1949, ACNP Records, Series II, Publicity Files (1942–1972), folder "Miscellaneous Publicity (1945–1966)," microfilm, roll 14, frames 617–18. Hancock concurred with the argument, stating, "It is my hope that a practical and satisfactory solution to the present problem which would attend the assignment of women officers to transports may be worked out." Pers-17 to Pers-21, 28 October 1949, memorandum, Assignment of WAVES to duty on Navy Transports, ACNP Records, "Miscellaneous Publicity," frame 613.

41. Wave Detailing to Assistant Chief for Women, via Head, Detailing Section, 11 April 1958, Memorandum, MSTS duty for women Hospital Corpsmen, suggestions concerning, ACNP Records, Series II, Publicity Files (1942–1972), folder "Miscellaneous Publicity (1945–1966)," microfilm, roll 14, frames 541–42.

42. "Sea-Going Waves? It's True—," *All Hands* (August 1958), ACNP Records, series II, Publicity Files (1942–1972), folder "Miscellaneous Publicity (1945–1966)," microfilm, roll 14, frames 543–44.

43. "*Mann's* Woman Is Navy's First," *Navy Times*, 15 July 1961, 2.

44. Ebbert and Hall, *Crossed Currents*, 167–68.

45. Ebbert and Hall.

46. "Although the proportion of women among college students fell during the postwar years, their numbers kept rising. This meant a far larger constituency of educated women, always the nucleus of feminist movements." Woloch, "Feminist Movement," 394.

47. ROC training was initially held at the Naval Training Center in Great Lakes, Michigan. The program was moved in 1952 to the U.S. Naval Training Center in Bainbridge, Maryland, and was subsequently superseded by the College Junior Program established at the Officer Indoctrination School in Newport, Rhode Island, in 1953. Rita Lenihan to Joy Bright Hancock, 14 February 1968, ACNP Records, Series I, Subject Files (1940–1970), folder "Historical Matters (1944–1968)," microfilm, roll 4/frame 4620.

48. Conference of District and Air Command Assistants (W), 16–18 May 1956, ACNP Records, Series I, p. 27, microfilm, roll 1, frame 211. The General Line School was originally established as the Naval Postgraduate School in Annapolis. The name changed when the school moved to Monterey, California, in 1952. The name was subsequently changed back to the Naval Postgraduate School, as it is known today. See http://www.npsfoundation .org/001_history.htm.

49. Ebbert and Hall, *Crossed Currents*, 162–64.

50. Conference of District and Air Command Assistants (W), 16–18 May 1956, ACNP Records, Series I, p. 60, microfilm, roll 1, frame 235.

51. "Bill to Relax Wave Grade Curbs OK'd," *Navy Times*, 31 March 1956, 6.

52. Conference of District and Air Command Assistants (W), 16–18 May 1956, ACNP Records, Series I, pp. 59–60, microfilm, roll 1, frames 234–35.

53. "Bill to Relax Wave Grade Curbs OK'd," 6.

54. Conference of District and Air Command Assistants (W), 16–18 May 1956, ACNP Records, Series I, p. 60, microfilm, roll 1, frame 235.

55. In October 1961, 2,500 male lieutenant commanders competed for 800 vacancies in the rank of commander, with approximately a 33 percent chance of

selection, while 41 women lieutenant commanders competed for 2 vacancies, a selection opportunity of 5 percent. Between 1964 and 1968, 80 percent of male lieutenants eligible for promotion were selected while only 13 percent of women were. Ebbert and Hall, *Crossed Currents*, 156.

56. Capt. Carlton Charles Lucas to Chief of Naval Personnel, 9 May 1961, Report of the Board to Study Existing Policies and Procedures Governing the Assignment of Officer and Enlisted Personnel Navy, ACNP Records, Series I, Subject Files 1940–1970, folder "Lucas Board," microfilm, roll 4, frame 4947.

57. Pers K to Pers A, 30 September 1964, ACNP Records, Series I, Subject Files (1940–1970), folder "Justification-Officer/Enlisted 1963–65," microfilm, roll 4, frame 4791. Emphasis added.

58. A. L. Ducey (Pers B-116) to Pers-B, 18 May 1961, Recommendations concerning assignment of women personnel; comments on, ACNP Records, Series I, Subject Files (1940–1970), folder "Lucas Board," microfilm, roll 4, frames 4966–68.

59. Chief of Naval Personnel to Distribution List, 11 July 1961, Report of Board to Study Existing Policies and Procedures Governing the Assignment of Officer and Enlisted Personnel Navy, ACNP Records, Series I, Subject Files (1940–1970), folder "Lucas Board," microfilm, roll 4, frames 4947–48.

60. Betty J. Morden, *The Women's Army Corps, 1945–1978* (Washington, DC: Center of Military History, U.S. Army, 1990), 203.

61. Holm, *Women in the Military*, 163.

62. CO, NAS NORVA to BuPers via ComFIVE, 9 May 1950, ACNP Records, Series I, Subject Files (1940–1970), folder "Marriage Policies (1942–1954)," microfilm, roll 4, frames 5022–23.

63. L. K. Wilde (Pers-13a) to Pers-A11, 7 June 1950, memorandum, Marriage of enlisted personnel in Pay Grades E-1, E-4 inclusive; recommendations concerning, ACNP Records, Series I, Subject Files (1940–1970), folder "Marriage Policies (1942–1954)," microfilm, roll 4, frames 5015–16.

64. Holm, *Women in the Military*, 163.

65. Morden, *Women's Army Corps, 1945–1978*, 203.

66. Stephen S. Jackson, Deputy Assistant Secretary of Defense, to Melvin Price, Chairman, Subcommittee on Manpower Utilization, House Armed Services Committee, House of Representatives, 8 July 1959, ACNP Records, Series I, Subject File (1940–1970), folder "Justification–Officer/Enlisted (1963–1965)," microfilm, roll 3, frames 4722–4833.

67. W. V. Combs, Assistant Chief of Naval Operations (Manpower), to Chief of Naval Operations, memorandum, 4 October 1965, Civilian Replacement Programs, ACNP Records, Series I, Subject File (1940–1970), folder "Justification–Officer/Enlisted (1963–1965)," microfilm, roll 3, frames 4722–4833.

68. Holm, *Women in the Military*, 164.
69. Holm, 199–200.
70. Holm, 190.
71. Chambers, *To Raise an Army*, 257.
72. Holm, *Women in the Military*, 191.
73. Holm, 194.
74. Holm, 201.

CHAPTER 5. SEA CHANGE IN THE SEVENTIES

1. Zumwalt, 265.
2. Andrew J. Bacevich, "Who Will Serve?" *Wilson Quarterly* 22, no. 3 (1998): 88.
3. Zumwalt, *On Watch*, 262.
4. CNO [Z-66] to NAVOP, 172054Z DEC 70, Subject: Equal Opportunity in the Navy, Naval Historical Center, https://www.history.navy.mil/content/history /nhhc/research/library/online-reading-room/title-list-alphabetically/z/list-z -grams/z-gram-66.html, 21 September 2016; CNO [Z-116] to NAVOP, 071115Z AUG 72, Subject: Equal Rights and Opportunities for Women in the Navy, Naval Historical Center, https://www.history.navy.mil/research/library /online-reading-room/title-list-alphabetically/z/list-z-grams/z-gram-116 .html, 6 January 2022 [hereafter Z-gram 116].
5. Z-gram 116.
6. "*Sanctuary* Undergoing 11-Month Conversion to 'Family Care' Ship," *Navy Times*, 29 March 1972, 10.
7. "*Sanctuary* Undergoing Conversion."
8. Georgia Clark Sadler, "Women in the Sea Services: 1972–1982," *Proceedings* 109 (May 1983): 140.
9. Zumwalt, *On Watch*, 264–65.
10. Zumwalt, 261.
11. Navy Office of Information, Internal Relations Division, Biographical Data, Robin L. Quigley, Captain USN (Ret.), 6 January 1971, in Captain Robin L. Quigley, USN (Ret.) oral history, conducted by Etta Belle Kitchen, 15 June 1976, San Diego, CA (Annapolis: U.S. Naval Institute) [hereafter Quigley oral history].
12. Quigley oral history, 249–50.
13. Quigley oral history.
14. Beth F. Coye, "The Restricted Unrestricted Line Officer: The Status of the Navy's Woman Line Officer," *Naval War College Review*, reprinted in U.S. Congress, House Committee on Armed Services, *Hearings before Special Subcommittee on the Utilization of Manpower in the Military*, 92nd Cong., 1st

and 2nd sess., HASC No 9251 (Washington, DC: GPO, 1972), 13, 26 October, 4, 19 November 1971; 6 March 1972, 12473–484.

15. Coye, "Restricted Unrestricted Line Officer," 12477.

16. Hancock, *Lady in the Navy*, 222.

17. Quigley oral history, 213; Rosemary Purcell, "Capt. Quigley versus 'Waves': Urges End to Misleading Term," *Navy Times*, 29 March 1972, 24.

18. Quigley oral history, 225–27.

19. Quigley oral history, 228, 230.

20. Quigley oral history, 231.

21. Purcell, "Capt. Quigley versus 'Waves'," 24.

22. Purcell.

23. Purcell.

24. Quigley oral history, 207–12.

25. Quigley oral history, 271.

26. Quigley oral history, 274.

27. Quigley oral history, 279.

28. Quigley oral history.

29. Quigley oral history, 280.

30. 0. Quigley oral history, 262.

31. Quigley oral history, 248.

32. Quigley oral history, 290.

33. Quigley oral history, 294.

34. Quigley oral history, 301.

35. Zumwalt, *On Watch*, 262–64.

36. Quigley oral history, 305. Quigley also noted that she had received a three-page letter "of chastisement" from Zumwalt "taking me to task for every single one of the philosophies I expressed in the memorandum." She was referring to her memorandum directing the abolition of the use of the term "Waves" and the Women's Representative system, 236.

37. Navy Office of Information, Biographical Data, Robin L. Quigley, Captain, USN (Ret.), 6 January 1971, Modern Biographical Files in the Navy Department Library, Naval History and Heritage Command.

38. Holm, *Women in the Military*, 282–85.

39. Gary E. Weir, "The American Sound Surveillance System: Using the Ocean to Hunt Soviet Submarines, 1950–1961," *International Journal of Naval History* 5, no. 2 (2006), https://www.ijnhonline.org/wp-content/uploads/2012/01/article_weir_aug06.pdf.

40. IUSS CAESAR Alumni Association, "Integrated Undersea Surveillance System (IUSS) History 1950–2010," http://www.iusscaa.org/history.htm, last updated 8 December 2017.

41. Naval Military Personnel Command (NMPC-62), *Women in the Navy Information Book* (Washington, DC: Department of the Navy, 1979) [hereafter *Women in the Navy Information Book*], 34–37.
42. *Women in the Navy Information Book*, 35–38.
43. *Women in the Navy Information Book*, 39–41.
44. *Women in the Navy Information Book*, 42–43.
45. *Women in the Navy Information Book*, 43.
46. *Women in the Navy Information Book*, 50.
47. *Women in the Navy Information Book*, 49.
48. U.S. Congress, House Committee on the Armed Services, *Hearings before the Special Subcommittee on the Utilization of Manpower in the Military*, 92nd Cong., 1st and 2nd sess., HASC No 9251 (Washington, DC: GPO, 1972), 12485.
49. U.S. Congress, House Committee on the Armed Services, *Hearings before the Special Subcommittee on the Utilization of Manpower in the Military*, 92nd Cong., 2nd sess., HASC No. 9258 (Washington, DC: GPO, 1972), 14631–32.
50. Holm, *Women in the Military*, 317.
51. "Women with Navy Wings," *All Hands* (April 1975): 32; "From Plane Captains to Pilots," *Naval Aviation News* (July 1977): 12.
52. John Whiteclay Chambers, "Conscription," in *The Reader's Companion to American History*, ed. Eric Foner and John A. Garraty (Boston: Houghton Mifflin, 1991), 219.
53. Martin Binkin and John D. Johnston, *All-Volunteer Armed Forces: Progress, Problems, and Prospects*, Report prepared for the Committee on Armed Services, U.S. Senate, 93rd Cong., 1st sess. (Washington, DC: GPO, 1973), 38.
54. *Women in the Navy Information Book*, 8.
55. Sadler, "Women in the Sea Services," 142–43.
56. *Women in the Navy Information Book*, 8; Ebbert and Hall, *Crossed Currents*, 188.
57. Quigley oral history, 253. Quigley stated that she had no direct role in the integration of OCS, which took place during her tenure as ACNP (W), but she pointed to it as an example of "how to do things right" concerning the integration of women.
58. *Women in the Navy Information Book*, 9; Sadler, "Women in the Sea Services," 146.
59. *Frontiero v. Richardson*, 411 U.S. 677 (1973), http://www.oyez.org/oyez/resource/case/128/, 11 February 2006.
60. Kerber, *No Constitutional Right to Be Ladies*, 276.

61. Defense Advisory Committee on Women in the Services, History of Recommendations, spring 1974, https://dacowits.defense.gov/Home/Documents/1974-Spring/.

62. "Military Academies: Should They Admit Women?" *Congressional Quarterly Weekly Report* 32, no. 28 (July 13, 1974): 1818–19.

63. "Military Academies: Should They Admit Women?" 1819–20.

64. "Military Academies: Should They Admit Women?" 1820.

65. "National Security: Women in Academies," *Congressional Quarterly Almanac* XXXI (1975), 94th Cong., 1st sess. (Washington, DC: Congressional Quarterly, 1976), 370.

66. Defense Advisory Committee of Women in the Services, History of Recommendations, https://dacowits.defense.gov/Home/Documents/1975-Spring/.

67. DACOWITS, History of Recommendations.

68. Kathleen Bruyere, *Women at Sea: 25 Years and Counting*, transcript of panel sessions of symposium sponsored by the Naval Historical Foundation and the Surface Navy Association, Washington, DC, 20 November 2003, 2–3. *Navy Regulations* (1973 ed.), articles 0836, 0837, 0839, 0857, 0859, and 0860, "require that officers detailed to or succeeding to command of Naval Districts, Naval Bases, ships, etc. be 'eligible for command at sea.'" Article 0902 defines the term "'elige\ible for command at sea' as applicable to all male officers of the Navy . . . except those designated for the performance of engineering, aeronautical engineering or special duties, and . . . limited duty officers . . . not authorized to perform all deck duties afloat." U.S. Navy Resource Management Center, Norfolk, VA, "Women in the Navy" Workshop booklet, n.d., 2, author's files.

69. Bruyere, *Women at Sea*, 6.

70. Bruyere, 6–7.

71. George C. Wilson, "Women Eyed for Fighting Ship Duty; Pentagon Eyes Women for Duty on Combat Ships," *Washington Post*, 18 May 1977, A1.

72. George C. Wilson, "Navy Chief's Vision: All-Woman Crew," *Washington Post*, 26 June 1977, A4.

73. NAVOP 074/78, "Potential Assignment of Navy Women to Duty at Sea," 29 June 1978, 1. The exact language of the amendment read: "Women may not be assigned to duty in vessels or aircraft that are engaged in combat missions nor may they be assigned to *other than temporary duty* on vessels of the Navy except hospital ships, transports, *and vessels of a similar classification not expected to be assigned to combat missions.*" The italicized text was the new language inserted into the original section 6015. "Women in the Navy" Workshop booklet, 5.

74. Timothy S. Robinson, "Barring Women from Navy Ships Is Struck Down; Law Barring Women from Ships Ruled Unconstitutional," *Washington Post*, 28 July 1978, A1.

75. Robinson.

76. Office of the Chief of Naval Operations, *Navy Study Group's Report on Progress of Women in the Navy* (Washington, DC: Department of the Navy, 1987) [hereafter Progress of Women in the Navy], 1-A-4.

77. NAVOP 130/78, 232018Z OCT 78, "Assignment of Women to Shipboard Duty," author's files.

78. NAVSEC Washington DC to COMNAVSURFPAC San Diego, CA, 042024Z OCT 78, "Visit Clearance Request Women aboard Ship Program," author's files.

79. DCNO MPT Washington DC, 281716Z FEB 79, "Revised Plan for the Assignment of Women to Shipboard Duty in FY 79," author's files.

80. Cdr. R. L. Hazard, OP-13E, 2 January 1980, Overview of Women in Ships Program, Files of the Office of the Assistant Chief of Naval Personnel for Women's Policy (PERS-00W) [hereafter PERS-00W files], Records of the Special Assistant for Women's Policy, Archives Branch, Naval History and Heritage Command, Washington, D.C.. Guided missile ships are specifically designed for the purpose of research, development, and operational evaluation testing of guided missile systems. They are not combatant vessels. See the history of USS *Norton Sound*, one of the ships originally chosen to receive women crewmembers, at https://www.history.navy.mil/research/histories/ship-histories/danfs/n/norton-sound.html.

81. CNO Washington DC, 031720Z MAR 79, "Women at Sea Monitoring Plan," author's files.

82. CNO Washington DC, R 131414Z JUN 79, "Standardized Orientation Training RE the Women in Ships Program," author's files.

83. USS *Jason*, Women to Sea Workshop Handout, n.d., author's files.

84. Workshop for Prospective USS *Canopus* Crewmembers (undated), PERS-00W files.

85. OP-01(W) was the organizational code for the position within the staff of the Office of the Chief of Naval Operations, also known as OPNAV. Within the Navy's Bureau of Personnel, her position was known by the code PERS-00W.

86. Surface Navy Association, Naval Historical Foundation, and Naval Historical Center Symposium, *Women At Sea: 25 Years and Counting*, Transcript of panel discussions, Washington, DC: 20 November 2003, 10.

87. Surface Navy Association, et al., 11

88. DACOWITS, History of Recommendations, Fall Conference 1975, https://dacowits.defense.gov/Home/Documents/1975-Fall/.

89. DACOWITS, 12–13. The impetus for the study probably came in part from a DACOWITS recommendation first made during the committee's fall 1975 conference calling for the development of nondiscriminatory physical standards to match an individual's physical capabilities to the specific job requirements.

90. Sadler, Women at Sea Symposium transcript, 15.

91. Sadler, Women at Sea Symposium transcript, 16.

92. *Progress of Women in the Navy*, 1–38, 1-A-7–8.

93. Sadler, "Women in the Sea Services," 142.

94. *Progress of Women in the Navy*, 1–16.

95. Navy Personnel Command, https://www.mynavyhr.navy.mil/Career -Management/Community-Management/Enlisted/Special-Operations/

96. *Progress of Women in the Navy*, 1–27, 1–30.

97. *Progress of Women in the Navy*, 1–29.

98. Secretary of the Navy to John C. Stennis, Chairman, Senate Committee on Armed Services, PERS-00W Files. The letter was apparently a draft written in anticipation of a formal request from SecNav to Congress to open more MSLF ships to women. There is no signature block and a handwritten date of November 1979; copy in author's files.

99. *Progress of Women in the Navy*, ES-5–6.

100. John R. Schindler, *A Dangerous Business: The U.S. Navy and National Reconnaissance during the Cold War* (Fort George G. Meade, MD: Center for Cryptologic History, National Security Agency, 2004), https://www.nsa .gov/History/Cryptologic-History/Historical-Publications/#cold-war.

101. *Progress of Women in the Navy*, 1–18, 1–20–1–21, 1–23.

102. *Progress of Women in the Navy*, 1–24.

103. "Women in the Military: Debate," *Congressional Quarterly Weekly Report* 37, no. 16 (21 April 1979): 741–43.

104. "Women in the Military: Debate," 742.

105. "Women in the Military: Debate," 743.

106. "Carter Gets His Draft Registration Plan," *Congressional Quarterly Weekly Report* 38, no. 26 (28 June 1980): 1819.

107. Linda Kerber interview with Richard Danzig, Washington, May 1991, quoted in *No Constitutional Right to Be Ladies*, 279.

108. Kerber, *No Constitutional Right to Be Ladies*, 281.

109. Ilene Rose Feinman, *Citizenship Rites: Feminist Soldiers and Feminist Anti-militarists* (New York: New York University Press, 2000), 127.

110. Kerber, *No Constitutional Right to Be Ladies*, 286–87.

111. Kerber, 268–69.

112. "Draft Registration Begins on Schedule," *Congressional Quarterly Weekly Report* 38, no. 30 (26 July 1980): 2138.
113. Dahlgren, *Thoughts on Female Suffrage*, 4.
114. *Statements and Speeches Monthly Report, Margaret Chase Smith, U.S. Senate*, vol. 5, 80th Cong., 1948, 68, MCSL Papers.
115. *Statements and Speeches*, vol. 39A, 92nd Cong., 1972, 95, MCSL Papers.
116. Feinman, *Citizenship Rites*, 137.
117. *Rostker v. Goldberg*, 453 U.S. 57 (1981), https://www.oyez.org/cases/1980/80–251.
118. Coye, "Restricted Unrestricted Line Officer," 12473.
119. Quoted in Feinman, *Citizenship Rites*, 128.
120. Sadler, "Women in the Sea Services," 154.
121. Sadler, "Women in the Sea Services," 142–43.

CHAPTER 6. FROM WAVES TO WARRIORS

1. Senate, Senator Kennedy of Massachusetts speaking for the Kennedy-Roth Amendment to the National Defense Authorization Act for Fiscal Years 1992 and 1993, S. 11412, 102nd Cong., 1st sess., *Congressional Record*, 31 July 1991, 137, no. 119, 20713.
2. *Progress of Women in the Navy*, 1–38.
3. *Progress of Women in the Navy*, 1–38, 1–46, 1–48, 1–52.
4. "Navy Takes Ship out of Operation Because of Key Personnel Shortage," *New York Times*, 12 April 1980, 14.
5. "Carrier Borrows 50 Sailors to Leave for Mediterranean," *New York Times*, 6 August 1980, 10.
6. "Navy Takes Ship out of Operation"; "Navy Shifting Manpower to Keep Ships Prepared," *New York Times*, 7 August 1980, 14.
7. Seth Cropsey, "Low Pay on the High Seas," *Fortune*, 3 November 1980, 67.
8. "*Norton Sound* PO Convicted on Sex Counts," *Navy Times*, 28 July 1980, 3.
9. "Navy Plans to Discharge 8 Accused as Lesbians," *New York Times*, 21 June 1980, 20.
10. Rosemary Purcell, "*Norton Sound* Probing 16 Female Crewmembers," *Navy Times*, 30 June 1980, 21.
11. "Navy Clears a Woman of Lesbianism Charges," *New York Times*, 8 August 1980, 17.
12. "Navy Lesbianism Hearings Are Closed to Reporters," *New York Times*, 13 August 1980, 18.
13. "Navy's Inquiry Finds Second Sailor Guilty of Sexual Misconduct," *New York Times*, 21 August 1980, 22.
14. Ebbert and Hall, *Crossed Currents*, 258–59.

15. Judy Mann, "Pledge of Woman Justice May Just Be More Bilge," *Washington Post*, 24 June 1981, C1; Monica Langley, "Reagan Men Learn What GOP Women Really Want: Jobs," *Wall Street Journal*, 7 July 1981, 1.

16. Mann, "Pledge of Woman Justice May Just Be More Bilge."

17. Langley, "Reagan Men Learn What GOP Women Really Want."

18. Mann, "Pledge of Woman Justice May Just Be More Bilge."

19. Mann.

20. "Navy Announces Plan to Double Number of Women aboard Ships," *New York Times*, 30 November 1980, 62.

21. Robert Lindsey, "Navy Sends More Women to Sea, Despite Problems," *New York Times*, 29 June 1980, 14.

22. Holm, *Women in the Military*, 387.

23. U.S. Senate, *Hearings before a Subcommittee of the Committee on Appropriations, Department of Defense Appropriations for Fiscal Year 1982*, Part 2, *Manpower*, 97th Cong., 1st sess. (Washington, DC: GPO), 15.

24. Feinman, *Citizenship Rites*, 140.

25. Holm, *Women in the Military*, 390.

26. Holm.

27. Holm, 393.

28. "Military Told to Lower Barriers to Women's Service," *New York Times*, 31 January 1982, 25.

29. George C. Wilson, "Reagan Agrees to Live with Budget Compromise; Panel Votes Freeze on Troop Numbers," *Washington Post*, 4 May 1983, A1; Richard Halloran, "Weinberger Criticizes Rejection of Plan to Strengthen Armed Forces," *New York Times*, 5 May 1983, A24; Richard Halloran, "The Pentagon: Smiles, Politesse and 400 Women," *New York Times*, 19 June 1984, A18.

30. Lorry M. Fenner, "'Either You Need These Women or You Do Not': Informing the Debate on Military Service and Citizenship," *Gender Issues* 16, no. 3 (1998): 15.

31. "Sex Harassment Called Widespread in Military," *Washington Post*, 12 February 1980, A5; "Sex Harassment Found in Military by Women," *New York Times*, 12 February 1980, B15.

32. U.S. Congress, House Committee on the Armed Services, *Hearings before the Military Personnel Subcommittee*, 96th Cong., 1st and 2nd sess., HASC No 9672 (Washington, DC: GPO, 1981), 328.

33. *Hearings*, 330.

34. *Hearings*, 333.

35. Defense Advisory Committee on Women in the Services, History of Recommendations, https://dacowits.defense.gov/Home/Documents/1980-Spring/.

36. Women's Research and Education Institute, "Sexual Harassment Chronology," author's files; *Progress of Women in the Navy*, 3–3.
37. Susan Marquez Owen, "Men and Women of "Sin City," *San Francisco Chronicle*, 5 August 1990, 8.
38. Mary Schumacher, "Women in the Navy," Kennedy School of Government Case Program, Harvard University (1988), 2, PERS-00W Files.
39. Schumacher, 3–4.
40. Schumacher, 18.
41. Ron Harris, "Sex Harassment in Navy, Marines Alleged; Scathing Reports Say Ship Captain Tried to 'Sell' Female Sailors," *Los Angeles Times*, 18 September 1987, 24.
42. Harris.
43. Editorial, "Harassment and Military Women," *Christian Science Monitor*, 18 September 1987, 15.
44. "Half of Women in Navy Study Complain of Sexual Harassment," *Los Angeles Times*, 21 December 1987, 1.
45. Paul Roush, "A Tangled Webb," *Proceedings* 123, no. 8 (August 1997): 42–45.
46. James Webb, "Women Can't Fight," *Washingtonian* (October 1979): 146.
47. George C. Wilson, "Navy Nominee to 'Reexamine' Academy's Pro Sports Policy; Webb Also Won't 'Roll Back the Clock' on Admitting Women," *Washington Post*, 7 April 1987, A15; "James Webb Wins Senate Approval as Navy Secretary," *New York Times*, 10 April 1987, 18.
48. "Navy Limits Recruitment of Women; Action Designed to Save Shore Jobs for Men," *San Diego Union-Tribune*, 3 February 1987, A2.
49. "Curb on Navy Women Halted by Weinberger," *Los Angeles Times*, 4 February 1987, 21; "Weinberger Reverses Navy Plan to Freeze Women," *San Diego Union-Tribune*, 4 February 1987.
50. Rep. Don Edwards, "Naval Duty Nearly Impossible for Women," editorial, *Los Angeles Times*, 15 April 1987, part 2, p. 5.
51. Richard Halloran, "Navy Expands the Role of Women," *New York Times*, 22 December 1987, D23; and Navy Study on Progress of Women in the Navy, *Progress Report*, 1-A-10.
52. Department of Defense report, *Task Force on Women in the Military* (January 1988), 10.
53. DOD, *Task Force on Women in the Military*, 9.
54. *Progress of Women in the Navy*, ES-5–ES-6.
55. DOD, *Task Force on Women in the Military*, iii–v.
56. "Special Gulf Escort Given to Ship with Women in Crew," *San Diego Union-Tribune*, 2 June 1987, A1. See also "Women to Be in *Stark* Repair Crew,"

San Diego Union-Tribune, 2 June 1987, A2; Tom Burgess, "Navy Women in Strange Waters," *San Diego Union-Tribune*, 7 June 1987, B3.

57. Tom Burgess, "Navy Angry over Policy; Lower Test Scores Allowed for Men to Win Promotion," *San Diego Union-Tribune*, 1 April 1989, A1; "Anchors Aweigh on Female Promotions," *San Diego Union-Tribune*, 7 April 1989, B10; "The Numbers Game," *San Diego Union-Tribune*, 8 April 1989, B14; Tom Burgess, "Navy Cuts Back on Unequal Demands for Promotions," *San Diego Union-Tribune*, 28 July 1989, A4.

58. Tom Burgess, "S. D. Officer Is First Woman in Line for Command of Naval Ship," *San Diego Union-Tribune*, 25 January 1989, B1; Robert Dietrich, "Gernes Becomes First Woman Eligible to Command Navy Ship," *San Diego Union-Tribune*, 26 January 1989, B3; "Ay, Ay, Ma'am," *San Diego Union-Tribune*, 30 January 1989, B6.

59. "Woman Gets Command of Navy Ship," *Washington Post*, 29 December 1990, A16.

60. Nora Zamichow, "For Her, the Sky Is No Limit; Command of Aviation Squadron Is Next Step in Cmdr Mariner's Pioneering Career," *Los Angeles Times*, 25 June 1990, A3.

61. Molly Moore, "Navy Officer Charged with Raping Shipmate: Male Lieutenant Allegedly Assaulted Female Ensign on USS *Suribachi*," *Washington Post*, 12 June 1990, A5; "Sailor Accused of Raping Enlisted Woman on Ship: Alleged Assault Is Second in Three Months," *Washington Post*, 23 July 1990, A4; "Navy Lieutenant Guilty of Raping Female Officer," *San Diego Union-Tribune*, A19; "Sailor Convicted of Shipboard Rape," *Louisville* (KY) *Courier-Journal*, 28 July 1990, 6A.

62. "Taunted, Woman Quits Academy," *New York Times*, 14 May 1990, B9; Felicity Barringer, "Harassment Case Shakes Annapolis," New *York Times*, 9 May 1990; Felicity Barringer, "4 Reports Cite Naval Academy for Rife Sexism: Harassment Often Seen as the Norm in Class," *New York Times*, 10 October 1990, A8.

63. Molly Moore, "Navy Failed to Prosecute in 6 Rapes: Probe Finds Laxity on Sex Offenses at Florida Base," *Washington Post*, 22 October 1990, A1.

64. Moore.

65. Jane Gross, "Admiral Praises Lesbians but Urges Their Dismissal," *New York Times*, 2 September 1990, 24.

66. Gross.

67. Jon Carroll, "Predatory Lesbians behind the Bulkheads," *San Francisco Chronicle*, 6 September 1990, F12.

68. Gross, "Admiral Praises Lesbians," 24.

69. Peter Cary, "Death at Sea," *U.S. News and World Report*, 23 April 1990, 20–30. The NIS's mission was to investigate criminal conduct of Navy service personnel and civilian employees as well as to conduct counterespionage operations. The NIS evolved from the District Intelligence Office organization of the Office of Naval Intelligence, becoming an independent command in 1972. DIO/NIS had a long history of investigating Navy personnel suspected of homosexuality, which constituted a significant part of agents' caseloads.

70. Juan J. Walte, "Female Sailors Are Shortchanged on Promotions," *USA Today*, 4 April 1991, 6A.

71. Molly Moore, "Sex Harassment Called Pervasive in Navy; Internal Study Recommends Changes in Policies Affecting Women," *Washington Post*, 4 April 1991, A4.

72. Moore.

73. Appendix R, "Role of Women in the Theater of Operations," in *Conduct of the Persian Gulf War: Final Report to Congress*, vol. 2 (Washington, DC: Department of Defense, 1992); Naval Historical Center, Frequently Asked Questions, http://www.history.Navy.mil.faqs/faq48–3f.htm.

74. Amanda Dolasinski, "MOAA Interview: How This Former Naval Aviator Made a Historic Landing as a Commercial Pilot," Military Officers Association of America, 4 March 2020, https://www.moaa.org/content/publications-and-media/news-articles/2020-news-articles/moaa-interview-this-aviators-military-training-helped-her-make-an-historic-landing/.

75. *Conduct of the Persian Gulf War*: "Because media attention was afforded to the relatively few cases in which women faced combat conditions, the public perceptions of the role of women in the Gulf War has tended to be skewed. . . . Navy women served on hospital, supply, oiler and ammunition ships afloat. Ashore they served in construction battalions, fleet hospitals and air reconnaissance squadrons, as well as in many support billets. No Navy women saw combat, either directly or indirectly."

76. Defense Advisory Committee on Women in the Services, https://dacowits.defense.gov/Home/Documents/1991-Spring/.

77. "Way Is Cleared for Women to Fly Combat Missions," *Congressional Quarterly Almanac*, vol. XLVII, 102nd Cong., 1st sess. (Washington, DC: Congressional Quarterly, 1992), 414.

78. "Majority Back Women in Combat," *USA Today*, 29 July 1991, 4A.

79. *Hearing of the Manpower and Personnel Subcommittee of the Senate Armed Services Committee on Women in Combat*, Federal News Service (Federal Information Systems Corporation, 1991), 20–21.

80. Statement of Gen. Robert Barrow, USMC (Ret.), to Senate Armed Services Committee, Manpower and Personnel Subcommittee, 18 June 1991, "Women in Combat Testimony from a Marine Corps General's Opinion," CSPAN video, 00:13:30, 18 June 1991, https://www.c-span.org/video/?c4454887 /user-clip-women-combat-testimony-marine-corps-generals-opinion.

81. Holm, *Women in the Military*, 488.

82. "The Senate adopted the Glenn-McCain amendment by a 96–3 vote immediately before rejecting the motion to kill the Kennedy-Roth proposal," in "Way Is Cleared for Women to Fly Combat Missions," 414; see also Holm, *Women in the Military*, 494–503.

83. Barton Gellman, "Panel Seeks to Limit Women in Combat; Presidential Commission Divided," *Washington Post*, 4 November 1992, A3.

84. "Commission Calls for Women on Warships," *Congressional Quarterly Almanac*, vol. XLVIII, 102nd Cong., 2nd sess. (Washington, DC: Congressional Quarterly, 1992), 519.

85. Gellman, "Panel Seeks to Limit Women in Combat."

86. Gellman.

87. Gellman.

88. Gellman.

89. Melissa Healy, "Ban Urged on Women in Most Combat Roles," *Los Angeles Times*, 4 November 1992, A1.

90. General Accounting Office, *Women in the Military: Attrition and Retention*, NSIAD-90–87BR (Washington, DC: General Accounting Office, July 1990), 3, 88.

91. General Accounting Office, *Women in the Military: Deployment in the Persian Gulf War*, GAO/NSIAD-93–93 (Washington, DC: General Accounting Office, July 1993), 3, 19.

92. GAO, *Women in the Military: Deployment in the Persian Gulf War*, 3, 27.

93. GAO, *Women in the Military: Deployment in the Persian Gulf War*, 40.

94. GAO, *Women in the Military: Deployment in the Persian Gulf War*, 47.

95. William H. McMichael, *The Story of the U.S. Navy's Tailhook Scandal: The Mother of All Hooks* (New Brunswick, NJ: Transaction Books, 1997), 2.

96. Derek J. Vander Schaaf, Deputy Inspector General, Memorandum for the Secretary of Defense, 12 April 1993, Report of Investigation: Tailhook 91- Part 2, Events of the 35th Annual Tailhook Symposium.

97. McMichael, *Mother of All Hooks*, 54–55.

98. McMichael, 89.

99. McMichael, 225.

100. Frontline, "The Navy Blues: Punishment after Tailhook," http://www.pbs .org/wgbh/pages/frontline/shows/Navy/tailhook/disc.html.

101. *Tailhook '91: Part 2* (Washington, DC: GPO, 1993), X-3.

102. *Tailhook '91: Part 2*, X-2.

103. *Tailhook '91: Part 2*, X-5. Among the misconduct singled out in the report was "ballwalking," the act of exposing one's testicles. Other activities cited in the DOD IG report included male aviators shaving the legs and pubic areas of women, and "belly/navel shots," drinking tequila from people's navels. "Chicken fights" in the pool involved women riding on the shoulders of male aviators and trying to remove each other's bathing suit tops. "Butt biting," or "sharking," involved biting people on the buttocks. "Zapping" was the practice of affixing a squadron's sticker onto the body or clothing of an individual. Aviators also engaged in oral sex and sexual intercourse in public areas, with other people watching. The most notorious incident was "the gauntlet," a premeditated assault organized by naval aviators who lined the hallway on the third floor of the hotel and physically accosted unsuspecting women who tried to pass through. *Tailhook '91: Part 2*, VI-1, VII-1–5.

104. John Burlage, "Someone Must Be the Sacrificial Lamb," *Navy Times*, 6 July 1992, 3.

105. House Armed Services Committee, *Defense Policy Panel and Military Personnel and Compensation Subcommittee Hearing on Gender Discrimination*, 30 July 1992, Federal News Service transcript, 3.

106. *House Hearing on Gender Discrimination*, 4.

107. *House Hearing on Gender Discrimination*, 10.

108. Secretary of Defense to the Secretary of the Army, Secretary of the Navy, Secretary of the Air Force, Chairman, Joint Chiefs of Staff, Assistant Secretary of Defense (Force Management and Personnel), and Assistant Secretary of Defense (Reserve Affairs), memorandum on Policy on the Assignment of Women in the Armed Forces, 28 April 1993, copy in author's files.

109. Elizabeth A. Palmer, "Officers Say Women in Battle Won't Change Standards," *Congressional Quarterly Weekly Report*, 15 May 1993, 1245.

110. Pat Towell, "Surprises Are Unlikely as Hill Tackles Defense Budget," *Congressional Quarterly Weekly*, 14 August 1993, 2233.

111. Eric Schmitt, "Navy Women Bringing New Era on Carriers," *New York Times*, 21 February 1994, A1.

CHAPTER 7. HAZE GRAY AND UNDER WAY

1. Peter J. Boyer, "Admiral Boorda's War," *New Yorker*, 16 September 1996, 68–69.

2. Gilbert Lewthwaite, "Tailhook: The Story Reaches a Conclusion," *Baltimore Sun*, 20 February 1994, E1; Eric Schmitt, "Navy Women Bringing New Era on

Carriers," *New York Times*, 24 February 1994, A1; Bradley Graham, "Coping on a Co-ed Carrier; Tailhook-Sensitive Navy Steers New Course," *Washington Post*, 27 June 1994, A1; George C. Wilson, "Stretching Their Wings; The Navy's Female Aviators Break the Carrier Barrier," *Washington Post*, 8 November 1994, E1.

3. Eric Schmitt, "Female Fighter Pilot Killed in Crash off California," *New York Times*, 27 October 1994, A18; Pat Flynn, "First Female Tomcat Pilot Lost at Sea," *San Diego Union-Tribune*, 27 October 1994, A1.

4. *Lohrenz v. Donnelly*, 223 F. Supp. 2d 25 (DDC 2002), 7.

5. Missy Cummings, *Hornet's Nest: The Experiences of One of the Navy's First Female Fighter Pilots* (New York: Writer's Showcase presented by Writer's Digest, iUniverse.com, 1999), 356.

6. Pat Flynn, "Attempt to Salvage Sunken F-14 Begins, "*San Diego Union-Tribune*, 5 November 1994, B1; Patricia Dibsie, "Navy Fails a 2d Time to Recover Lost F-14A; Hultgreen's Jet within Reach When Main Line Snaps in Roiling Seas," *San Diego Union-Tribune*, 11 December 1994, B1; Patricia Dibsie, "Female Pilot's Body Recovered," *San Diego Union-Tribune*, 15 November 1994, A1; Pat Flynn, "Hultgreen Cleared of Blame in F-14 Crash; Female Pilot's Mom Gets Navy Briefing," *San Diego Union-Tribune*, 28 February 1995, A1; Pat Flynn, "F-14's Fate Sealed in Split Seconds; Videotape Captured Pilot's Last Moments," *San Diego Union-Tribune*, 1 March 1995, A1; "Lies about Lt. Hultgreen Fly in the Face of Facts," *San Diego Union-Tribune*, 6 March 1995, A2; Vice Adm. Robert J. Spane, "Anatomy of a Plane Crash; Evaluating, Explaining the Results of Two Different Navy Investigations," *San Diego Union-Tribune*, 13 April 1995, B9.

7. George C. Wilson, "Navy Orders Female Pilot Off Carrier; Review Board Cites Landing Difficulties," *Washington Post*, 21 January 1995, A12; Eric Schmitt, "Navy's First Female Combat Pilot Loses Sea Duty," *New York Times*, 23 January 1995, A10; Tom Bowman, "Navy Orders Female Pilot to Fly Cargo," *Buffalo News*, 1 March 1995, 6; James Crawley, "Navy Grounds Female F-14 Pilot for Evaluation of Flying Skills," *San Diego Union-Tribune*," 30 June 1995, B1.

8. Evan Thomas and Gregory L. Vistica, "Falling out of the Sky: For the Navy's First Female Combat Pilots, the Problem Wasn't Sexual Harassment—It Was the Silent Treatment," *Newsweek*, 17 March 1997, 26–29.

9. Steve Vassalo, "Missionary Misfits: Meet a Former Fighter Pilot, Current Autonomous Vehicles Road Warrior," *Forbes*, 17 October 2020, https://www.forbes.com/sites/stevevassallo/2020/10/17/missionary-misfits-meet-a-former-fighter-pilot-current-autonomous-vehicles-road-warrior/?sh=7489ef6e5f15.

10. Center for Military Readiness, https://www.cmrlink.org/MissionStatement, 28 May 2006. The current version of the mission statement reads, "Sound personnel policies should be based on empirical evidence, reality, and actual experience, not sociological theories rooted in flawed ideology and political correctness."

11. Center for Military Readiness. A printout of the 2006 CMR board members is in the author's files.

12. Rowan Scarborough, "Female Pilot Leaves Navy after Suit: Settles for $150,000 in Privacy Case," *Washington Times*, 31 October 1998.

13. Rowan Scarborough, "Navy Boss Censures Officers on Records," *Washington Times*, 19 March 1998, 10.

14. *Lohrenz v. Donnelly*, 7.

15. *Lohrenz v. Donnelly*, 16.

16. *Lohrenz v. Donnelly*, 22.

17. Scott Huddleston, "Then and Now: Forging the Way," *San Antonio Express-News*, 14 November 2004, posted on the Arlington National Cemetery website, "Kara Spears Hultgreen, Lieutenant, United States Navy," http://www.arlingtoncemetery.net/hultgrn.htm.

18. John W. Dean, "Justice Scalia's Thoughts, and a Few of My Own, on *New York Times v. Sullivan*," *FindLaw*, http://writ.news.findlaw.com/dean/20051202.html, 31 May 2006. Dean discussed Scalia's disagreement with the 1964 landmark ruling that "held that when a plaintiff in a defamation lawsuit is a public figure, such as a government official, the plaintiff can only prevail if he or she can show the statement was made with 'actual malice'—a problematic phrase." Dean used *Lohrenz v. Donnelly* as a case in point.

19. "Another Aircraft Mishap on *Lincoln*," *Navy Times*, 2 October 1995, 2; Dale Eisman, "Navy Dumps F-14 Squad Chief after Crash: Last Week's Nashville Accident Was the Third Bad Accident since He Took Charge in '95," *Norfolk Virginian-Pilot*, 5 February 1996, A1; Bradley Graham, "Navy Blames Pilot in Crash in Nashville," *Washington Post*, 13 April 1996, A1.

20. Dale Eisman, "Report on Women Pilots Faults Navy; Inspector Raps Training Tactics Used at Sea in Stinging Terms," *Norfolk Virginian-Pilot*, 2 July 1997, A1.

21. Otto Kreisher, "Admiral Boorda's Goal: Women on Every Ship," *San Diego Union-Tribune*, 4 May 1994, A1; Eric Schmitt, "New Top Admiral to Push Wider Combat Role for Women," *New York Times*, 4 May 1994, A20; "Gender Equality a Goal; New Chief Says Navy Needs More Women," *St. Louis Post-Dispatch*, 4 May 1994, A4.

22. Boyer, "Admiral Boorda's War," 78–79.

23. Boyer, 79.
24. Boyer, 80.
25. Boyer.
26. Boyer, 82.
27. Ernest Blazar, "Why? Questions Haunt Those Left Behind," *Navy Times*, 27 May 1996, 14; Larry Di Rita, "Reflections on a Naval Career," *Proceedings* 121, no. 8 (1995): 8, 10.
28. James Webb, "Our Navy Is Struggling for Its Soul," *Navy Times*, 13 May 1996, 33.
29. Webb.
30. Webb.
31. Boyer, "Admiral Boorda's War," 82–83.
32. Name withheld, "CNO Should Resign," *Navy Times*, 20 May 1996.
33. Boyer, "Admiral Boorda's War," 83–84.
34. Blazar, "Why?," *Navy Times*, 14.
35. George C. Wilson, "Boorda Saw Death as Aiding Navy," *Navy Times*, 10 June 1996, 7.
36. Chairman, Board for the Correction of Naval Records, to Secretary of the Navy, Review of Naval Record of [name redacted] (Deceased), Docket No. 6956-98, 18 December 1998, https://web.archive.org/web/20080227203135/http://boards.law.af.mil/NAVY/BCNR/CY1998/06956–98.pdf.
37. Carolyn H. Becraft, Assistant Secretary of the Navy (Manpower and Reserve Affairs), memorandum for the Executive Director, Board for the Correction of Naval Records, 21 June 1999, Petition on Behalf of [name redacted] (Deceased), https://web.archive.org/web/20080227203135/http://boards.law.af.mil/NAVY/BCNR/CY1998/06956–98.pdf.
38. Rowan Scarborough, "Push on to Put Tailhook in Past: 2 Senators Cite Navy Morale," *Washington Times,* 28 May 1996; Dale Eisman, "5 Years after Tailhook, a Changed Navy," *Norfolk Virginian-Pilot,* 7 September 1996, A1.
39. Capt. Paul Ryan, "Much Ado about Nothing," *Proceedings* 123, no. 6 (1997): 66–68, "Straight from the Top," *Proceedings* 123, no. 6 (1997): 9; Chief Petty Officer Joseph T. Monaghan, "Nobody Asked Me but . . . Warriors Are Meant to Fight," *Proceedings* 123, no. 6 (1997): 69; Cdr. Gerard D. Roncolato and Lt. Cdr. Stephen F. Davis Jr., "A View from the Gender Fault Line," *Proceedings* 124, no. 3 (1998): 102–4; Richard Boyle, "Women Should Not Serve in Submarines," *Proceedings* 125, no. 12 (1999): 96.
40. Associated Press, "U.S. Navy Assigns First Women to a Combat-Equipped Ship," *New York Times,* 1 March 1992, 24.

41. *Norfolk Virginian-Pilot*, "USS Love Boat Returns to Port Some Male and Female Crew Members of the Carrier *Eisenhower* Were Disciplined for Having Sex." The article originated in the *Norfolk Virginian-Pilot* and was republished in the *Orlando Sentinel*, 19 March 1995, A6; "Love Boat II," *Washington Times*, 28 March 1995, A18.

42. Jack Dorsey, "Troubled Waters Entangle the *Ike*; 2 Removed for Having Sex, 14 Sent Home for Pregnancy at Sea, 1 Put on Bread and Water for Dating," *Norfolk Virginian-Pilot*, 18 March 1995, A1; William H. McMichael, "Just One of the Guys, Say Women on History-Making Carrier Mission," 13 April 1995, *Newport News Daily Press*, A1.

43. U.S. Navy, My Navy HR, Active Duty Pregnancy, References, OPNAVINST 6000.1 (Series), https://www.mynavyhr.navy.mil/Career-Management /Detailing/Deployability/Active-Duty-Pregnancy/.

44. "Sailing into Motherhood," *New York Times*, 11 February 1995, 14; Bradley Graham, "Navy Adopts a Gentler Response to Service Pregnancies," *Washington Post*, 7 February 1995, A4.

45. Dave Mayfield, "Novelty of Females aboard Gone as *Ike* Returns to Sea," *Norfolk Virginian-Pilot*, 18 February 2000, A1.

CHAPTER 8. SITREP

1. Dolasinski, "MOAA Interview."

2. Scott C. Truver, "The U.S. Navy in Review," *Proceedings* 125, no. 5 (1999): 76.

3. Scott C. Truver, "The U.S. Navy in Review," *Proceedings* 127, no. 5 (2001): 79–84.

4. *CHIPS* magazine, "Interview with Vice Adm. Patricia Ann Tracey Director, Navy Staff," October–December 2004, https://www.doncio.Navy.mil/CHIPS /ArticleDetails.aspx?ID=3272.

5. Ebbert and Hall, *Crossed Currents*, 331; Terry L. Buckman, "Gender Integration: What's Next?" *Proceedings* 125, no. 2 (1999): 31; Graeme Zielinski, "Kathleen McGrath," *Washington Post*, obituaries, 29 September 2002, https:// www.washingtonpost.com/archive/local/2002/09/29/kathleen-mcgrath /cf8f7147-a024-42ca-a708-e179809873a6/.

6. Naval History and Heritage Command, *Gunston Hall* (LSD 44), 1999 Command History Report, https://www.history.Navy.mil/content/dam /nhhc/research/archives/command-operation-reports/ship-command -operation-reports/g/gunston-hall-lsd-44/pdf/1999.pdf; Naval History and Heritage Command, *Carter Hall* (LSD 50), 1999 Command History Report, https://www.history.Navy.mil/content/dam/nhhc/research

/archives/command-operation-reports/ship-command-operation-reports/c
/carter-hall-lsd-50-ii/pdf/1999.pdf; Naval History and Heritage Command,
FOIA Reading Room, USS *Rushmore*, 1999 Command History Report,
https://www.history.Navy.mil/content/dam/nhhc/FOIA/USS%20RUSH
MORE%20(LSD-47)%20CHR%20for%201999.pdf.

7. "The Military Medals Database," Bronze Star Citation, Hall of Valor, https://
valor.militarytimes.com/hero/56723.

8. C-Span, "Q&A with Michelle Howard," Washington, DC, 22 November
2015, https://www.c-span.org/video/?328741–1/qa-michelle-howard.

9. Jack Sweetman, *American Naval History: An Illustrated Chronology of the U.S.
Navy and Marine Corps, 1775–Present*, 3rd ed. (Annapolis: Naval Institute
Press, 2002), 301; Mark L. Evans and Roy A. Grossnick, *United States Naval
Aviation, 1910–2010*, vol. 2 (Washington, DC: Department of the Navy, 2015),
453.

10. "USS *Cole* (DDG-67)," Naval History and Heritage Command, https://www
.history.Navy.mil/browse-by-topic/ships/modern-ships/uss-cole.html.

11. Sharon H. Disher, "Women Can Fight," *Proceedings* 132, no. 9 (2006): 12.

12. Scott C. Truver, "The U.S. Navy in Review," *Proceedings* 128, no. 5 (2002):
74–82; "Navy Releases Names of Crew Members," 2 April 2001, Associated
Press, https://apnews.com/article/826ddb30e25a147e5fdda9c58f7140a4.

13. "Remembering Those We Lost," *The National 9/11 Pentagon Memorial*,
https://www.defense.gov/Experience/Pentagon-Memorial/.

14. "'Intelligence Matters' Presents: Remembering 9/11 with Andy Card,"
updated 18 August 2021, 7:11 a.m. CBS News, https://www.cbsnews.com
/news/intelligence-matters-presents-911-andy-card/.

15. Scott C. Truver, "The U.S. Navy in Review," *Proceedings* (May 2003): 89.

16. "Carrier Crew Includes 1000 Female Sailors," *Mercury* (Hobart, Tasmania,
Australia), 20 January 2001, 7, *Gale OneFile: News*, link.gale.com/apps/doc
/A100921065/GPS?u=aacpl_itweb&sid=bookmark-GPS&xid=7b9f3402; Dave
Hirschman, "Military: Women Fly as Regulars in Air War," *Atlanta Journal-
Constitution*, 14 October 2001, A10. *Gale OneFile: Business*, link.gale.com/apps
/doc/A79107418/GPS?u=aacpl_itweb&sid=bookmark-GPS&xid=a5780df9.

17. "Military Women Take a Back Seat in Saudi Arabia," *Record* (Bergen
County, NJ), 5 December 2001, L11, *Custom Newspapers*, https://link.gale
.com/apps/doc/A80587922/SPN.SP00?u=aacpl_itweb&sid=bookmark-SPN
.SP00&xid=915426de; "No Veils for US Soldiers in Saudi; Servicewomen
Will Not Be Ordered to Wear Abaya," *Herald* (Glasgow, Scotland), 16 May
2002, 13, *Custom Newspapers*, https://link.gale.com/apps/doc/A85975337
/SPN.SP00?u=aacpl_itweb&sid=bookmark-SPN.SP00&xid=93beb85f.

18. "No Veils for US Soldiers," 13.
19. "No Veils for US Soldiers."
20. "Saudi Arabian Dress Code Isn't for U.S. Servicewomen," *Norfolk Virginian-Pilot*, 21 May 2002, B8, *Custom Newspapers*, https://link.gale.com/apps/doc/A86183222/SPN.SP00?u=aacpl_itweb&sid=bookmark-SPN.SP00&xid=15d7757e.
21. "Military Injustice," *Arizona Daily Star*, 5 July 2002, B10, *Custom Newspapers*, https://link.gale.com/apps/doc/A88812309/SPN.SP00?u=aacpl_itweb&sid=bookmark-SPN.SP00&xid=06b78fa0.
22. "Woman to Head A-10 Unit," *Arizona Daily Star*, 1 May 2004, A1, *Custom Newspapers*, https://link.gale.com/apps/doc/A116471750/SPN.SP00?u=aacpl_itweb&sid=bookmark-SPN.SP00&xid=17f82527.
23. Scott C. Truver, "U.S. Navy in Review," *Proceedings* 130, no. 5 (2004): 84; Naval History and Heritage Command, *Saipan* (LHA 2), 2003 Command History Report, https://www.history.Navy.mil/content/dam/nhhc/research/archives/command-operation-reports/ship-command-operation-reports/s/saipan-lha-2-ii/pdf/2003.pdf.
24. Ryan Gallucci, "Women in Service: Marine Corps Lioness Program," *American Veterans* (blog), 30 March 2010, https://americanveteranmagazine.blogspot.com/2010/03/women-in-service-marine-corps-lioness.html.
25. "*Lioness*: There for the Action Missing from History," https://rocofilms.com/films/lioness/.
26. Rick Jervis, "Despite Rule, U.S. Women on Front Line in Iraq War," *USA Today*, 27 June 2005, 8A, *Custom Newspapers*, link.gale.com/apps/doc/A133596413/SPN.SP00?u=aacpl_itweb&sid=bookmark-SPN.SP00&xid=e4c872bb.
27. *Military Times*, "Honor the Fallen," https://thefallen.militarytimes.com/Navy-culinary-specialist-1st-class-regina-r-clark/943336.
28. Megan Katt, "Blurred Lines: Cultural Support Teams in Afghanistan," *Joint Forces Quarterly* 75, 4th quarter 2014, 109.
29. Katt.
30. Margaret C. Harrell, Laura Werber, Peter Schirmer, Bryan W. Hallmark, et al., *Assessing the Assignment Policy for Army Women* (Santa Monica, CA: RAND Corporation, 2007), https://www.rand.org/pubs/monographs/MG590–1.html.
31. Department of the Army, Army Regulation 600-8-22, Military Awards, 5 March 2019, 110.
32. Kristy N. Kamarck, *Women in Combat: Issues for Congress*, Washington, DC: Congressional Research Service, 13 December 2016, 8.
33. U.S. Navy, Office of Women's Policy, "Women in the U.S. Navy," PowerPoint brief (August 2005), slides 19–20. Copy in author's files.

34. Nelson Hernandez, "At the Naval Academy, a Lyrical Change," *Washington Post*, 20 May 2004, B5, https://www.washingtonpost.com/wp-dyn /articles/A41410–2004May19.html; *FEDweek*, Armed Forces News, Sweeping Changes for Navy Uniforms, 16 September 2004, https://www.fedweek .com/armed-forces-news/sweeping-changes-for-Navy-uniforms/; Kati Hill, "Nobody Asked Me but . . . Goodbye Bucket Cover," *Proceedings* 142, no. 12 (2016), https://www.usni.org/magazines/proceedings/2016/december /nobody-asked-me-goodbye-bucket-cover.

35. Michael D. Shear and Tim Craig, "Va. Senate Race Goes Negative on 1979 Essay," *Washington Post*, 14 September 2006, https://www.washingtonpost .com/wp-dyn/content/article/2006/09/13/AR2006091302301.html?itid=lk _interstitial_manual_38; Paul West, "Allen versus Webb: Referendum on the War?" *Proceedings* 132, no. 10 (2006): 18–21; Seth McLaughlin, "Military Women Support Webb as a 'Man of Integrity,'" *Washington Times*, 18 October 2006, B1.

36. Dan LaMothe, "Under Pressure, Jim Webb Declines to Be Recognized as a Distinguished Naval Academy Graduate," *Washington Post*, 28 March 2017, https://www.washingtonpost.com/news/checkpoint/wp/2017/03/28 /jim-webb-has-been-named-a-distinguished-naval-academy-graduate-and -some-alumni-are-furious/.

37. LaMothe.

38. Jennifer Grogan, "Navy to Allow Women to Serve on Submarines," *New London* (CT) *Day*, 29 April 2010, *Custom Newspapers*, https://link.gale.com /apps/doc/A225111224/SPN.SP00?u=aacpl_itweb&sid=bookmark-SPN .SP00&xid=c02f3fa9.

39. Steven Lee Myers, "New Debate on Submarine Duty for Women," *New York Times*, 15 November 1999, A1, https://www.nytimes.com/1999/11/15/us /new-debate-on-submarine-duty-for-women.html?searchResultPosition=2.

40. "ROTC Women Allowed to Train in Submarines," *Palm Beach Post*, 26 June 1999, 20A, *Custom Newspapers*, https://link.gale.com/apps/doc/A62784950/ SPN.SP00?u=aacpl_itweb&sid=bookmark-SPN.SP00&xid=8ed96a77.

41. Myers, "New Debate on Submarine Duty for Women."

42. Carlisle A. Trost, "Not in Our Submarines," *Proceedings* 126, no. 9 (2000): 2.

43. Lory Manning, "Comment and Discussion," *Proceedings* 126, no. 10 (2000): 28.

44. K. H. Wieschoff, "Comment and Discussion," *Proceedings* 127, no. 1 (2001): 28.

45. James McLain, "Comment and Discussion," *Proceedings* 127, no. 2 (2001): 29.

46. Cameron Stoner, "Women in Submarines: 10 Years Later," SUBLANT Public Affairs, https://www.navy.mil/Press-Office/News-Stories/Article/2671640 /women-in-submarines-10-years-later/.

47. "8 Years on, It's Been Smooth Sailing for Female Submariners; by Jennifer McDermott," *Florida Times Union*, 9 March 2018, A1, *Custom Newspapers* (accessed 25 September 2021), https://link.gale.com/apps/doc/A530732532 /SPN.SP00?u=aacpl_itweb&sid=bookmark-SPN.SP00&xid=9ddb783a.

48. Kris Osborn, "Female Sailors Secretly Videotaped Showering on Submarines," Military.com, 3 December 2014, https://www.military.com/daily-news /2014/12/03/female-sailors-secretly-videotaped-showering-on-submarines .html.

49. Gordon Jackson, "Final Sailor Sentenced in *Wyoming* Trials," *Brunswick* (GA) *News*, 25 July 2015, *Custom Newspapers*, https://link.gale.com /apps/doc/A423073885/SPN.SP00?u=aacpl_itweb&sid=bookmark-SPN .SP00&xid=ed6a95a7.

50. Jennifer McDermott, "Second Group of Women Chosen for Submarine Service," *New London* (CT) *Day*, 10 June 2011, *Custom Newspapers*, https://link.gale .com/apps/doc/A258518749/SPN.SP00?u=aacpl_itweb&sid=bookmark-SPN .SP00&xid=3ab565e8.

51. Kate Wiltrout, "In a Fleet of Firsts, She's Second to None," *Norfolk Virginian-Pilot*, 9 May 2011, A1, *Custom Newspapers,* https://link.gale.com/apps/doc/A255947194 /SPN.SP00?u=aacpl_itweb&sid=bookmark-SPN.SP00&xid=dad96442.

52. Ben Werner, "Vice Adm. Nora Tyson Retires from Command of U.S. 3rd Fleet," USNI News, 18 September 2017, https://news.usni.org/2017/09/18/ vice-adm-nora-tyson-retires-command-u-s-3rd-fleet; Wiltrout, "In a Fleet of Firsts"; Bill Sizemore, "First Woman to Lead Carrier Strike Is Taking Helm," *Norfolk Virginian-Pilot*, 28 July 2010, B3, *Custom Newspapers*, https://link. gale.com/apps/doc/A232866773/SPN.SP00?u=aacpl_itweb&sid=bookmark -SPN.SP00&xid=4e9e7e47; Corinne Reilly, "Promotion Has a Special Guest: Former President," *Norfolk Virginian-Pilot*, 3 August 2011, B3, *Custom Newspapers*, https://link.gale.com/apps/doc/A263320836/SPN.SP00?u=aacpl _itweb&sid=bookmark-SPN.SP00&xid=8557561c.

53. Donna Fenn, "5 Tough Leadership Lessons from the Navy's Top Female Commander," *Fortune*, 25 May 2015, https://fortune.com/2015/05/25/5 -tough-leadership-lessons-from-the-Navys-top-female-commander/.

54. Michelle Howard, "Admiral Michelle Howard: Leading the Navy into a New Era," interview by Moira Forbes, Forbes Women's Summit, May 2014, video, 6:26, https://www.youtube.com/watch?v=F8nip7jv_mo.

55. *The MacNeil/Lehrer NewsHour*, 23 April 1993, NewsHour Productions, American Archive of Public Broadcasting, Boston and Washington, http://americanarchive.org/catalog/cpb-aacip-507-gq6qz2361c.

56. Richard Goldstein, "Rosemary Mariner, Trailblazing Navy Pilot and Commander, Dies at 65," *New York Times*, 1 February 2019, https://www.nytimes.com/2019/02/01/obituaries/rosemary-mariner-dead.html.

57. Goldstein.

58. Jacey Fortin, "Navy Honors Trailblazer with All-Female Flyover," *New York Times*, 2 February 2019, https://www.nytimes.com/2019/02/02/us/captain-rosemary-mariner-funeral.html.

59. Diana Jean Schemo, "Air Force Ignored Sex Abuse at Academy, Inquiry Reports," *New York Times*, 23 September 2003, 16.

60. George Edmonson, "Military Sex Assault Inquiry Ordered; 88 Cases Reported of Misconduct against Servicewomen in War Zones, Pentagon Says," *Austin* (TX) *American-Statesman*, 7 February 2004, A5, *Custom Newspapers*, https://link.gale.com/apps/doc/A113025913/SPN.SP00?u=aacpl_itweb&sid=bookmark-SPN.SP00&xid=7573e6a6; "Military Commanders Must Stop Sexual Assaults," *Wisconsin State Journal*, 29 February 2004, B3, *Custom Newspapers*, https://link.gale.com/apps/doc/A113786621/SPN.SP00?u=aacpl_itweb&sid=bookmark-SPN.SP00&xid=32477ea9.

61. Defense Advisory Committee on Women in the Services, 2004 Report, https://dacowits.defense.gov/Reports/.

62. Kristy N. Kamarck and Barbara Salazar Torreon, *Military Sexual Assault: A Framework for Congressional Oversight*, updated February 26, 2021, Congressional Research Service, https://crsreports.congress.gov R44944.

63. Todd South, "US Supreme Court Ruling Reverses Military Statute of Limitations on Rape Cases," *Military Times*, 15 December 2020, https://www.militarytimes.com/news/your-military/2020/12/15/us-supreme-court-ruling-reverses-military-statute-of-limitations-on-rape-cases/; *United States v. Briggs*, 19–108, 10 December 2020.

64. Nancy Montgomery, "Report: Lieutenant Colonel in Sex Assault Case to Retire as Major," *Stars and Stripes*, 17 October 2013, https://www.stripes.com/branches/air_force/report-lieutenant-colonel-in-sex-assault-case-to-retire-as-major-1.247732; Richard Lardner, "Air Force Sexual Assault Case to Be Reviewed," *Norfolk Virginian-Pilot*, 12 March 2013, A6, *Custom Newspapers*, https://link.gale.com/apps/doc/A322258846/SPN.SP00?u=aacpl_itweb&sid=bookmark-SPN.SP00&xid=129e6516.

65. Craig Whitlock, "General Retiring after Uproar over Handling of Sexual Assaults," *Washington Post*, 9 January 2014, *Proquest Global Newsstream*, https://

www.proquest.com/newspapers/general-retiring-after-uproar-over-handling/docview/1475310083/se-2?accountid=2739.

66. Tom Vanden Brook, "Air Force Chief of Sex-Assault Prevention Accused of Groping," *USA Today*, 7 May 2013, 01A, *Custom Newspapers*, https://link.gale.com/apps/doc/A328974372/SPN.SP00?u=aacpl_itweb&sid=bookmark-SPN.SP00&xid=ba67ac2c.

67. Gillibrand Statement on Inclusion of Military Justice Improvement and Increasing Prevention Act in NDAA, 22 July 2021, https://www.gillibrand.senate.gov/news/press/release/gillibrand-statement-on-inclusion-of-military-justice-improvement-and-increasing-prevention-act-in-ndaa.

68. Doug Criss, "The Media's Version of #MeToo Is Unrecognizable to the Movement's Founder, Tarana Burke," CNN, 30 November 2018, https://www.cnn.com/2018/11/30/us/tarana-burke-ted-talk-trnd/index.html; Jodi Kantor and Megan Twohey, "Harvey Weinstein Paid Off Sexual Harassment Accusers for Decades," *New York Times*, 5 October 2017, https://www.nytimes.com/2017/10/05/us/harvey-weinstein-harassment-allegations.html?_r=0.

69. Jessica Bennett, "The Me Too Movement: When the Blinders Come Off," *New York Times*, 30 November 2017, https://www.nytimes.com/2017/11/30/us/the-metoo-moment.html.

70. Dave Phillips, "Military Missteps Allowed Soldier Accused of Murder to Flee, Report Says," *New York Times*, 30 April 2021, https://www.nytimes.com/2021/04/30/us/vanessa-guillen-fort-hood-aaron-robinson.html.

71. U.S. Secretary of the Army, Report of the Fort Hood Independent Review Committee, 6 November 2020, https://www.Army.mil/forthoodreview/.

72. Gillibrand statement, 22 July 2021.

73. Jennifer Steinhauer, "Old-Guard Senators Defy Changes in How Military Treats Sex Assault Cases," *New York Times*, 3 June 2021, updated 14 July 2021, https://www.nytimes.com/2021/06/03/us/politics/gillibrand-military-sexual-assault.html.

74. Editorial Board, "The Two Men Blocking Military Sexual Assault Reform," *New York Times*, 19 June 2021, https://www.nytimes.com/2021/06/19/opinion/sunday/inhofe-reed-military-sexual-assault-gillibrand.html.

75. Mike Turner, Press release, Speier, Turner Introduce Bipartisan Vanessa Guillén Military Justice Improvement and Increasing Prevention Act to Remove Sexual Assault Prosecution Decisions from the Chain of Command, https://turner.house.gov/2021/6/speier-turner-introduce-bipartisan-vanessa-guill-n-military-justice-improvement-and-increasing-prevention-act-to-remove-sexual-assault-prosecution-decisions-from-the-chain-of-command.

76. Todd Lopez, "Sexual Assaults Will No Longer Be Prosecuted by Commanders," *DOD News*, 2 July 2021, https://www.defense.gov/News/News-Stories

/Article/Article/2681848/sexual-assaults-will-no-longer-be-prosecuted-by
-commanders/.

77. U.S. Department of Defense, news release, "Commencing Department of Defense Actions and Implementation to Address Sexual Assault and Sexual Harassment in the Military. Independent Review Commission Recommendation-Implementation Roadmap," 22 September 2021, https:// www.defense.gov/News/Releases/Release/Article/2785437/commencing -department-of-defense-actions-and-implementation-to-address-sexual-a/.

78. John M. Donnelly, "Senators Hit Pentagon's 'Lax' Response to Sexual Assault," *Congressional Quarterly Roll Call,* 26 October 2021, https://www.rollcall. com/2021/10/26/senators-hit-pentagons-lax-response-to-sexual-assault/.

79. Gillibrand Statement on the Gutting of Bipartisan Military Justice Reforms by House and Senate Armed Services Leadership, 7 December 2021, https:// www.gillibrand.senate.gov/news/press/release/gillibrand-statement-on-the -gutting-of-bipartisan-military-justice-reforms-by-house-and-senate-armed -services-leadership.

80. Congressional Research Service, *CRS Report: Expanding the Selective Service: Research Issues Surrounding Women and the Draft,* updated 14 September 2020, 2, https://crsreports.congress.gov, LSB10491.

81. "CRS Report: Expanding the Selective Service," 3.

82. *History, Art & Archives,* U.S. House of Representatives, "RANGEL, Charles B.," https://history.house.gov/People/Listing/R/RANGEL,-Charles-B— (R000053)/; Brian Tumulty, "Rangel Wants Women to Register for Selective Service," *USA Today,* 15 February 2013, https://www.usatoday.com/story /news/nation/2013/02/15/rangel-selective-service-women/1923631/.

83. "CRS Report: Expanding the Selective Service," 3.

84. "CRS Report: Expanding the Selective Service."

85. *Kyle-Labell v. Selective Service,* 364 F. Supp. 3d 394 (D.N.J. 2019) at 31.

86. Amicus curiae of General Michael Hayden et al., *National Coalition for Men v. Selective Service System,* 593 U.S. (2021) (No. 20–298), https://www.supremecourt .gov/search.aspx?filename=/docket/docketfiles/html/public/20–928.html.

87. Amicus curiae brief of the Modern Military Association of America et al., *National Coalition for Men v. Selective Service System.*

88. Amicus curiae brief of the National Organization for Women Foundation et al., *National Coalition for Men v. Selective Service System.*

89. Amicus curiae brief of the Center for Military Readiness et al., *National Coalition for Men v. Selective Service System.*

90. Statement of Justice Sotomayor, *National Coalition for Men v. Selective Service System.*

91. Rebecca Kheel, "Congress Drops Effort to Add Women to the Draft," *Military Times*, 7 December 2021, https://www.military.com/daily-news/2021/12/07/congress-drops-effort-add-women-draft.html.
92. Nate Hudson, "Congresswoman Hartzler Wants to Abolish the Draft," Ozark Radio News, 15 November 2021: https://www.ozarkradionews.com/local-news/congresswoman-hartzler-wants-to-abolish-the-draft.
93. "Remarks on Women-in-Service Review," as delivered by Secretary of Defense Ash Carter, 3 December 2015, https://www.defense.gov/News/Speeches/Speech/Article/632495/remarks-on-the-women-in-service-review/.
94. Edward Gibbon, *The History of the Decline and Fall of the Roman Empire*, vol. 6, https://www.gutenberg.org/files/736/736-h/736-h.htm.

— BIBLIOGRAPHY —

Library of Congress
  Rare Books Collection
  Serial and Government Publications Division
Margaret Chase Smith Library, Skowhegan, Maine
National Archives
  Name Index Cards to the Correspondence of the Military Intelligence Division of the War Department General Staff, 1917–1941. Microfilm Publication M1194, Washington, DC: National Archives and Records Service, General Services Administration, 1981.
  Record Group 24. Records of the Bureau of Naval Personnel, 1798–1991.
  Record Group 38.4. Records of the Office of Naval Intelligence (ONI), Office of the Deputy Chief of Naval Operations (Operations), 1875–1956.
  Record Group 45. Naval Records Collection of the Office of Naval Records and Library Subject File, 1911–1927.
  Record Group 165. Records of the War Department, General and Special Staffs. War College Division, Army War College, General Correspondence, 1903–1919.
Naval History and Heritage Command. Records of the Special Assistant for Women's Policy, 1947–1991. Operational Archives Branch.
Princeton University, Seeley G. Mudd Manuscript Library. Department of Rare Books and Special Collections, Ferdinand Eberstadt Papers.
United States Naval Academy, Nimitz Library. Special Collections and Archives Division.

BOOKS AND JOURNALS

Bacevich, Andrew J. "Who Will Serve?" *Wilson Quarterly* 22, no. 3 (1998): 80–92.
Boyle, Richard. "Women Should Not Serve in Submarines." U.S. Naval Institute *Proceedings* [hereafter *Proceedings*] 125, no. 12 (1999): 96.
Buckman, Terry L. "Gender Integration: What's Next?" *Proceedings* 125, no. 2 (1999): 31.

Butler, Mrs. Henry F. *I Was a Yeoman (F)*. Washington, DC: Naval Historical Foundation, 1967.

Campbell, D'Ann. "Fighting with the Navy: The WAVES in World War II." In *New Interpretations in Naval History: Selected Papers from the Tenth Naval History Symposium*, ed. Jack Sweetman. Annapolis: Naval Institute Press, 1993.

———. "Servicewomen of World War II." *Armed Forces and Society* 16, no. 2 (1990): 251–70.

"Carter Gets His Draft Registration Plan." *Congressional Quarterly Weekly Report* 38, no. 26 (28 June 1980): 1819.

Chambers, John Whiteclay. *To Raise an Army: The Draft Comes to Modern America*. New York: Free Press, 1987.

CHIPS Magazine. "Interview with Vice Adm. Patricia Ann Tracey Director, Navy Staff," October–December 2004, https://www.doncio.navy.mil/CHIPS /ArticleDetails.aspx?ID=3272.

"Commission Calls for Women on Warships." *Congressional Quarterly Almanac* XLVIII, 102nd Cong., 2nd sess. Washington, DC: Congressional Quarterly, 1992, 519–20.

Compere, Tom, ed. *The Navy Blue Book*. Vol. 1. New York: Military Publishing Institute, by Bobbs-Merrill, 1960.

Coye, Beth F. "The Restricted Unrestricted Line Officer: The Status of the Navy's Woman Line Officer." *Naval War College Review* 25, no. 3, art. 6, 1972, https:// digital-commons.usnwc.edu/nwc-review/vol25/iss3/6.

Cummings, Missy. *Hornet's Nest: The Experiences of One of the Navy's First Female Fighter Pilots*. New York: Writer's Digest, iUniverse.com, 1999.

Dahlgren, Madeline Vinton. *Thoughts on Female Suffrage and in Vindication of Women's True Rights*. Washington, DC: Blanchard and Mahoun, 1871.

Daniels, Jonathan. *The End of Innocence*. New York: De Capo Press, 1972.

Daniels, Josephus. *The Cabinet Diaries of Josephus Daniels, 1913–1921*. Ed. David Cronon. Lincoln: University of Nebraska Press, 1963.

———. *The Wilson Era: Years of War and After, 1917–1923*. Chapel Hill: University of North Carolina Press, 1946.

Davies, Margery W. *Woman's Place Is at the Typewriter: Office Work and Office Workers, 1870–1930*. Philadelphia: Temple University Press, 1982.

Dean, John W. "Justice Scalia's Thoughts, and a Few of My Own, on *New York Times v. Sullivan*." *FindLaw* Legal News and Commentary, https://supreme .findlaw.com/legal-commentary/justice-scalias-thoughts-and-a-few-of-my -own-on-new-york-times-v-sullivan.html, 31 May 2006.

DePauw, Linda Grant. *Battle Cries and Lullabies: Women in War from Prehistory to Present*. Norman: University of Oklahoma Press, 1998.

Dessez, Eunice C. *The First Enlisted Women, 1917–1918.* Philadelphia: Dorrance, 1955.

Di Rita, Larry. "Reflections on a Naval Career." *Proceedings* 121, no. 8 (1995): 8, 10.

Disher, Sharon Hanley. *First Class: Women Join the Ranks at the Naval Academy.* Annapolis: Naval Institute Press, 1998.

Dorwart, Jeffery M. *Conflict of Duty: The U.S. Navy's Intelligence Dilemma, 1919–1945.* Annapolis: Naval Institute Press, 1983.

"Draft Registration Begins on Schedule." *Congressional Quarterly Weekly Report* 38, no. 30 (26 July 1980): 2138.

Dyer, G. P. "Navy Supply Department in War Time." *Proceedings* 46, no. 3 (1920): 379–92.

Ebbert, Jean, and Marie-Beth Hall. *Crossed Currents: Navy Women from World War I to Tailhook.* Washington, DC: Brassey's, 1993.

Ebbert, Jean, and Marie-Beth Hall. *Crossed Currents: Navy Women from World War I to Tailhook.* 3rd ed. Washington, DC: Brassey's, 1999

Evans, Mark L., and Roy A. Grossnick. *United States Naval Aviation, 1910–2010.* Vol. 2. Washington, DC: Department of the Navy, 2015.

Feinman, Ilene Rose. *Citizenship Rites: Feminist Soldiers and Feminist Antimilitarists.* New York: New York University Press, 2000.

Fenner, Lorry M. "'Either You Need These Women or You Do Not': Informing the Debate on Military Women and Citizenship." *Gender Issues* 16, no. 3 (1998): 5–32.

Foner, Eric, and John A. Garraty, eds. *The Reader's Companion to American History.* Boston: Houghton Mifflin, 1991.

Gavin, Lettie. *American Women in World War I: They Also Served.* Niwot: University Press of Colorado, 1997.

Gibbon, Edward. *The History of the Decline and Fall of the Roman Empire.* Vol. 6, https://www.gutenberg.org/files/736/736-h/736-h.htm.

Godson, Susan H. *Serving Proudly: A History of Women in the U.S. Navy.* Annapolis: Naval Institute Press, 2001.

———. "The WAVES in World War II." *Proceedings* 107, no. 12 (1981): 46–51.

Greenwald, Maurine Weiner. *Women, War and Work: The Impact of World War I on Women Workers in the United States.* Contributions in Women's Studies 12. Westport, CT: Greenwood Press, 1980.

Hancock, Joy Bright. *Lady in the Navy: A Personal Reminiscence.* Annapolis: Naval Institute Press, 1972.

Hill, Kati. "Nobody Asked Me but . . . Goodbye Bucket Cover." *Proceedings* 142, no. 12 (2016), https://www.usni.org/magazines/proceedings/2016/december/nobody-asked-me-goodbye-bucket-cover.

Holm, Jeanne. *Women in the Military: An Unfinished Revolution*. Rev. ed. Novato, CA: Presidio Press, 1992.

Holmes, W. J. *Double-Edged Secrets: U.S. Naval Intelligence Operations in the Pacific during World War II*. Annapolis: Naval Institute Press, 1998.

Karsten, Peter. *The Naval Aristocracy: The Golden Age of Annapolis and the Emergence of Modern American Navalism*. New York: Free Press, 1972.

Katt, Megan. "Blurred Lines: Cultural Support Teams in Afghanistan." *Joint Forces Quarterly* 75, 4th quarter (2014): 109.

Kerber, Linda K. *No Constitutional Right to Be Ladies*. New York: Hill and Wang, 1998.

———. *Women of the Republic: Intellect and Ideology in Revolutionary America*. Chapel Hill: University of North Carolina Press, 1980.

Layton, Edwin T. *And I Was There: Pearl Harbor and Midway—Breaking the Secrets*. New York: William Morrow, 1985.

Manning, Lory. "Not in Our Submarines." Comment and Discussion. *Proceedings* 126, no. 10 (2000): 28.

McEnaney, Laura. "Atomic Age Motherhood: Maternalism and Militarism in the 1950s." In *Women's America: Refocusing the Past*, 5th ed., ed. Linda K. Kerber and Jane Sherron De Hart, 448–54. New York: Oxford University Press, 2000.

McLain, James. "Not in Our Submarines." Comments and Discussion. *Proceedings* 127, no. 2 (2001): 29–30.

McMichael, William H. *The Story of the U.S. Navy's Tailhook Scandal: The Mother of All Hooks*. New Brunswick, NJ: Transaction, 1997.

McNamee, Luke. "Keep Our Navy Strong." *Proceedings* 49, no. 5 (1923): 801–10.

"Military Academies: Should They Admit Women?" *Congressional Quarterly Weekly Report* 32, no. 28 (13 July 1974): 1818–19.

Miller, Douglas T., and Marion Nowak. "The Happy Home Corporation and Baby Factory." In *The Fifties: The Way We Really Were*, chapter 14. Garden City, NY: Doubleday, 1977.

Miller, Kelly. *Kelly Miller's History of the World War for Human Rights*. Washington, DC: Austin Jenkins, 1919.

Monaghan, Joseph T. "Nobody Asked Me but . . . Warriors Are Meant to Fight." *Proceedings* 123, no. 6 (1997): 69.

Morden, Betty J. *The Women's Army Corps, 1945–1978*. Washington, DC: Center of Military History, U.S. Army, 1990.

Mundy, Liza. *Code Girls: The Untold Story of the American Women Code Breakers of World War II*. New York: Hachette Books, 2017.

"National Security: Women in Academies." *Congressional Quarterly Almanac* XXXI, 94th Cong., 1st sess. Washington, DC: Congressional Quarterly, 1976, 369–70.

Nelson, Anna Kasten. "Anna M. Rosenberg, an 'Honorary Man.'" *Journal of Military History* 68 (January 2004): 133–62.

Palmer, Elizabeth A. "Officers Say Women in Battle Won't Change Standards." *Congressional Quarterly Weekly*, 15 May 1993, 1245.

Prados, John. *Combined Fleet Decoded: The Secret History of American Intelligence and the Japanese Navy in World War II*. Annapolis: Naval Institute Press, 1995.

Rappaport, Armin. *The Navy League of the United States*. Detroit: Wayne State University Press, 1962.

Reynolds, Clark G. *Admiral John H. Towers: The Struggle for Naval Air Supremacy*. Annapolis: Naval Institute Press, 1991.

Roncolato, Gerard D., and Stephen F. Davis Jr. "A View from the Gender Fault Line." *Proceedings* 124, no. 3 (1998): 102–4.

Roush, Paul. "A Tangled Webb." *Proceedings* 123, no. 8 (1997): 42–45.

Ryan, Paul. "Much Ado about Nothing." *Proceedings* 123, no. 6 (1997): 66–68.

Sadler, Georgia Clark. "Women in the Sea Services: 1972–1982." *Proceedings* 109, no. 5 (1983): 140–55.

Schindler, John R. *A Dangerous Business: The U.S. Navy and National Reconnaissance during the Cold War*. Fort George G. Meade, MD: Center for Cryptologic History, National Security Agency, 2004.

Schumacher, Mary. "Women in the Navy." Kennedy School of Government Case Program, Harvard University (1988), 2, PERS-00W Files.

Sherman, Janann. *No Place for a Woman: A Life of Senator Margaret Chase Smith*. New Brunswick, NJ: Rutgers University Press, 2000.

———. "'They Either Need These Women or They Do Not': Margaret Chase Smith and the Fight for Regular Status for Women in the Military." *Journal of Military History* 54 (January 1990): 47–78.

"Straight from the Top." *Proceedings* 123, no. 6 (1997): 9.

Sweetman, Jack. *American Naval History: An Illustrated Chronology of the U.S. Navy and Marine Corps, 1775–Present*, 3rd ed. Annapolis: Naval Institute Press, 2002.

Towell, Pat. "Surprises Are Unlikely as Hill Tackles Defense Budget." *Congressional Quarterly Weekly*, 14 August 1993, 2233.

Treadwell, Mattie E. *The Women's Army Corps*. The United States Army in World War II, Special Studies. Washington, DC: Office of the Chief of Military History, Department of the Army, 1954.

Trost, Carlisle A. "Not in Our Submarines." *Proceedings* 126, no. 9 (2000): 2.

Truver, Scott C. "The U.S. Navy in Review." *Proceedings* 125, no. 5 (1999): 76–80, 82.

———. "The U.S. Navy in Review." *Proceedings* 127, no. 5 (2001): 79–84.

———. "The U.S. Navy in Review." *Proceedings* 128, no. 5 (2002): 74–82.

————. "The U.S. Navy in Review." *Proceedings* 129, no. 5 (2003): 88–92, 94.

————. "The U.S. Navy in Review." *Proceedings* 130, no. 5 (2004): 80–82, 84–86.

Turnbull, Archibald Douglas. "Seven Years of Daniels." *North American Review* 212 (1920): 606–17.

"Way Is Cleared for Women to Fly Combat Missions." *Congressional Quarterly Almanac* XLVII, 102nd Cong., 1st sess. Washington, DC: Congressional Quarterly, 1992, 414.

Weatherford, Doris. *American Women and World War II*. History of Women in America. New York: Facts on File, 1990.

Weir, Gary E. "The American Sound Surveillance System: Using the Ocean to Hunt Soviet Submarines, 1950–1961." *International Journal of Naval History* 5, no. 2 (2006), https://www.ijnhonline.org/wp-content/uploads/2012/01/article_weir_aug06.pdf.

Welter, Barbara. "The Cult of True Womanhood: 1820–1860." *American Quarterly* 18, no. 2 (1966): 151–74.

West, Paul. "Allen versus Webb: Referendum on the War?" *Proceedings* 132, no. 10 (2006): 18–21.

Wieschoff, K. H. "Not in Our Submarines." Comment and Discussion. *Proceedings* 127, no. 1 (2001): 28–29.

Wilcox, Jennifer. *Sharing the Burden: Women in Cryptology during World War II*. Fort George G. Meade, MD.: Center for Cryptologic History, National Security Agency, 1998.

Williams, Kathleen Broome. *Improbable Warriors: Women Scientists and the U.S. Navy in World War II*. Annapolis: Naval Institute Press, 2001.

"Women in the Military: Debate in House Panel Focuses on Legal Questions, Combat Role." *Congressional Quarterly Weekly Report* 37, no. 16 (21 April 1979): 741–43.

Wu, Judy Tzu-Chun. *Doctor Mom Chung of the Fair-Haired Bastards: The Life of a Wartime Celebrity*. Berkeley: University of California Press, 2005.

————. "Mom Chung of the Fair-Haired Bastards: A Thematic Biography of Doctor Margaret Chung (1889–1959)." PhD diss., Stanford University, 1998.

Zumwalt, Elmo R. Jr. *On Watch: A Memoir*. New York: Quadrangle, 1976.

MAGAZINES

Bogle, Lori Lyn, and Joel L. Hewitt. "The Best Quote Jones Never Wrote." *Naval History*, April 2004, 18–23.

Boyer, Peter J. "Admiral Boorda's War." *New Yorker*, 16 September 1996, 68–86.

Cary, Peter. "Death at Sea." *U.S. News and World Report*, 23 April 1990, 20–30.

Cropsey, Seth. "Low Pay on the High Seas." *Fortune*, 3 November 1980, 67.

"The Draft: Reluctant Call-up." *Newsweek,* 26 September 1955, 37–38.

Fenn, Donna. "5 Tough Leadership Lessons from the Navy's Top Female Commander." *Fortune,* 25 May 2015, https://fortune.com/2015/05/25/5-tough -leadership-lessons-from-the-navys-top-female-commander/.

"From Plane Captains to Pilots." *Naval Aviation News,* July 1977, 12.

Holliday, Kate. "Are Women in Uniform Immoral?" *Woman's Home Companion,* August 1952, 32–33, 47–48.

"The Last Frontier." *Independent Woman,* January 1953, 8–10.

Lehman, Milton. "Why Are They Quitting?" *Saturday Evening Post,* 30 July 1955, 34.

"Military Has New Strategy in Battle of the Sexes." *Insight on the News* 18, no. 13, 15 April 2002, 48.

Morris, Mary. "What's behind the Girls behind the Men?" *Mademoiselle,* July 1951.

"Navy Fishes for Volunteers—Drafts, Too." *Business Week,* 24 September 1955, 30.

"Opportunities for Women." *Parent* magazine, April 1952, 123.

Richards, Guy. "Waves Find Stricter Moral Code in Boot Camp Than in Own Homes." *New York Journal American,* June 1962.

"Role in Defense Described to Advisory Council." *Independent Woman,* January 1953, 25.

"Sea-Going Waves? It's True—." *All Hands,* August 1958, 20–21.

"Services: Luring the Ladies." *Newsweek,* 5 November 1951, 27–28.

"Services: Women Wanted." *Newsweek,* 29 October 1951, 26.

"Skirting the Military." *Independent Woman,* October 1953, 348.

Stratton, Dorothy C. "Our Great Unused Resource—Womanpower." *New York Times Magazine,* 1 October 1950.

Thomas, Evan, and Gregory L. Vistica. "Falling out of the Sky: For the Navy's First Female Combat Pilots, the Problem Wasn't Sexual Harassment—It Was the Silent Treatment." *Newsweek,* 17 March 1997, 26–29.

Webb, James. "Women Can't Fight." *Washingtonian,* October 1979, 144–46.

"Women with Navy Wings." *All Hands,* April 1975, 32.

GOVERNMENT SOURCES

Amicus Curiae Brief of the Center for Military Readiness et al. National Coalition for *Men v. Selective Service System,* 593 U.S. (2021) (No. 20-298), https:// www.supremecourt.gov/search.aspx?filename=/docket/docketfiles/html /public/20-928.html.

Amicus Curiae Brief of General Michael Hayden et al. *National Coalition for Men v. Selective Service System,* 593 U.S. (2021) (No. 20-298), https:// www.supremecourt.gov/search.aspx?filename=/docket/docketfiles/html /public/20-928.html.

Amicus Curiae Brief of the Modern Military Association of America et al. *National Coalition for Men v. Selective Service System*, 593 U.S. (2021) (No. 20-298), https://www.supremecourt.gov/search.aspx?filename=/docket /docketfiles/html/public/20-928.html.

Amicus Curiae Brief of the National Organization for Women Foundation et al. *National Coalition for Men v. Selective Service System*, 593 U.S. (2021) (No. 20-298), https://www.supremecourt.gov/search.aspx?filename=/docket /docketfiles/html/public/20-928.html.

Barrow, General Robert, USMC (Ret.). Statement to Senate Armed Services Committee, Manpower and Personnel Subcommittee. "Women in Combat Testimony from a Marine Corps General's Opinion." CSPAN video, 00:13:30, 18 June 1991, https://www.c-pan.org/video/?c4454887/user-clip -women-combat-testimony-marine-corps-generals-opinion.

Becraft, Carolyn H., Assistant Secretary of the Navy for Manpower and Reserve Affairs. Memorandum for the Executive Director, Board for the Correction of Naval Records, 21 June 1999, Subj: Petition on Behalf of [name redacted] (Deceased), https://web.archive.org/web/20080227203135/http://boards.law .af.mil/NAVY/BCNR/CY1998/06956–98.pdf.

Binkin, Martin, and John D. Johnston. *All-Volunteer Armed Forces: Progress, Problems, and Prospects*. Report prepared for the Committee on Armed Services, Senate, 93rd Cong., 1st sess. Washington, DC: U.S. GPO, 1973.

Chairman, Board for the Correction of Naval Records to Secretary of the Navy. Subj: Review of Naval Record of [name redacted] (Deceased). Docket No. 6956-98, 18 December 1998, https://web.archive.org/web/20080227203135 /http://boards.law.af.mil/NAVY/BCNR/CY1998/06956–98.pdf.

Code of Federal Regulations: Title 3—The President, 1943–1948 compilation. Washington, DC: Federal Register Division, National Archives and Records Service, 1957.

Congressional Research Service. *CRS Report: Expanding the Selective Service: Research Issues Surrounding Women and the Draft* (updated 14 September 2020), 2, https://crsreports.congress.gov LSB10491.

Defense Advisory Committee on Women in the Services. History of Recommendations, https://dacowits.defense.gov/Reports/Recommendations/.

———. History of Recommendations. Spring 1974, https://dacowits.defense .gov/Home/Documents/1974-Spring/.

———. History of Recommendations. Spring 1975, https://dacowits.defense .gov/Home/Documents/1975-Spring/.

———. History of Recommendations. Spring 1980, https://dacowits.defense .gov/Home/Documents/1980-Spring/.

———. History of Recommendations. Spring 1991, https://dacowits.defense.gov/Home/Documents/1991-Spring/.

———. 2004 Report, https://dacowits.defense.gov/Reports/.

Eberstadt, Ferdinand. *Report to the Commission on the National Security Organization.* Volume 3, chapter 12: Personnel Administration, Policies and Practices, section 14 (1948), "Women in the National Security Establishment."

General Accounting Office. *Women in the Military: Attrition and Retention.* NSIAD-90-87BR. Washington, DC: General Accounting Office, July 1990.

———. *Women in the Military: Deployment in the Persian Gulf War.* GAO/NSIAD-93-93. Washington, DC: General Accounting Office, July 1993.

Gillibrand Statement on the Gutting of Bipartisan Military Justice Reforms by House and Senate Armed Services Leadership, 7 December 2021, https://www.gillibrand.senate.gov/news/press/release/gillibrand-statement-on-the-gutting-of-bipartisan-military-justice-reforms-by-house-and-senate-armed-services-leadership.

Harrell, Margaret C., Laura Werber, Peter Schirmer, Bryan W. Hallmark, et al. *Assessing the Assignment Policy for Army Women.* Santa Monica, CA: RAND Corporation, 2007, https://www.rand.org/pubs/monographs/MG590-1.html.

Historical Office of the Secretary of Defense. Histories of the Secretaries of Defense, https://history.defense.gov/DOD-History/Secretaries-of-Defense/.

Kamarck, Kristy N. *Women in Combat: Issues for Congress.* Washington, DC: Congressional Research Service, R42075, December 13, 2016.

Lebonick, Cara Moore. "Mustering Out: The Navy's First Black Yeowomen." *Rediscovering Black History* (blog). NARA, 9 November 2020, https://rediscovering-black-history.blogs.archives.gov/2020/11/09/golden-14/

Naval History and Heritage Command. *Carter Hall* (LSD 50) 1999 Command History Report, https://www.history.navy.mil/content/dam/nhhc/research/archives/command-operation-reports/ship-command-operation-reports/c/carter-hall-lsd-50-ii/pdf/1999.pdf.

———. *Gunston Hall* (LSD 44) 1999 Command History Report, https://www.history.navy.mil/content/dam/nhhc/research/archives/command-operation-reports/ship-command-operation-reports/g/gunston-hall-lsd-44/pdf/1999.pdf.

———. *Saipan* (LHA 2) 2003 Command History Report, https://www.history.navy.mil/content/dam/nhhc/research/archives/command-operation-reports/ship-command-operation-reports/s/saipan-lha-2-ii/pdf/2003.pdf.

———. "USS *Hopper* Commissioning (1997). Part 1." YouTube video, 9:25, posted 5 March 2010, https://www.youtube.com/watch?v=_qD5HC_PxfM.

————. USS *Rushmore* 1999 Command History Report, https://www.history
.navy.mil/content/dam/nhhc/FOIA/USS%20RUSHMORE%20(LSD-47)%20
CHR%20for%201999.pdf.

"Remembering Those We Lost." *The Pentagon Memorial,* https://www.defense
.gov/Experience/Pentagon-Memorial/.

Report of the Fort Hood Independent Review Committee, 6 November 2020,
https://www.army.mil/forthoodreview/.

Statement of Sotomayor, J. *National Coalition for Men v. Selective Service System.* 593 U.S. (2021) (No. 20-298), https://www.supremecourt.gov/search
.aspx?filename=/docket/docketfiles/html/public/20-928.html.

Stoner, Cameron. "Women in Submarines: 10 Years Later." SUBLANT Public
Affairs, https://www.navy.mil/Press-Office/News-Stories/Article/2671640
/women-in-submarines-10-years-later/.

Tailhook '91: Part 2. Washington, DC: GPO, 1993.

Truman, Harry S. Executive Order 9981. "Desegregation of the Armed Forces."
Establishing the President's Committee on the Equality of Treatment and
Opportunity in the Armed Services. *Code of Federal Regulations:* Title 3—The
President, 1943–1948 compilation. Washington, DC: Federal Register Division,
NARA, 1957.

Turner, Mike. Press release. Speier, Turner Introduce Bipartisan Vanessa Guillén Military Justice Improvement and Increasing Prevention Act to Remove
Sexual Assault Prosecution Decisions from the Chain of Command, https://
turner.house.gov/2021/6/speier-turner-introduce-bipartisan-vanessa-guill
-n-military-justice-improvement-and-increasing-prevention-act-to-remove
-sexual-assault-prosecution-decisions-from-the-chain-of-command.

Umfleet, LaRae. "1898 Wilmington Race Riot Report." North Carolina Office
of Archives and History Research Branch, https://digital.ncdcr.gov/digital/
collection/p249901coll22/id/5842 (31 May 2006).

U.S. Congress. *Congressional Record.* 65th Cong., 2nd sess., 1918. Vol. 56.

U.S. Congress. *Congressional Record.* House. 79th Cong., 2nd sess., Naval Affairs
Committee. Hearings on H.R. 5915, "To Amend the Naval Reserve Act of
1938, as Amended, so as to Establish the Women's Reserves on a Permanent
Basis, and for Other Purposes." 21 May 1946, 3319–39.

U.S. Congress. *Congressional Record.* House. Proceedings and Debates of the
80th Congress, 2nd sess. Women's Armed Services Act of 1948, 12 May
1948–2 June 1948.

U.S. Congress. House Committee on the Armed Services. *Defense Policy Panel
and Military Personnel and Compensation Subcommittee Hearing on Gender
Discrimination.* 30 July 1992. Federal News Service.

U.S. Congress. House Committee on the Armed Services. *Hearings before the Military Personnel Subcommittee.* 96th Cong., 1st and 2nd sess., HASC No 9672. Washington, DC: GPO, 1981.

U.S. Congress. House Committee on the Armed Services. *Hearings before the Special Subcommittee on the Utilization of Manpower in the Military.* 92nd Cong., 1st and 2nd sess., HASC No 9251. Washington, DC: GPO, 1972.

U.S. Congress. House Committee on the Armed Services. *Hearings before the Special Subcommittee on the Utilization of Manpower in the Military.* 92nd Cong., 2nd sess., HASC No 9258. Washington, DC: GPO, 1972.

U.S. Congress. *Proceedings and Debates.* 77th Cong., 2nd sess. Vol. 88, part 2, 23 February 1942–25 March 1942. Washington, DC: GPO, 1942.

U.S. Congress. *Statements and Speeches, Monthly Report, Margaret Chase Smith, U.S. Senate.* 80th Cong., 1948, vol. 5, 6 April 1948.

U.S. Congress. *Statements and Speeches, Monthly Report, Margaret Chase Smith, U.S. Senate.* 92nd Congress, 1972, vol. 39A.

U.S. Congress. Senate. "Establishing A Women's Auxiliary Reserve in the Navy." Report No. 1511. 77th Cong., 2nd sess., 1942. CIS U.S. Serial Set, Miscellaneous Senate Reports, S. Rep. 4, no. 1415-1631, microfiche.

U.S. Congress. Senate. *Hearing of the Manpower and Personnel Subcommittee of the Senate Armed Services Committee, Women in Combat.* Federal News Service. Federal Information Systems Corporation, 1991.

U.S. Department of the Army. Army Regulation 600-8-22. Military Awards (5 March 2019), 110.

U.S. Department of Defense. "Commencing Department of Defense Actions and Implementation to Address Sexual Assault and Sexual Harassment in the Military. Independent Review Commission Recommendation-Implementation Roadmap." News release, 22 September 2021, https://www.defense .gov/News/Releases/Release/Article/2785437/commencing-department-of-defense-actions-and-implementation-to-address-sexual-a/.

———. *2020 Demographics Profile of the Military Community,* https://download .militaryonesource.mil/12038/MOS/Reports/2020-demographics-report.pdf.

———. "George C. Marshall, September 21, 1950–September 12, 1951, 3rd Secretary of Defense, Truman Administration." Secretaries of Defense Biographies, https://history.defense.gov/DOD-History/Secretaries-of-Defense/.

———. "Role of Women in the Theater of Operations." *Conduct of the Persian Gulf War: Final Report to Congress.* Vol. 2, appendix R. Washington, DC: Department of Defense, 1992.

———. Secretary of Defense Speech. "Remarks on Women-in-Service Review." Delivered by Secretary of Defense Ash Carter, 3 December 2015, https://www

.defense.gov/News/Speeches/Speech/Article/632495/remarks-on-the
-women-in-service-review/.

———. *Task Force on Women in the Military*. Report. January 1988.

U.S. Department of Labor. Women's Bureau. *The New Position of Women in American Industry*. Bulletin 12. Washington, DC: GPO, 1920.

———. Women's Bureau. *The Occupational Progress of Women: An Interpretation of Census Statistics of Women in Gainful Occupations*. Bulletin 27. Washington, DC: GPO, 1922.

U.S. Department of the Navy. Bureau of Naval Personnel. Assistant Chief of Naval Personnel for Women. *The WAVES: Records of the Assistant Chief of Naval Personnel for Women, 1942–1972*. Wilmington, DE: Scholarly Resources, 1991. Microform collection available at Nimitz Library, U.S. Naval Academy, Annapolis, MD. Original files are held in the Naval Historical Center's Operational Archives in Washington, DC.

———. Naval Military Personnel Command (NMPC-62). *Women in the Navy Information Book*. Washington, DC: Department of the Navy, 1979.

———. Office of the Chief of Naval Operations. *Navy Study Group's Report on Progress of Women in the Navy*. Washington, DC: Department of the Navy, 1987.

———. Office of Women's Policy. "Pregnancy Policy: OPNAVINST 6000.1B." PowerPoint brief presented to the Defense Advisory Committee on Women in the Services, May 2004, www0.dtic.mil/dacowits/agendadoc/ppts/Navy _Pregnancy_Brief_140504.ppt.

———. Office of Women's Policy. "Women in the U.S. Navy." PowerPoint brief, August 2005, www.cgwla.org/symposiumStuff/Women%20in%20the%20 Navy%20Standard%20Brief%20-%20August%202005.ppt (accessed 20 March 2006).

U.S. House of Representatives. Committee on Armed Services. Subcommittee No. 3, Organization and Mobilization. Hearings on S. 1641, "To Establish the Women's Army Corps in the Regular Army, to Authorize the Enlistment and Appointment of Women in the Regular Navy and Marine Corps and the Naval and Marine Corps Reserve, and for Other Purposes." 80th Cong., 2nd sess., 18, 23, 25, 27 February, 2, 3, March 1948: 5563–5747.

U.S. House of Representatives. History, Art & Archives. "RANGEL, Charles B.," https://history.house.gov/People/Listing/R/RANGEL,-Charles-B--(R000053)/.

U.S. House of Representatives. Office of the Clerk. *Biographical Directory of the United States Congress, 1774–Present*, http://bioguide.congress.gov/scripts /biodisplay.pl? index=H000934.

U.S. House of Representatives. Office of the Clerk. "Women in Congress: Congresswomen's Biographies," http://bioguide.congress.gov/congresswomen /index.asp.

U.S. Navy Regulations, 1920. Reprint. Washington, DC: GPO, 1941.

U.S. Senate. *Hearings before a Subcommittee of the Committee on Appropriations, Department of Defense Appropriations for Fiscal Year 1982*. Part 2, Manpower. 97th Cong., 1st sess. Washington, DC: GPO, 1–400.

U.S. Senate. Senator Kennedy of Massachusetts speaking for the Kennedy–Roth Amendment to the National Defense Authorization Act for Fiscal Years 1992 and 1993 to the Committee on the Armed Services. S. 11412. 102nd Cong., 1st sess. *Congressional Record*, 31 July 1991, vol. 137, no. 119.

U.S. Statutes at Large, 41 (May 1919–March 1921).

"USS *Cole* (DDG 67)." Naval History and Heritage Command, https://www .history.navy.mil/browse-by-topic/ships/modern-ships/uss-cole.html.

Vander Schaaf, Derek J. Deputy Inspector General. Memorandum for the Secretary of Defense, 12 April 1993. Report of Investigation: Tailhook 91. Part 2, Events of the 35th Annual Tailhook Symposium.

UNPUBLISHED MATERIAL

CNO Washington DC, 031720Z MAR 79. "Women at Sea Monitoring Plan." Author's files.

CNO Washington DC, R 131414Z JUN 79. "Standardized Orientation Training RE the Women in Ships Program." Author's files.

DCNO MPT Washington DC, 281716Z FEB 79. "Revised Plan for the Assignment of Women to Shipboard Duty in FY 79." Author's files.

Surface Navy Association, Naval Historical Foundation, and Naval Historical Center Symposium, Women At Sea: 25 Years and Counting, Transcript of panel discussions, Washington, DC: 20 November 2003.NAVOP 074/78. 29 June 1978. "Potential Assignment of Navy Women to Duty at Sea." Author's files.

NAVOP 130/78, 232018Z OCT 78. "Assignment of Women to Shipboard Duty." Author's files.

NAVSEC Washington, DC, to COMNAVSURFPAC San Diego, CA, 042024Z OCT 78. "Visit Clearance Request Women aboard Ship Program." Author's files.

Quigley, Capt. Robin L. USN (Ret.). Oral history interview by Etta Belle Kitchen, 15 June 1976, San Diego, CA. U.S. Naval Institute, Annapolis.

Smith-Hutton, Capt. Henri H. USN (Ret.). Oral history interview by Paul B. Ryan, 1976. U.S. Naval Institute, Annapolis.

USS *Jason*. Women to Sea Workshop Handout. N.d. Author's files.

Workshop for Prospective USS *Canopus* Crewmembers. N.d. PERS-00W Files.

ONLINE SOURCES

"Admiral Michelle Howard: Leading the Navy into a New Era." Interview by Moira Forbes, Forbes Women's Summit, May 2014, video, 6:26, https://www.youtube.com/watch?v=F8nip7jv_mo.

C-Span. "Q&A with Michelle Howard." Washington, DC: 15 October 2015, https://www.c-span.org/video/?328741-1/qa-michelle-howard.

Center for Military Readiness, http://www.cmrlink.org/.

Criss, Doug. "The Media's Version of #MeToo Is Unrecognizable to the Movement's Founder, Tarana Burke." CNN, 30 November 2018, https://www.cnn.com/2018/11/30/us/tarana-burke-ted-talk-trnd/index.html.

Dolasinski, Amanda. "MOAA Interview: How This Former Naval Aviator Made a Historic Landing as a Commercial Pilot." Military Officers Association of America, 4 March 2020, https://www.moaa.org/content/publications-and-media/news-articles/2020-news-articles/moaa-interview-this-aviators-military-training-helped-her-make-an-historic-landing/.

Donnelly, John M. "Senators Hit Pentagon's 'Lax' Response to Sexual Assault." *Congressional Quarterly Roll Call,* 26 October 2021, https://www.rollcall.com/2021/10/26/senators-hit-pentagons-lax-response-to-sexual-assault/.

Gallucci, Ryan. "Women in Service: Marine Corps Lioness Program." *American Veterans* (blog), 30 March 2010, https://americanveteranmagazine.blogspot.com/2010/03/women-in-service-marine-corps-lioness.html.

"'Intelligence Matters' Presents: Remembering 9/11 with Andy Card." Updated 18 August 2021, 7:11 a.m., CBS News, https://www.cbsnews.com/news/intelligence-matters-presents-911-andy-card/.

IUSS CAESAR Alumni Association. "Integrated Undersea Surveillance System (IUSS) History 1950–2010," http://www.iusscaa.org/history.htm.

Lioness: There for the Action. Missing from History. "About the Film," https://rocofilms.com/films/lioness/./

"The Military Medals Database." Bronze Star Citation, Grace Mehl, Hall of Valor, https://valor.militarytimes.com/hero/56723.

Military Times. "Honor the Fallen," https://thefallen.militarytimes.com/navy-culinary-specialist-1st-class-regina-r-clark/943336.

Public Broadcasting Service. Frontline. "The Navy Blues: Punishment after Tailhook," http://www.pbs.org/wgbh/pages/frontline/shows/navy/tailhook/disc.html.

Vassalo, Steve. "Missionary Misfits: Meet a Former Fighter Pilot, Current Autonomous Vehicles Road Warrior." *Forbes*, 17 October 2020, https://www.forbes.com/sites/stevevassallo/2020/10/17/missionary-misfits-meet-a-former-fighter-pilot-current-autonomous-vehicles-road-warrior/?sh=7489ef6e5f15.

— INDEX —

281

ABOUT THE AUTHOR

RANDY CAROL GOGUEN was born in Fitchburg, Massachusetts. She received her undergraduate degree from the College of New Rochelle in New York and earned a master's degree in international relations from the Patterson School of Diplomacy and International Commerce, University of Kentucky. She earned a PhD in diplomatic and military history from Temple University in Philadelphia. She served in the enlisted ranks in the U.S. Marine Corps Reserve and the U.S. Navy Reserve. She was commissioned as an intelligence officer in the U.S. Navy Reserve in 1987, retiring at the rank of commander in 2010 with thirty-two years of service. She served as a history instructor at the U.S. Naval Academy from 1998 to 2000. In the aftermath of the terrorist attacks of 11 September 2001 she was mobilized to the Office of Naval Intelligence in Suitland, Maryland. Following her release from active duty, she served as the civilian historian for that organization until her retirement in 2022. She resides in Fairhaven, Maryland.